Electrical Contractor
Start and run a money-making business

Dan Ramsey

TAB Books
Division of McGraw-Hill

New York San Francisco Washington, D.C. Auckland Bogotá
Caracas Lisbon London Madrid Mexico City Milan
Montreal New Delhi San Juan Singapore
Sydney Tokyo Toronto

Dedication

*The quality of life
is of greater value
than the quantity.*

pbk   3 4 5 6 7 8 9 10 11 12   FGR/FGR   9 9 8 7 6

Library of Congress Cataloging-in-Publication Data

Ramsey, Dan, 1945–
    Electrical contractor : start and run a money-making business / by
Dan Ramsey.
        p.   cm.
    Includes index.
    ISBN 0-8306-4467-9 (p)
    1. Electric contracting—Management. 2. New business enterprises-
-Management.   I. Title.
HD9716.E432R36 1993
621.319'24'068—dc20   93-23867
                                                              CIP

Acquisitions editor: Kimberly Tabor
Editorial team: Steve Bolt, Executive Editor
                Sally Anne Glover, Editor
                Stacey R. Spurlock, Indexer
Production team: Katherine G. Brown, Director
                Rose McFarland, Layout
                Nancy K. Mickley, Proofreader
Design team: Jaclyn J. Boone, Designer
                Brian Allison, Associate Designer
Cover design: Carol Stickles, Allentown, Pa.   HT1
Cover photography: Brent Blair, Harrisburg, Pa.   4436

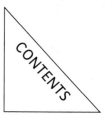

Acknowledgments

A child is a composite of not only its parents, but also of its friends. A book is much like a child in that it's conceived, grows inside the author's mind, is born to paper, and soon takes its place in the world.

Among this book's relatives and friends are: Kimberly Tabor and Stacy V. Pomeroy of TAB Books/McGraw-Hill, Inc.; George Lord, J.C. Mascari, and Beatrice Dare of the Service Corps of Retired Executives, Portland District Office; Roy L. Fietz and Lori Capps of the Business Development Center at Southwest Oregon Community College; The U.S. Small Business Administration Office of Business Development; Ron Hoyt of the Oregon Technology Access Program; Angela Talbot of Independent Electrical Contractors, Inc.; Daniel G. Walter and William J. Normand of the National Electrical Contractors Association; James L. Bennett of McBee Systems, division of ROMO Corporation; Eric J. Faltraco of the Faltraco Group; Kent Yunk of McCormick Systems, Inc.; Jan France and Bob Adams of TRF Systems, Inc.; The U.S. Department of Commerce, Office of Business Liaison. Some business forms in this book were produced using KeyForm Designer Plus from SoftKey Software Products, Inc. Thanks, too, to the staff of Communication Solutions for their work on the manuscript for this book.

Electricity is an essential part of modern life. Imagine what your day would be like without lighting, air conditioning, refrigeration, climate control, security, television, radio, telephones, microwaves, and electrical appliances. Few of us remember the days before electrical service—and fewer still want to return to those "dark" days.

Electricians are indispensable in the power chain. They apply their knowledge of electricity to bring us the goodies of the twentieth century, but you probably already know that. Chances are that you are an electrician or that you have a compelling interest in the trade. What you're looking for is the knowledge you need to turn this trade into a business.

Maybe you're a journeyman electrician with years of experience from which you want to profit; maybe you're an apprentice electrician with a long-term goal of controlling your own electrical contracting business, or you could be someone currently working in a related trade with a dream of becoming a competent electrical contractor someday in the future.

Along the way, as you built your skills and goals, you decided that what you need is some training in business. You want to understand how to start, operate, build, and profit from your own enterprise, but you don't have a master's degree in business. Thankfully, you don't need one. This book is written for you.

The challenges of electrical contracting

There are many reasons why an otherwise rational person would want to become an electrical contractor. The most popular is, "I want to be my own boss." What that typically means is, "I want to be able to better control what I do, how I do it, and for whom I do it." While many experienced electrical contractors will argue that a "boss" has limited control over people and situations, being your own boss at least gives you the illusion of power. Actually, those who become their own boss sometimes give up control to others for a variety of reasons. This book will show you not only how to be your own boss, but also how to retain the control you need to be an effective electrical contractor. It will give you "power" tools.

Others want to become electrical contractors because their day is otherwise dull and they want new and exciting challenges. Maybe they spend eight or more hours a day pulling wire, repairing motors, installing co-ax lines, or other tedious tasks—with no challenges in sight. They want to go to work each day saying, "Surprise me!" This book will help these people find new challenges and help them make each new day an enjoyable learning experience.

Some electricians move from job to job, unsuccessfully searching for a boss that will appreciate their skills and their work ethics, but the boss says, "Just do it quickly and move on." While efficiency is good, these electricians know that the best way is not always the fastest. They also take pride in their work. They'd love to work for themselves—the only bosses that appreciate what electricians do. It's a matter of pride and professionalism. This book will show these electricians how to put their ethics to work and develop a profitable business where quality is important.

A few electricians are nearing the end of their careers, but they aren't ready to quit. The boss has fewer and fewer jobs for the "old guy." These long-time electricians want to apply what they know in the areas that best fit their physical limitations. No more snaking conduit through attics or lifting heavy equipment. They want to work a few hours a week at the jobs that are still fun and profitable. This book will help them find the appropriate jobs and guide them in setting up a profitable business that won't require huge start-up costs and professional fees.

A select number of electricians say, "I haven't learned it all yet; bring me more challenges." They not only want to learn all there is to know about electrical work, but they also want to learn as much as they can about marketing, business accounting, computers and software, negotiations, pricing, and communications. This book will give them an overview of all of this and more. It will continue them on their quest for challenge.

Other electricians, because of an accident or ill health, must leave their trade, but they don't want to retrain for another occupation; they want to put their knowledge to work in electrical contracting. This book will show them how to set up and run a successful electrical contracting business without having to do any of the physical work. It will teach them how to manage employees, work with subcontractors, efficiently schedule jobs, collect accounts, and many more skills to help them succeed as nonworking supervisors.

In the first chapter of this book, you'll take a close look at yourself. You'll look for the qualities, skills, assets, goals, and temperament needed to become a successful electrical contractor. You'll also learn the single most important key to the success—or failure—of your electrical contracting business. Maybe you've never thought of it, or maybe you have, but I'll explain this key to you in the first chapter and teach it to you throughout the book. I really want you to succeed!

You'll also learn about the dozens of opportunities there are for electrical contractors—and how to find out which one is right for you. I'll review the tools and equipment you'll need, show you where to get free help with your business, introduce you to some professional organizations that will help, and cover some of the technology tools that will make your job easier and your business more profitable.

Next, I get down to how to actually start your electrical contracting business. I'll talk about customers and where to find them, where to locate your business, how to name it, how to license it, how to set up your business bank account, and what legal form your business should take for greatest efficiency and lowest taxes.

The next few chapters cover important things like contracting, office equipment and software, how to find and keep money, how to set your fees and estimate costs, how to bid jobs, how to sell value when your competitors are selling price, and how to sell your services to the government.

If keeping records is drudgery to you, chapter 5 will make it . . . well, not fun, but at least a lot easier. You'll learn how other electrical contractors keep track of income and expenses, pay the appropriate amount of taxes, give and get credit, make collections, work with suppliers, and much more.

Chapter 6 might be the most important one in this comprehensive book. Chapter 6 explains in clear terms how to get and keep customers. Of all the problems that plague new contracting businesses, the lack of good customers is the one that locks more doors. Fortunately, it's also the one that's the easiest to cure. Skim the rest of this book if you must, but read every word of this vital chapter.

Income is great—except if the outgo is greater. Many new contractors face their biggest challenge in keeping expenses down. How do I get quantity discounts? How much materials should I buy at a time? How can I schedule work so I don't have employees standing around or drawing excessive overtime? How can I keep the taxes from taking all my profits? How can I know that I'm spending too much/too little money before I spend it?

Business is actually legalized gambling. The idea is that you should only play games that have the best odds in your favor; you want to reduce risks. Chapter 8 covers all the risks you take as an electrical contractor—legal, taxes, fire, liability, worker's comp, on-the-job accidents, bank failure, recessions—with specifics on how to keep your losses to a minimum. The chapter also shows you how to make sure you're not overinsured.

Hopefully, as your contracting business grows, you'll refer to the next few chapters often. They cover renting equipment, working with the weather, organizing your job truck and job site, how to negotiate, how to find and keep the best employees, how to profit from apprenticeship programs, and how to deal with employee dishonesty and substance abuse.

Every day in your new business, you'll communicate with clients, prospects, employees, government officials, partners, and other influential people. Knowing how to communicate with them is so important to your success as an electrical contractor that I've included a whole chapter on it. It might sound like a dull or simplistic topic for a book such as this, but don't believe it. This single chapter might do more for the success of your business than any other. Give it a try.

All living things grow, and your new business is no exception. The final chapter in this book will guide you through dozens of ideas and proven examples of how to make your electrical contracting business much better than anyone else's. You'll learn how to manage the numerous problems that will continue to crop up in the years to come. Most important, this chapter will remind you how to have fun at what you do, and, if you're interested, it will show you how to build your business toward a satisfying and profitable retirement.

One more thing: Throughout this book you'll find forms and charts to illustrate the principles I discuss. However, the appendix includes the largest number of usable work-sheets designed especially for the electrical contracting business. You can easily copy them out of the book to use in estimating jobs and costs, keeping track of income and expenses, measuring profits and losses, managing employees, and bidding on jobs.

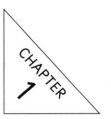

Success as an electrical contractor

AN ELECTRICAL CONTRACTOR wears a number of hard hats. He or she is a qualified and experienced electrician, a business person, an employer, a buyer, a bidder, a credit manager, a bookkeeper, a tax collector, a customer relations representative, a problem-solver, a communicator, and—hopefully—a successful business person.

Is this the right life for you? Is this the way you want to earn your living? Before you answer, read this chapter. Maybe you're exactly the right person for the job. Maybe you're not, but you do have the determination to learn what you need to know to be a success. In either case, this initial chapter will help you look deeper into the job title—its rewards and frustrations—to see if you can see yourself wearing the many hard hats that the trade requires.

An electrical contractor seems like a specific job title, but it's actually fairly broad. An electrical contractor is someone who contracts or works for others and applies knowledge and skills concerning electricity to a specific job. The assignment might be unique, such as installing an industrial control system in a paper mill, or it might be repetitive, like wiring 300 identical condo units in a new development.

The contractor might be "independent" in that he or she works for himself or herself. However, the contractor is not fully independent because the customer is also the boss. If the contractor doesn't please the "boss," then the job is over. Still, there's usually more independence in operating your own electrical contracting business than in working for a regular employer.

Contractors who specialize in a specific phase of construction are often called "subcontractors." However, the distinction is subtle. Those who furnish their services under a contract with a client are actually "contractors."

What does it take?

To start your own electrical contracting business, you'll need a number of resources. First, of course, you'll need to have extensive knowledge, skill, and experience as a journeyman electrician in at least the field in which you'll specialize. Most electrical contractors have a minimum of 15 years' experience in their aspect of electrical work before starting their contracting business. A few have less, but many have much more. The reason is simple: you'll be paid very well for what you know. So, the more you know, the more you'll be paid.

Gaining journeyman status is distinct for most types of electrical work: residential, commercial, and industrial. There are numerous trade associations, such as the Independent Electrical Contractors group and the National Electrical Contractors Association, that set up standards and certification programs for electricians. Also, regional and local groups—who are often members of national associations—establish standards for determining skill levels within the trade. I'll cover these in depth later in the book. The point is that the aspiring electrical contractor must first become recognized as a crafts-person within the trade before successfully selling advanced knowledge and skills.

Not all journeymen electricians should or even want to become electrical contractors. There's more to running a successful business than being a successful employee. Business requires additional skills and attitudes. Ask yourself these questions—then get a friend or relative to answer them for you as well:

- Do I sincerely like people?
- Do others turn to me for help in making decisions?
- Do I get along well with others, even those with whom I don't agree?
- Do I like to make decisions?
- Do I enjoy competition?
- Do I have self-discipline?
- Do I plan ahead?

- Am I a leader?
- Am I willing to work long hours?
- Do I have the physical stamina to handle a busy schedule and heavy work load if necessary?
- Am I willing and able to temporarily lower my standard of living in order to firmly establish my business?
- Is my family or others close to me willing and able to go along with the struggle for business success?
- How much money am I willing to gamble on this venture, knowing that I might be risking all of it?
- Do I have sufficient experience in this field to know what's required to be successful?
- Have I had any training in the basics of business? If not, am I willing to take some time to learn them?

As you step through this book, other questions will occur to you:

- Is there a need for this service in my area?
- Is my goal of becoming an electrical contractor in my area realistic and attainable?
- Who else is offering such a service in this area?
- Why will my service be of greater value to customers?
- How can I let prospects know the value of my service?
- Who will my customers be?
- What do they want?
- How much will they pay?
- How will I keep these customers happy?
- Where will I set up my business?
- How will I keep my business going when the economy changes?
- How can I make my business more profitable without diminishing the quality of my work?

Of course, you won't have the answers to all of these questions yet. The intent of this book is to help you get the right answers to these and other questions that are important to your success. In addition to knowledge and experience, you'll need some physical assets in order to succeed as an electrical contractor. Most are obvious:

- Hand tools (pliers, screwdrivers, hack saw, etc.).
- Testing instruments (volt-ohmmeter, circuit tester, etc.).
- A work vehicle.
- Materials as required by the job (wire, cable, cords, connectors, conduit, outlet and junction boxes, switches, receptacles, fixtures, fuses, circuit breakers, motor parts, etc.).
- NEC handbook.

I'll cover the final selection of these physical assets later in this book.

You'll also need one of the most important assets: cash. Most new businesses fail within a couple of years and often for the same reason; they run out of money. You don't have to be rich to go into business for yourself, but you do need some cash and at least a few assets (home equity, cars, investments) that can be quickly turned into cash if necessary. In later chapters, this book will help you determine exactly how much money you'll need and explain abundant ways to get it.

Another vital part of building your business will be building your credit. Even if you lack some of the cash you need, your credit can make start-up easier. In fact, you'll learn how to profitably use your credit and save your cash for emergencies. So, if your credit's poor or nonexistent, you'll learn how to build it up to where it becomes a valuable asset to your business and your success.

Let me talk about another essential asset—one that doesn't always get discussed in business books: work ethics. Ethics are rules of conduct. So, work ethics are the rules you set for yourself for performing the work that you do. If you'll set—and stick to—the "golden rule" in your business dealings, you'll find, as thousands of others have, that gold comes to those who follow the rules. This isn't preaching. It's just good business. Treat your customers the way you want to be treated, and you'll be so far ahead of the "anything-for-a-buck" contractors that you'll prosper. More important, you'll feel good about yourself and what you do. Your customers will also be your friends, and they'll help you to prosper. Remember the first rule of good business: use money to make friends—not the other way around.

Another vital asset to your business success is related: your relatives. If you've family and close friends who will help you and support you, you've already succeeded. If your family is not supportive of your business ideas, start now in your search to find common ground where you and they can be comfortable with this new adventure. Maybe they're concerned about your health, about your possibly failing, about your being away so much, or maybe they're honestly jealous of your success. Take time to talk with them and get them to share their real feelings about your ideas. Don't talk; just listen. Believe me, success is much more satisfying if you have people with whom to share it.

You might find that you have relatives or friends who want very much to see you succeed and have skills or assets they'll share with you. Make them a part of your journey and your success. Maybe your wife or a parent has business skills you might need; maybe they can help with office duties, or maybe they have other resources that will help you build your business. Ask for participation, for ideas, for suggestions. You certainly don't have to accept all of them, but you might find just the right pieces to make this puzzle become a complete picture.

The point of this discussion is that there are many assets required to start your own electrical contracting business. However, don't let the lack of any of them completely discourage you. In the coming pages, you'll learn how to make the most of what you do have and how to increase these assets until they're sufficient for success.

The statistics about business failure are enough to make you quit before you start: many close the doors within the first year, and most within five years. Why?

Why businesses fail

Not all businesses who close their doors have failed. Some actually merge with other firms, or sell off their assets at a profit. Unfortunately, too many do fail, losing money in the process.

So why do people continue to open businesses? Because most of us feel that we can beat the odds. If this weren't so, Las Vegas would be a small desert community instead of Glitter City. The ones who win in Vegas or in business are those who know the odds, learn how to master them, and know when to quit.

Many business experts will tell you that the reason why businesses fail is "undercapitalization." They don't have enough money to survive. However, if they're in the business of making—not spending—money, the actual problem is that they didn't make enough money. How does a business—any business—make money? By supplying a product or service to those who need it. So, the real reason why businesses fail is that they fail to communicate the benefits that people will receive by using their product or service. Businesses fail because they fail to communicate.

Communication is the distribution of information. That information might be fact, or opinion, or emotions. To transfer information to another person is to communicate. This book communicates information to you. It does so with black marks on paper that your mind recognizes and translates into ideas. Information can also be communicated by the sound of words heard by your ears and translated into thoughts in your mind.

So what does "communication" have to do with electrical contracting? Much more than you might have thought. Wire "communicates" electricity from its source to a receiver. If the wire fails in its job, the fixture or motor or other apparatus doesn't receive its power and nothing happens. There must be a source, a communicator, and a receiver in order to make things happen.

It will be the same in your business. You're the source of knowledge about electricity. In a way, your hands and tools communicate this knowledge to the job you're performing.

- If you want to get prospects to know about your skills and use them, you must communicate with prospects.
- If you want employees to perform their jobs accurately and efficiently, you must communicate with your employees.
- If you want bankers to lend you money—and be glad to do so—you must communicate with these bankers.
- If you want your family to be proud and supportive of what you do, you must communicate with them.

Communicate what? Communicate accurate information that you want them to know in terms that they want to hear. That is, communicate "benefits." A benefit is simply an advantage or a reward that one product or action has over another or over not doing anything.

The benefit of this book to you is that, if you'll put out a little time, effort, and money, you'll learn what you need to know to be successful as an electrical contractor. That's the clear and understood reward you can receive for applying what you learn here.

So what benefits do you offer that you can communicate to prospects, customers, employees, bankers, family, and others? Start thinking about the benefits, and write them down on a sheet of paper as they occur to you. I'll be discussing them throughout this book as I help you design your business, market your services, and communicate with others. I'll also tell you about the smartest rock in the world.

Maybe you've been in your line of electrical work for many years and want to specialize in it as you become an electrical contractor; maybe you want to move into a closely related field that better fits your interests, or maybe you want to transport your electrical knowledge and skills into an entirely new field such as installing computer systems.

Opportunities for electrical contractors

In the next few pages, I'll summarize many of the fields of electrical contracting that have been successful for contractors. It might confirm to you that your chosen specialty is the right one for you, or it might give you new ideas that can lead you into a specialty that will be more enjoyable and more profitable for you.

Within each of the following markets, you can further specialize in power installation; lighting installation; outlets, switches and controls; electrical heating and controls; alarm and signal systems; high voltage and line work; electrical materials and equipment; telephone and intercom systems; and/or wiring for electronic and computer systems. You can then further specialize in areas such as burglar alarm installation, electrical cable splicing, communication equipment installation, fire alarm installation, sound equipment installation, telephone installation, and computer system installation.

Residential electrical contractors

The largest percentage of electrical contractors specialize in residential work. They might offer all types of residential electrical services, or they might specialize in new construction, remodeling, mobile homes, or farms.

New construction

Some electrical contractors only work in new construction, installing service heads, meter panels, and circuit breaker panels; installing conduit; running wiring; installing junction and outlet boxes; installing switches and outlets; installing lighting fixtures; installing stationary fans or power vents. New construction electrical contractors also install electric ranges and ovens, water heaters, space heaters, garage door openers, or related appliances.

In most cases, the work is physically less difficult than other types of electrical work because the walls and ceilings in which the contractors work are uncovered. An efficient, new-construction residential electrician can completely wire a home in just a few days. Of course, this requires that—to reduce driving time—the contractor find more jobs either for new construction that's nearby or at least in the area.

Remodeling

Some residential electrical contractors specialize in remodeling. They might be called on to install wiring and fixtures in an addition to an existing home, or to install lighting or fan fixtures in a room that has already been sheathed. It makes the work somewhat more difficult and often more physically demanding, climbing through attics and under houses. However, the jobs tend to last longer. Unfortunately, there are typically no other homes on the block that might require an electrician during the same period, so driving to and from the job must be factored in.

In some areas, enterprising electrical contractors will specialize in hooking up mobile homes to existing power sources. This is quite an exclusive specialty, as it requires that numerous new mobile homes be installed within the area in order to keep the electrician busy. Some contractors will build a secondary service doing this job when business is slower or when there's a local eruption of mobile home sales and installations.

Mobile homes

In rural areas, many successful electrical contracting businesses have been built by exclusively servicing farms and agricultural businesses. They wire barns for equipment and lighting; they install and maintain electric fencing, and they work under contract to rural electric utility districts for line maintenance and repair.

Farms and ranches

A growing electrical service business is developing around commercial businesses as they compete for the consumer's dollar with greater efficiency and technology. Commercial electrical contractors might specialize in retail stores, warehouses, offices, or even in a specific technology such as computers.

Commercial electrical contractors

Shops are being replaced by strip malls, minimalls and supermalls. Old stores are being renovated and updated. These retail outlets require new fixtures, expanded service boxes, signage, and related electrical services. Even within this specialty, some electrical contractors are niche marketing to firms who renovate older stores or to contractors who remodel grocery stores. These specialties might require more travel or require living within a large metropolitan area, but the jobs typically last longer than many projects. Also, specialist

Retail stores

contractors often get a higher hourly rate than general electrical contractors.

Warehouses With transportation costs climbing, many large industrial firms are building regional warehouses to be closer to their customers. These extensive, new warehouses require electrical services and electrical contractors. In some installations, the contractors should have high-lift equipment to wire and install lighting and security fixtures. However, such equipment can often be rented locally, allowing any enterprising electrical contractor to bid on a warehouse installation.

Offices Office buildings and stand-alone offices require electrical services similar to those of the retail store. Lighting requirements are somewhat different, and most offices require special considerations for computers. However, an electrical contractor who wants to specialize in office systems can often build up a profitable business in larger cities.

Computer systems You don't have to know anything about computers in order to specialize in installing systems, but it will help. Remember, the more you know, the more you profit. Electrical contractors are used to run network cable and power lines, install fixtures, and even assist with the installation of larger computers. If you move into this specialty, you'll need to learn about uninterruptible power supplies (UPS) and related equipment that can ensure that vital computer data is not lost during a power outage.

Industrial electrical contractors Surprisingly, industrial electrical contracting might be one of the most lucrative of the specialties outlined here. Why? Because customers are typically large factories and plants that can't afford to be without electrical service for very long. They must have well-trained and experienced electricians on staff or on call who know the special requirements of industry. Also, each industry is somewhat unique. Specialties within this field include motors, controls, and high voltage.

Industrial motors are vital to the operation of any plant. They grind the flour, debark the logs, convey the packages, and help form the product. Motors range from one-fourth to hundreds of horsepower. Yet they all work on the same principles of electromagnetism. Industrial electrical contractors who, specializing in installing and maintaining motors, will require extensive training and experience in this field. However, a resourceful contractor can hire retired industrial employees who are familiar with the motors, and they can maintain them under contract.

Motors

Many industrial machines are hydraulic, but their controls are often electrical—especially those modernized by computers. Electrical contractors with experience in industrial controls can build a profitable and satisfying service business in this specialty. Depending on the local industrial market, such a business can be built with minimal travel.

Controls

Electrical contractors who specialize in high-voltage systems are a different breed. Most injuries on residential and commercial electrical jobs are minor. However, many accidents on high-voltage systems are fatal. Those who know how to eliminate the danger can develop a needed service where word-of-mouth is all the advertising that's necessary. Additional training and certifications are required.

High voltage

By now you might have narrowed the field down to one or two specialties where your knowledge, skills, experience, and interests come together. However, you're still not sure which would offer you the best chance for success as an electrical contractor. After all, the success ratio for a farm electrical service in Los Angeles or an industrial service in southern Florida is small. You're either going to have to change specialties or move. No matter what you decide to do, the next step is to evaluate the local need for your service.

Determining local need

The first step in measuring local need is to check the local telephone book's yellow pages under "Electric Contractors" and related headings. Count the number of listings under each heading. Then count the number of listings that indicate by

Yellow pages

name or wording that they would be a competitor. If you're in a large metropolitan area, you could mark the location of each potential competitor on a map to determine if there's a geographic area that's unserved. Maybe there's a reason for an area with no electrical contractors: wrong area for the specialty, or maybe it's a gold mine waiting to be worked. It's worth further investigation.

Permit office

Next, visit your local governmental office that issues building or electrical service permits. You'll spend some valuable time there, so bring a notebook. You might have to get permission to go through files, or the data you need might be available in summary documents produced by this department. You'll look for information about those competitors you found in the local yellow pages to find out which are busiest and whether larger ads in the phone book reflect the success of the contractor.

You'll also determine the number of permits issued monthly during the past couple of years. This information is important because it will tell you whether there's an increasing or decreasing need for your services in your area. It will also tell you which months you should expect to be the busiest and which months you probably won't be busy. Does this information match your own experience?

Dig a little bit deeper into the permits records—or ask someone there to help you. If there are slower months for permits in your specialty, are these same months better for other specialties? Could you build your business wiring new homes during the summer and installing commercial signage or remodeling retail stores during the winter?

Friendly contractors

You can also determine local need for your electrical contracting service by discussing your business goal with contractors in related fields. A general contractor whom you interview might not only be an excellent source of information about local need, but also a prospective client. You might someday subcontract your services to him or her.

So, interview a few general and specialty contractors (plumbing, painting, roofing, signage, etc.) whom you know or would like to know. Buy them lunch or bring them a new client or job, telling them that you're considering becoming an electrical contractor and you need some advice from them. Most—but not all—will be appreciative and flattered.

Before your interview, outline the questions you want to ask them and put the questions in a logical order. Start with open-ended questions that allow them to talk about themselves: Why is it that your contracting business is so successful? Then move to the specific questions that will help you make your own business successful: If you were giving advice to new electrical contractors, what three things would you tell them? Once they're comfortable with you and you feel like they might help you build your own business, ask: Would you consider recommending me for future electrical contracting work? It's okay if they say "no" or "I'm not sure yet." If they do, say, "May I ask why?" Then listen. A contractor who is hesitant is more honest with you than one who says yes and means no.

Here's another idea. If you know any electrical contractors in other regions, or if you know someone who could introduce you to them, interview them as well. These noncompeting electrical contractors might give you additional information that will help you build your new business. Be aware, though, that conditions in their market might be different from yours. However, any information can be useful.

Okay, you've done some research to find out if there's a local need for your service. You've studied area phone books, reviewed permits issued for the last year or two, and interviewed contractors for information and opportunities. Now let's look at the market itself.

Defining your market

To clearly define who you are to your customers, you first need to define who you are to them. You have to understand what it is that you'll offer them. At this point, you only have to express it in broad terms.

- "I'm an electrical contractor who specializes in one-person jobs that can be performed with minimal tools."
- "I'm an industrial electrical contractor who works primarily with large stationary motors."

- "I'm a contractor who uses my knowledge of the trade to hire specialized subcontractors for almost any type of electrical job there is."
- "I'm an electrical contractor who prefers to spend my time working rather than marketing, so I want larger jobs from long-term clients, even if they aren't as profitable."
- "I'm a well-known electrical contractor with extensive experience who would prefer to find a young, energetic partner who will do much of the work so I can spend time fishing."

Get the point? By defining your own skills and interests, you can better define those who might hire you—your market.

Defining your process

A process is a series of actions performed to get a specific result. An automotive assembly line is a process where a series of actions are performed—bodies attached to frames, doors and dashboards installed—to get a specific result: a car. Makes sense.

However, did you ever think that what you do is a process? It is. Your process might be the assembly of correctly wired service boxes, or the repair of industrial controls, or the installation of a security system. Like the automobile assembly process, it requires specific tools, materials, procedures, and knowledge. It also has a specific result. The point is that no one gets paid unless they perform a needed process for someone else. A tailor makes suits; McDonald's makes hamburgers; Boeing makes commercial aircraft.

By now I hope you've decided what type of electrical contracting business you'll build—residential, commercial, industrial—and what services you'll specialize in. In fact, you might have two or three ideas on what type of contracting business you'll build.

To define the process you'll perform, first define the end product or products you'll sell to your customers. For example, an industrial electrical contractor might be selling motors that are maintained well enough to never break down on the job. A residential remodeling contractor might be selling an updated home wiring system that's both safe and economical, or a security contractor might be offering clients an electrical system that will assure them of total and trustworthy security in which price is not the primary concern. Clearly defining the end product you'll furnish will help you and the client to maintain clear expectations of the end result. It will also help ensure that your business stays focused.

For an electrical contractor, the process might be simple or it might be complex. However, it has many things in common with other tasks performed by electrical contractors—and by other service firms.

First, it has tools. These might be simple hand tools or complex electrical testing tools, or it might simply be your hands. What are the tools you need in your process?

A process also has raw materials. It could be wiring, or junction boxes, or lighting ballasts, or other materials. What are the raw materials you need in your process?

A process requires skill or the application of certain knowledge. It might be the skill of winding motor armatures, or installing servo-motors, or wiring overhead lighting. It's probably a combination of many skills and extensive, specialized knowledge. What are the skills and the knowledge you need in your process?

Finally, how do others profit from your process? Is your process a convenience for them, or do they actually make money from it? How much money? The more someone else profits from your process, the more you'll profit.

Knowing the answer to these questions will help you become more efficient—and more profitable—at what you do. You'll know exactly what tools and materials you'll need, understand what you do to these materials, and what the end result will be for your customer. This might sound pretty basic to you, but understanding your "process" will help you become more successful at it. Defining your process will also help you from getting sidetracked on jobs that really don't fit you and won't be as profitable for you.

How much should you make?

One of your primary motives for aspiring to become an electrical contractor is monetary. You want to make a profit. It's the American way!

How much money should you expect to make as a successful electrical contractor? Of course, much depends on your local market, your specialty, your capital, your time in business, your management skills, and many other factors. However, the following table shows a "typical" breakdown of costs as a percentage of sales for a "typical" electrical contractor.

Typical breakdown of costs

Material cost	35%
Labor cost	33%
Job expense	14%
Overhead	15%
Profit	3%

That's it? I'll only receive a 3 percent profit? Yes, and be happy with it—because it's 3 percent of total sales. That is, if your firm sells $1 million in services in the coming year, your profit is $30,000. That's after paying salary to yourself and any partners. Obviously, as your sales grow and you learn more about your business, your profits will increase. However, it isn't realistic to expect a net profit of more than 5 percent. In fact, most large successful contractors earn a net profit of much less.

As most contracting businesses sell at least 5 times as much per year as their net worth, your capital is actually earning 15 percent or more (5 × 3%). If annual sales become 7 times your firm's net worth, you're now earning 21 percent!

In a later chapter, I'll go over the tools you'll need for your electrical contracting business and how to get the ones you don't already have. An electrical contractor wears many hard hats. Each must fit well. You must know what opportunities are available, who your customers are, and what you plan to offer them. Most important, you need to know your own goals and aspirations. Then you can find success as an electrical contractor.

CHAPTER 2

Starting your electrical contracting business

THE FIRST CHAPTER of this book gave you a whirlwind excursion through many of the pieces of the electrical contracting puzzle. In this and future chapters, I'll elaborate on each of these pieces of the puzzle.

This chapter will help you to define and apply the pieces needed to start your electrical contracting business. I'll cover goals, getting good advice, defining your prospects and clients, how to name your business, where to locate it, getting required licenses, setting up bank accounts, and the legal form your business will take. You'll also learn about professional associations, the SBA, SCORE, and other business resources that will help you start your business off well.

Every business has a goal of being successful, but what is success to you? Here are some goals set by electrical contractors. Select any of those that seem to apply to you, and make them yours:

What are your goals?

- Become a well-respected business person in my community.
- Build an electrical contracting business that will furnish me with a comfortable living and an ample retirement.
- Establish a successful contracting business that I can sell for at least $500,000 within ten years.
- Help electricians in my area by offering a well-paying and satisfying job while I build my own business.
- Build a successful business than I can pass to one or more of my children when they reach adulthood.
- See my name on the side of a dozen contractors' trucks.

- Build a large electrical contracting business by offering good service and eventually taking over unprofitable contracting businesses in the area.
- Take on a partner with more marketing knowledge who can help me build this business.

Those are just a few of the goals that electrical contractors set for themselves as they start their business. Of course, goals might change along the way. However, goals give you a target to aim for.

Your business plan

Your business goals, your process, and your assets all come together in a single document called a *business plan*. For large corporations, a business plan might be as large as the Denver phone book. However, for your new enterprise, a business plan is simply a few pages of ideas and numbers that help you to focus on the future. Your business plan should include:

- A definition of your "process," describing what you do, how you do it, and what tools and materials you require to produce an end product.
- A description of the type of business that would be most likely to purchase this service from you, including their background, location, typical annual sales, association memberships, and other precise information.
- Information on the name of your business, location, required licenses and bonds, form of ownership, the names and qualifications of members or partners, and related structural information.
- A list of the assets (what you own) and liabilities (what you owe) that you bring to the business, including a list of the professional skills, certifications, and training you have.

Of course, you're not going to be able to complete this business plan today. However, you can start it today with a spiral-bound or loose-leaf notebook. Start by defining your process and your business goals as we just discussed. Then make a section for each of the other categories: prospects, business structure, and assets. As you read through this book and come up with new ideas, write them down in your notebook and you'll soon have a business plan. In chapter 11, I'll show you how to turn this notebook into a document that will help you get additional funding from your bank, your suppliers, and others. Start making notes right now because you're going to move right into defining your customers.

Who would ever want to hire you? Hopefully, lots of people. You're skilled, ambitious, knowledgeable, honest, brave, thrifty, etc. The more you know about those who will hire you, the more work you'll get.

Demographics is the study of statistics about people: where they live, how much they make, how they buy, their favorite brands. Retailers use census information to build demographics that help them in deciding where to build a store. Electrical contractors can use demographics, too. They can learn who would use their services and, then, where to find them.

For example, a commercial electrical contractor specializing in installing security systems in shopping malls would want to learn the difference between a strip mall and a regional mall or a festival mall. How do regional mall retailers typically buy security systems? Is there one brand of security system that they seem to prefer? What does a regional mall retailer typically spend on a security system? This and additional information is available from a number of sources, including trade journals and magazines dealing with security, shopping malls, construction, and electrical systems. You might know of some of these sources yourself. If not, I'll tell you later about where to find this information at low cost.

Psychographics is a two-dollar word that means studying why people buy. You'd think that most people buy for logical reasons. However, in many cases, even in the business world, people buy for emotional reasons and justify their decision with logical reasons. So, knowing why your clients buy will help you sell to them more effectively.

A general contractor building condos might hire you because you're efficient and can get a quality job done in the least amount of time. Price, while certainly important, is a secondary consideration.

A side note: price isn't all it's cracked up to be. In fact, most customers who argue price with you are actually asking you to sell them value. I'll show you how to do this later in the book, so you won't have to haggle prices with every customer.

Back to psychographics: if you've built a solid reputation in your area as an electrical contractor whose name means quality, you can sell that name. People want to go with a winner, so you'll get some jobs just because people know you're involved. So learn what makes your customers buy and help them to buy from you.

Prospecting for clients

A *prospect* is someone who might become a customer. Why "might?" Because the prospects don't know you, your services, or the benefits of becoming your customer. I'll later cover how to turn prospects into customers. However, for now, let's start looking for prospects.

If you've defined who your customers will be, then you have a pretty good idea of who your prospects are. If you know that your customers will be industrial plants in your area that have electric controls, those are your prospects. Many successful electrical contractors start prospecting for clients by building a list of those who might someday purchase their services. From local chambers of commerce, state industrial handbooks, and related directories, you can compile a list of industrial plants in your area, including information on employees, primary industry, products, managers of maintenance departments, and other important facts. You can augment this information with data from phone calls to these prospects. You can also apply the same process to build up a list of prospects for your residential, commercial, or specialty electrical contracting business.

I'll talk about the many uses for computers and technology in your business later in this book. One type of program you should consider for your new business is called *contact management software*. These programs are available for $100 to $500, with the lower end adequate for smaller businesses. Contact management programs can help you build a prospect file or database where you can store information on prospects you gather from these sources. As you call these prospects and develop them into customers, your database will keep track of contacts you make, letters you've sent, requests you've made, and call-backs needed. Some contact management programs will even help you write letters, develop proposals and bids, take orders, and schedule jobs. More on computer tools—and toys—later.

Naming a business is much like naming a baby. In some ways, it will give direction to its growth. A well-named business will seem more successful to prospects, and will then become so.

Naming your business

A business name should make it clear to hearers what the firm does, or at least the industry the firm is in. If the owner or a partner is well-known in the area or the trade, his or her name could be incorporated into the business name. Here are some examples:

- Prairie Electric (denotes the region and the industry).
- Bob's Electric (identifies the industry, but sounds like a small business).
- Haskell Electric, Inc. (sounds bigger; surnames are better than first names, and "Inc." says it's a larger firm).
- Atlas Electrical Contractors (specifically identifies the service, though "Atlas" isn't a modern business name).
- Ryetown Electric Service (is probably a contractor, but might be an electric distribution company).
- Quality Electric Contractors (clearly identifies the industry and the owner's attitude).

When selecting a business name, many firms write a defining motto or slogan that's used in all stationery and advertisements to further clarify what the firm does:

- "Specializing in new wiring and rewiring homes and stores."
- "Specializing in mobile home services."
- "Commercial and industrial electrical contracting services."
- "Electrical maintenance and repair."
- "On-call 24 hours a day."

- "Since 1959."
- "Your one-stop electrical contracting service."

In your business plan notebook, write out a few possible business names and slogans. Of course, check the local phone book to make sure that someone else doesn't already use the name or the slogan.

Locating your business

The next question is: where will you locate your business? At home? From a vehicle? In a service shop? In a shared office? In your own office? The answer depends on how much business you expect to initially contract, what your space requirements are, your budget, and whether you plan to have clients visit your place of business.

Here are some factors you should consider as you determine the location of your business:

- Customer convenience.
- Availability of materials.
- Availability of transportation.
- Quality and quantity of employees in the area.
- Requirements and availability of parking facilities.
- Adequacy of utilities.
- Tax burden.
- Opportunities for signage.
- Quality of police and fire services.
- Environmental factors.
- Physical suitability of building.
- Opportunities for future expansion.
- Personal convenience.
- Cost of operation.

Considering these factors, let's look at your options.

Many small, service businesses begin their life at home. The entrepreneur sets up a small office at the dining table, in a walk-in closet, an extra bedroom, or a shop. For obvious reasons, this is an ideal situation for new electrical contractors.

First, there will be little or no additional rent expense. It's also more convenient for you to have all your records at home where you can review them at any time. In addition, you could have a family member, roommate, or someone living with you help by answering the telephone while you're away on jobs. Finally, you might be able to deduct some of your household costs as legitimate expenses and reduce your tax obligation.

However, the best reason is that it saves you time. A general contractor or other client can call you in the evening to ask about a specific job, and you can quickly check your records or make notes in the job file without leaving your home. The most popular initial location for a home-based contracting business is a desk in a bedroom. Tools and materials are kept in a locked canopy on the back of the firm's pickup truck or in a van.

A vehicle office is another practical office that you can use instead of, or in addition to, your home office. The vehicle can be a car, a pickup truck, or a van. A van is preferred because it can be secured and, if necessary, more easily alarmed. It also offers two large side panels where the business' name can be painted to advertise your business wherever you go.

Keep in mind that your vehicle will represent you and should be in good physical and mechanical condition. Breaking down at the side of the road or at a job site will be poor advertising for your business. If your climate doesn't require it, stay away from vehicles with air conditioning and other optional equipment that might require additional maintenance and costs. Basic is good.

If you don't plan on carrying more than one passenger, a full-size pickup can be equipped with a rack on the middle seat, where you can place a briefcase or a file box for papers, contract forms, plans, and other important papers. Another option is to take out the rear cab window and build a shallow box above the bed, where you can store papers from inside the cab. You can also build this "office" to the two sides of the bed and make compartments for tools or plans. Just make sure that you have a way of locking up your "office."

Service shop Depending on the specialty you select and the availability of business space, you might be able to rent a small service shop reasonably. This becomes a requirement if you're repairing or rebuilding a client's electrical equipment off-site. You'll then need a work area where you can disassemble, test, repair, and assemble equipment. There might not be sufficient room for such jobs in your garage or work vehicle. You might also need to keep an inventory of parts or materials.

A service shop could also be your best choice if you have numerous work vehicles and are concerned about security. Renting a large garage or shop will allow you to keep your vehicles securely indoors. Or maybe you live in the colder climates of the U.S. or Canada. An indoor storage site for vehicles will help ensure that they'll start every morning for the day's job.

Shared office You might have friends or relatives who are also contractors or subcontractors. You could share an office or a shop with them, reducing your costs and bringing them some rental income. Of course, don't share an office with anyone who might, in any way, be a competitor or be associated with a competitor. Prospects calling for you could be diverted. If you're specializing in a single aspect of electrical contracting, look for an office-mate who might be able to bring you prospects, and vice versa. You might even decide to strike up a partnership and join forces. I'll cover the pluses and minuses of partnerships later in this chapter.

Your own office As your electrical contracting business grows, you might want to move to your own office. The biggest disadvantage of such a move is the cost. However, there are many advantages. First, your own office will give you an image of being a large, successful, and permanent firm. Second, if your business requires that prospects, clients, or other contractors visit your facility, an office of your own will give them a better first impression of your business. Third, it will give you control over your business that you can't have if you're working out of the back of a truck or a shared office. Few electrical contractors start out from day one with their own office, but most aspire to someday growing into an office and shop of their own.

Your business location might be limited by local zoning laws. Before deciding where you'll set up your electrical contracting business, even in your truck, talk to the local zoning office about restrictions. You might find that so-called "cottage" or home businesses are allowed in your neighborhood as long as no clients come to your home and no equipment or job trucks are parked on the street overnight.

Zoning laws

Some zoning regulations might allow you to set up an electrical contracting office, but not repair electrical equipment under certain zoning classifications. If you work with heavy equipment, you'll also want to make sure you can legally bring such equipment into and out of your shop without breaching any regulations. Ask questions about zoning and restrictions before you set up your shop.

Here's one last, but important, question you should ask as you decide where you'll locate your business: where are your jobs and your suppliers located? To ask the question more specifically, is your office close enough to typical jobs that you won't be wasting time and gas getting to and from them each day? Also, if your contracting business requires frequent runs for supplies, is your office close to your primary suppliers? If you aren't close to them, consider the cost of fuel and time in your estimate of costs for the site.

Clients and suppliers

Unfortunately, the licensing requirements for electrical contracting businesses aren't universal. In some communities, all you'll need is a local business license. In other locations, you must apply for a state contracting license; file for a fictitious

Licensing your business

business name; apply for state, county, and local business licenses; pass professional requirements; furnish a bond; and jump through a flaming hoop on a hot day.

The best way to learn what requirements are for your area is to contact your state government. Some states have a "one-stop" business telephone number where you can find out what the requirements are, or at least the phone numbers of governing offices. You might be required to include a state license number on all correspondence, bids, estimates, advertisements, and vehicles. Tattoos are optional.

Starting a bank account

Money is so important to your business that I'll devote chapter 4 to working with money. In that chapter, you'll learn about capitalization, credit, interest, buying equipment and supplies, setting fees, estimating jobs, and more. However, right now you're making a list of the things you'll need to start your electrical contracting business. So let's consider your bank account.

Some new small businesses set up a commercial account at the bank where they have their personal account. If you have a good relationship with the bank, this is a good idea. However, many long-time contractors complain of bankers suddenly changing policy and withdrawing credit from otherwise trustworthy customers. They then begin to shop around for a new banker. The point is that the best time to shop for a second banker is when you begin your business. As your business grows, you might want to have accounts at two or more banks. Why? Because, as your business becomes more successful, both banks will probably solicit your complete business and make you offers that you might not get from a single suitor.

One more reason for separate banks for personal and business accounts: fewer errors. Small businesses who have both types of accounts at a single bank might find that checks were deposited to the wrong account, especially deposits made to a cash machine. Doing business with two banks gives you twice as many options.

To start a business account, you'll have to have some "seed" money, typically a hundred dollars or more. Also, most banks require a copy of your Registration of Fictitious Name form approved by the appropriate government office. If you make large night deposits—and most contracting businesses don't— you'll want a night deposit bag and key. With the proliferation of cash machines, your deposits can be made anytime and almost anywhere. You'll also need to furnish a federal ID number (discussed later) or your Social Security number. The tax collectors have friends everywhere—though I'm not sure why.

One of the most important decisions you'll make as you start your electrical contracting business is what legal form it will take. Why so important? Because how you record expenses, how you build your business, how you pay taxes, and how you manage liability all depend on the structure you give your business.

Forming your business

Of course, as your business grows, you'll be able to move from one type of structure to another, but sometimes there will be a cost. The cost will primarily be paid to the tax collector as he or she decides whether you changed structure to avoid paying your "fair share" of taxes. One of the reasons you might later change structure is because you want to legally reduce tax liability—and that's okay. It's the abuse of tax laws that brings the wrath of the IRS.

There are three common types of business structures: proprietorship, partnership, and corporation. Each has certain advantages and disadvantages, but they must all be considered against your specific circumstances, goals, and needs. Before considering each of them, consider the following questions:

- What's the ultimate goal and purpose of the enterprise, and which legal structure can best serve its purposes?
- What's the investors' liability for debts and taxes?
- What would the life of the firm be if something happened to one or more of the owners?
- What legal structure would ensure the greatest flexibility in managing the firm?

- What are the possibilities for soliciting additional capital?
- Would one type of business structure attract additional expertise over another?
- What are the costs and procedures in starting?

Sole proprietorship

The *sole proprietorship* is usually defined as a business that's owned and operated by one person. However, in many states a business owned jointly by a husband and wife is considered a proprietorship rather than a partnership. This is the easiest form of business to establish. You only need to obtain whatever licenses you need and begin operation. For its simplicity, the proprietorship is the most widespread form of small business organization and is especially popular with new electrical contractors.

Advantages of sole proprietorship

The first and most obvious advantage of a proprietorship is ease of formation. There's less formality and fewer legal restrictions associated with establishing a sole proprietorship. It needs little or no governmental approval and is usually less expensive to start than a partnership or a corporation.

Another advantage of a proprietorship is that it doesn't require that you share profits with anyone. Whatever is left over after you pay the bills (including taxes) is yours to keep. You'll report income, expenses, and profit to the IRS using Schedule C and your standard 1040 form, and you'll probably make quarterly instead of annual estimated tax payments to the IRS so you don't get behind.

Control is important to the successful contractor. A proprietorship gives that control and decision-making power to a single person—you. Proprietorships also give the owner flexibility that other forms of business don't. A partner must usually get agreement from other partners. A corporation must get agreement from other members of the board of directors or corporate officers. A proprietor simply makes up his or her mind and acts.

One more plus: the sole proprietor has relative freedom from government control and special taxation. Sure, the government has some say in how you operate and what taxes you'll pay. However, the government has less to say to the sole proprietor.

Yes, there's a downside to being the only boss. The most important downside is unlimited liability. The individual proprietor is responsible for the full amount of business debts, which might exceed the proprietor's total investment. This liability extends to all the proprietor's assets, such as house and car. One way around this is for the proprietor to obtain sufficient insurance coverage to reduce the risk of loss from physical loss or personal injury. However, if your suppliers aren't getting paid, they can come after your house.

Disadvantages of sole proprietorship

When the business is a single individual, the serious illness or death of that person can end the business. Also, individuals typically can't get the credit and capital that partnerships and corporations can. Fortunately, most electrical contractors don't require extensive capital. However, when they do, they seriously consider the advantages of taking on a partner or becoming a corporation.

Finally, as a sole proprietorship you have a relatively limited viewpoint and experience because you're only one person. You're more subject to "tunnel vision" or seeing things in a narrow way based on your experiences. You don't have someone with a commitment to your business who can give you a fresh viewpoint or new ideas.

The Uniform Partnership Act (UPA) adopted by many states defines a *partnership* as "an association of two or more persons to carry on as co-owners of a business for profit." How the partnership is structured, the powers and limitations of each partner, and their participation in the business are written into a document called the Articles of Partnership. The articles or descriptions can either be written by the partners, found in a legal form from a stationery store, or written by an attorney. Obviously, using an attorney is the best option because it will ensure that the document is binding and will reduce disputes that typically come up once the business is growing.

Partnership

Your firm's Articles of Partnership should include:

- The name, location, length, and purpose of the partnership.
- The type of partnership (covered in the next paragraph).
- A definition of the partners' individual contributions.
- Agreement on how business expenses will be handled.
- An outline of the authority of each partner.
- A summary of the accounting methods that will be used.
- Definition of how profits and losses will be distributed among the partners.
- The salaries and capital draws for each partner.
- An agreement of how the partnership will be modified or terminated. This includes dissolution of the partnership by death or disability of a member or by the decision of partners to disband.
- Description of how the members will arbitrate and settle disputes as well as change terms of the partnership agreement.

There are many types of partners within a partnership. An *active partner* is one who actively participates in the day-to-day operation of the business and is openly identified as a partner in the business. A *secret partner* is an active partner who is not openly identified as a partner for whatever reason. A *dormant partner* is one who is inactive and not known as a partner; a dormant partner usually participates by furnishing money or advice. A *silent partner* is one who doesn't actively participate in the business, but might have his or her name on the partnership. An example of a silent partner is a retired owner or figurehead. If the silent partner is only lending his or her name to the business and is not actually a true partner, then he or she is a nominal partner. Finally, a *limited or special partner* is one who agrees to furnish financial assistance but doesn't participate in the ongoing business decisions. Why would someone want to do that? Because a limited partner can only lose their investment in the business; creditors can't go after other assets, so his or her liability is limited.

Partnerships are easier and less costly to form than corporations. All that's really needed is Articles of Partnership, as previously discussed. In fact, that isn't always a legal requirement. If you want to form a partnership with a handshake, you can in many states.

A partner is naturally more motivated to apply his or her best abilities to the job than if the same person worked for an employer or a corporation. An active partner is more directly rewarded.

A partnership can typically raise capital more easily than a proprietorship. This is because there are more people whose assets can be combined as equity for the loan. Also, lenders will look at the credit ratings of each partner. So make sure that your business partners have good credit.

Partnerships are frequently more flexible in the decision-making process than a corporation, but less flexible than a proprietorship, as discussed earlier. Also, like proprietorships, partnerships offer relative freedom from government control and special taxation. A partnership doesn't pay income tax. Rather, all profits and losses flow through the partnership to the individual partners, who pay income and other taxes as if they were sole proprietors.

Of course, there are some minuses to partnerships. Like sole proprietorships, at least one partner will be a "general" partner and will assume unlimited liability for the business. Obtain sufficient insurance coverage to reduce the risk of loss from physical loss or personal injury. However, the general partner is still liable.

A partnership is as stable or as unstable as its members. Elimination of any partner often means automatic dissolution of the partnership. However, the business can continue to operate if the agreement includes provisions for the right of survivorship and possible creation of a new partnership. Partnership insurance can assist surviving partners in purchasing the equity of a deceased partner.

Though a partnership has less difficulty in getting financing than a sole proprietorship, the fragile nature of partnerships sometimes makes it difficult to get long-term financing. The best source, as discussed earlier, is using the combined equity of the partners from assets that they own as individuals. In fact, many partnerships are started because an active partner needs equity or financing that he or she can't get without a partner with more assets or better credit.

Depending on how the partnership agreement is drawn up, any partner might be able to bind all of the partners to financial obligations. Make sure your Articles of Partnership accurately reflect your intent regarding how partners can or can't obligate the partnership.

A major drawback to partnerships is the difficulty faced when arranging the exit of a partner. Buying out the partner's interest might be difficult unless terms have been specifically worked out in the partnership agreement.

As you can see, there are numerous pluses and minuses to partnerships. Many of the disadvantages can be taken care of in your Articles of Partnership. This is why I recommend that you use an attorney experienced in such agreements as you construct your partnership. The cost is usually worth it.

Corporation

We've been moving from the simplest to the more complex forms of business: proprietorship, partnership, and now the corporation. As they grow, businesses often become corporations, which are identified by an extension to their name: "Corp.," "Inc.," or, in Canada, "Ltd."

So, what is a corporation? More than 150 years ago, the U.S. Supreme Court defined a corporation as "an artificial being, invisible, intangible, and existing only in contemplation of the law." In other words, a corporation is a distinct legal entity, distinct from the individuals who own it. It's a legal being.

A corporation is usually formed by the authority of a state government. Corporations that do business in more than one state must comply with the federal laws regarding interstate commerce as well as with the individual state laws. The steps to forming a corporation begin with writing incorporation papers and issuing capital stock. Then, approval must be obtained from the Secretary of State in the state in which the corporation is being formed. Only then can the corporation act as a legal entity separate from those who own its stock.

The primary advantage to incorporation is that it limits the stockholders' liabilities to only their investment. If you buy $1,000 of stock in a corporation and it fails, you can only lose up to the $1,000 investment. The corporation's creditors can't come back to you demanding more money. The exception is when you put up some of your own assets as collateral for the corporation.

Advantages of the corporation

Ownership of a corporation is a transferable asset. In fact, the New York Stock Exchange and other exchanges make a big business out of transferring "stock" or partial ownership in corporations from one investor to another. If your electrical contracting business is a corporation, you can sell partial ownership or stock in it whenever you want, within certain limits. In fact, this is how many corporations get capital to grow. A corporation can also issue long-term bonds to gain cash required to purchase assets or build the business.

Your corporation has a separate and legal existence. Your corporation is not you or anybody else. It is itself. For example, in the case of illness, death, or other cause for loss of a corporate officer or owner, the corporation continues to exist and do business.

The corporation can also delegate authority to hired managers, although they're often one and the same. Also, the corporation can draw on the expertise and skills of more than one individual.

The corporation's state charter might limit the type of business it does to a specific industry or service. However, other states allow broad charters that permit corporations to operate in any legal enterprise.

Disadvantages of the corporation

Corporations face more governmental regulations on all levels: local, state, and federal. That means your business will spend more time and money fulfilling these requirements as a corporation than it would as a proprietorship or a partnership. Also, if your corporate manager is not also a stockholder, he or she will have less incentive to be efficient than if he or she had a share in your business.

As you can imagine, a corporation is more expensive to form than other types of businesses. Even if you don't use an attorney, there are forms and fees that will quickly add up. However, an attorney is a good investment when incorporating your electrical contracting business.

Finally, corporations allow the federal and some state governments to tax income twice: once on the corporate net income and once as it's received by the individual stockholders in the form of salary or dividends. A Subchapter S Corporation allows small businesses to tax the business as if it were a partnership (no income tax) and pass the tax liability on to the individual stockholders. Talk with your attorney about this option.

Professional associations

As an electrical contractor, you're a professional. Fortunately, there are national and regional associations of professionals just like you who can help your business grow through knowledge. Obviously, they aren't going to share their trade secrets, but most will help your business become more professional and more profitable.

The National Electrical Contractors Association or NECA (7315 Wisconsin Ave., Bethesda, MD 20814) is a 4800-member organization founded in 1901. It's an association of contractors who erect, install, repair, service, and maintain electric wiring, equipment, and appliances. The association provides management services and labor relations for electrical contractors, and conducts seminars for contractor sales and training. It also develops related educational programs. NECA publishes a monthly magazine called *Electrical Contractor* as well as other publications. In addition, it holds an annual exposition in a different major city in October of each year.

The Independent Electrical Contractors, or IEC (P.O. Box 10379, Alexandria, VA 22310) was founded in 1957 and currently has more than 2700 members. The IEC represents large and small electrical contractors, primarily open shop. It promotes the interests of its members in the areas of labor relations, taxation, business practices, and related topics. The IEC sponsors electrical apprenticeship programs and produces educational programs on estimating procedures, cost control, and personnel motivation. The IEC represents electrical contractors to the National Electrical Code panel. It also publishes Independent Electrical Contractor and the IEC Membership Directory.

There are other associations such as the National Electrical Contractors Council, a council of the Associated Builders and Contractors (729 15th St. NW, Washington, DC 20005). Independent motor repair firms have their own organization: Electrical Apparatus Service Association (1331 Baur Blvd., St. Louis, MO 63132). There's also the National Fire Protection Association (Batterymarch Park, Quincy, MA 03369), which has sponsored the National Electrical Code (NEC) since 1911.

Government resources

There are branches of federal and state governments that can also help you start your electrical contracting business. The most widely known and widely used government resource is the SBA, or Small Business Administration. The SBA (1441 L Street N.W., Washington, DC 20416) has offices in most major cities across the U.S., with a charter to help small businesses start and grow. The SBA offers counseling, booklets on business topics, and administers a small business loan guarantee program. In addition, it sponsors the Service Corps of Retired Executives (SCORE), Active Corps of Executives (ACE), Business Development Centers, and Technology Access Centers.

Publications

The SBA offers a number of valuable publications and videotapes for starting and managing small business. VHS videotapes on business plans, marketing, and promotions can be purchased from the SBA or borrowed through many public libraries. Publications are available on products/ideas/ inventions, financial management, management and planning, marketing, crime prevention, personnel management, and other topics. The booklets can be purchased for one or two dollars each at SBA offices or from SBA Publications, P.O. Box 30, Denver, CO 80201. Ask first for SBA Form 115A, The Small Business Directory, which lists available publications.

The SBA recently added a computer bulletin board service for business people who want to retrieve business information over a computer modem. Your regional SBA office can provide you with the current bulletin board number and requirements.

SBA loans

SBA loans have helped thousands of small companies get started, expand, and prosper. Here are some facts about SBA loans, current as of the writing of this book (early 1993):

SBA 7(a) guaranteed loans

The SBA 7(a) guaranteed loans are made by private lenders and can be guaranteed up to 80 percent by the SBA. Most SBA loans are made under this guaranty program. The maximum guaranty of loans exceeding $155,000 is 85 percent. SBA has no minimum size loan amount and can guarantee up to $750,000 of a private-sector loan. SBA provides special inducements to lenders providing guaranteed loans of $50,000 or less. The lender must be a financial institution who "participates" with the SBA. The small business submits a loan application to the lender, who makes the initial review; if the lender can't provide the loan directly, the lender might request an SBA guaranty. The lender then forwards the application and their analysis to the local SBA office. If approved by the SBA, the lender closes the loan and disburses the funds.

SBA direct loans

Loans of up to $150,000 are available only to applicants unable to secure an SBA guaranteed loan. Direct loan funds are available only to certain types of borrowers such as handicapped individuals, nonprofit sheltered workshops, Vietnam-era veterans, disabled veterans, businesses in high-unemployment areas, businesses owned by low-income individuals, or businesses located in low-income neighborhoods. The applicant must first seek financing from at least two banks in their area.

Working capital loans generally have maturities of five to seven years unless they're used to finance a fixed asset such as the purchase or major renovation of business real estate. The SBA requires that available assets be pledged to adequately secure the loan. Personal guaranties are required from all principles owning 20 percent or more of the business and from the chief executive officer with any share in the business. SBA loans aren't available to electrical or other special-trade contractors with average annual receipts more than $7 million during the last three years. If you're interested in applying for an SBA guaranteed or direct loan, call your regional office of the Small Business Administration.

Loan terms

The Service Corps of Retired Executives (SCORE, 1441 L Street N.W./Room 100, Washington, DC 20416) is a national nonprofit association with a goal of helping small business. SCORE members include retired men and women as well as those who are still active in their own business (ACE) who donate their time and experience to counseling individuals regarding small business. SCORE is sponsored by the U.S. Small Business Administration, and the local office is usually in or near that of the local SBA office.

SCORE

To take advantage of the counseling services of a SCORE counselor, complete a SCORE REQUEST FOR COUNSELING WORKSHEET (see the full page illustrations on page 39 and 40) and return them to the local office in person or by mail. The interview will be in person at a mutually agreed-upon time. The questionnaire will ask your type of business, whether you're starting, buying, or currently operating the business, how much experience you have in this business, and how much knowledge you have of accounting. The form will also ask you to classify your questions into one or more of the following categories:

- Accounting/taxes.
- Patents/copyrights.
- Construction.
- Insurance.
- Marketing.

- Distribution.
- Legal matters.
- Manufacture.
- Importing/exporting.
- Business plans.
- Home industry.
- Sales projections.
- Customer service.
- Other:_____.

SCORE counselors are typically highly experienced business people; some might have direct experience in the contracting business. There's no charge for their time and assistance, nor are you required to follow their advice. However, the more counselors you have, the greater your opportunity for success as an electrical contractor.

Business Development Centers

Business Development Centers (BDCs) are regional centers funded by the Small Business Administration and managed in conjunction with regional colleges. A BDC offers free and confidential counseling for small business owners and managers, new businesses, home-based businesses, and people with business ideas, including retail, service, wholesale, manufacturing, and farm businesses. BDCs sponsor seminars on various business topics, assist in developing business and marketing plans, inform entrepreneurs of employer requirements, and teach cash flow budgeting and management. BDCs also gather information sources, assist in locating business resources, and make referrals. Call your local SBA office or college campus to determine if there's a Business Development Center near you and, if so, what services they'll provide as you build your electrical contracting business.

Technology access centers

Technology access centers are a new and little-known service provided by the Small Business Administration and the National Institute of Standards and Technology (NIST), a division of the U.S. Department of Commerce. There are now just six Technology Access Centers in the U.S., and your SBA can tell you if there's one near you and how to contact it.

U.S. SMALL BUSINESS ADMINISTRATION

REQUEST FOR COUNSELING

A. NAME OF COMPANY	B. YOUR NAME (Last, First, Middle)	C. TELEPHONE (H) (B)

D. STREET	E. CITY	F. STATE	G. COUNTY	H. ZIP

I. TYPE OF BUSINESS (Check one)	J. BUS. OWNSHP./GENDER	K. VETERAN STATUS
1. ☐ Retail 4. ☐ Manufacturing 2. ☐ Service 5. ☐ Construction 3. ☐ Wholesale 6. ☐ Not in Business	1. ☐ Male 2. ☐ Female 3. ☐ Male/Female	1. ☐ Veteran 2. ☐ Vietnam-Era Veteran 3. ☐ Disabled Veteran

L.
- INDICATE PREFERRED DATE AND TIME FOR APPOINTMENT DATE _____ TIME _____
- ARE YOU CURRENTLY IN BUSINESS? YES ____ NO ____
- IF YES, HOW LONG? _____
- TYPE OF BUSINESS (USE THREE TO FIVE WORDS)
_____

M. ETHNIC BACKGROUND

a. Race:	b. Ethnicity:
1. ☐ American Indian or Alaskan Native	1. ☐ Hispanic Origin
2. ☐ Asian or Pacific Islander	2. ☐ Not of Hispanic Origin
3. ☐ Black	
4. ☐ White	

N. INDICATE, BRIEFLY, THE NATURE OF SERVICE AND/OR COUNSELING YOUR ARE SEEKING
_____

O.
- IT HAS BEEN EXPLAINED TO ME THAT I MAY USE FURTHER SERVICES SPONSORED BY THE U.S. SMALL BUSINESS ADMINISTRATION   YES ____ NO ____
- I HAVE ATTENDED A SMALL BUSINESS WORKSHOP   YES ____ NO ____
- CONDUCTED BY _____

P. HOW DID YOU LEARN OF THESE COUNSELING SERVICES?
1. ☐ Yellow Pages	3. ☐ Radio	5. ☐ Bank	7. ☐ Word-of-Mouth
2. ☐ Television	4. ☐ Newspapers	6. ☐ Chamber of Commerce	8. ☐ Other _____

Q. SBA CLIENT (To Be Filled Out By Counselor)
1. ☐ Borrower	2. ☐ Applicant	3. ☐ 8(a) Client	4. ☐ COC	5. ☐ Surety Bond

R. AREA OF COUNSELING PROVIDED (To Be Filled Out By Counselor)

1. Bus. Start-Up/Acquisition	5. Accounting & Records	9. Personnel
2. Source of Capital	6. Finan. Analysis/Cost Control	10. Computer Systems
3. Marketing/Sales	7. Inventory Control	11. Internat'l Trade
4. Government Procurement	8. Engineering R&D	12. Business Liq./Sale

I request business management counseling from the Small Business Administration. I agree to cooperate should I be selected to participate in surveys designed to evaluate SBA assistance services. I authorize SBA to furnish relevant information to the assigned management counselor(s) although I expect that information to be held in strict confidence by him/her.

I further understand that any counselor has agreed not to: (1) recommend goods or services from sources in which he/she has an interest and (2) accept fees or commissions developing from this counseling relationship. In consideration of SBA's furnishing management or technical assistance, I waive all claims against SBA personnel, SCORE, SBDC and its host organizations, SBI, and other SBA Resource Counselors arising from this assistance.

SIGNATURE AND TITLE OF REQUESTER	DATE

FOR USE OF THE SMALL BUSINESS ADMINISTRATION		
RESOURCE	DISTRICT	REGION

SBA FORM 641 (7-91) PREVIOUS EDITION IS OBSOLETE

WHITE: COUNSELOR
YELLOW: SBI OR SCORE OR SBDC SUB.
PINK: DO OR NSO OR SBDC LEAD

Small Business Administration request for counseling.

SCORE REQUEST FOR COUNSELING WORKSHEET

Name _____(Tel.)_____
Address _____

So that the **Service Corps of Retired Executives (SCORE)** can be more
helpful when assigning you a counselor, please include this
information sheet with the enclosed "Request for Counseling" form.

Kind or Type of Business:_____

I/We have been in business for _____ years; plan to start _____ ,
_____ buy a business

         a) ____ Retail
         b) ____ Construction
         c) ____ Manufacture
         d) ____ Service
         e) ____ Other business _____

I/We have _____ experience in this type of work.

I/We have managed this type of business _____ years _____ months.

I/We have _____ accounting knowledge.

I/We want most help in _____
_____

I/We want to talk with a Counselor having specialized experience
in:

Accounting Taxes		Marketing		Manufacture		Home Industry
Patents Copyrights		Distribution		Importing Exporting		Sales Projections
Construction		Legal Matters		Business Plans		Customer Service
Insurance		Other:_____				

Please mail this information sheet and the "Request for Counseling"
form to:
SCORE
222 S.W. Columbia St., Suite 500
Portland, Oregon 97201-6605
(503) 326-3441, (503) 326-2500

Sponsored by the U.S. Small Business Administration

[SCORE.WKS-07/31/92-JED]

SCORE request for counseling work-sheet.

Technology Access Centers use the power of the computer to access information from large computer databases. You pick the topic and the TAC will search these computerized libraries for information about the topic. In fact, some of the information for this book was discovered through a regional TAC.

For example, you can ask for articles and data on electrical contracting, information on your competitors, information about codes and regulations in your region, and related topics. Depending on which databases they have access to, TACs can find data that will help you make your business or marketing plan better identify profitable opportunities for your specialty.

The process is simple. A TAC representative will interview you to determine what information you need. He or she will then write your questions into terms that can be searched in computer databases. If the search is successful, you'll get a printed report of the results mailed to you. There's often a charge, but it's only a fraction of the cost charged by the database firm. The TAC sponsors pay the rest to encourage small business development. My search was just $20, and I gained a folder full of useful information.

One more federal resource is the U.S. Department of Commerce (Washington, DC 20230). It's Office of Business Liaison is the initial contact point for questions about business assistance. The Bureau of the Census is part of the Commerce Department, and it has detailed statistics on people and businesses in the U.S. There's even a contact for Construction Statistics and Housing Data to help you determine the size of your local market.

Other government resources

The Commerce Department's Economic Development Administration (EDA) provides financial and technical assistance to businesses who are willing to locate in economically distressed areas of the nation, and the department's Minority Business Development Agency (MBDA) encourages the development of minority-owned businesses. It provides management, marketing, financial, and technical assistance through business development centers (previously discussed), minority business trade organizations, and MBDA field offices.

States, too, want to encourage small businesses. Check with your state corporation division, your state legislator, or similar sources to find out what resources are available to you. After all, government is a partner in your business. In fact, they'll take their profit (taxes) before you get yours.

Technology and electrical contractors

Technology is the application of science to the needs of people. A hundred years ago, technology was making the gasoline-powered engine, and great things came from it. Today, technology is using microelectronics to expand the knowledge and power of the human brain. In both cases, technology brought greater service to people and greater profits to businesses.

Electrical contractors benefit from technology as new materials make electrical jobs easier and safer. Technology can also help your business become more efficient and more profitable—if you know how to use it.

The next chapter will help you in equipping your electrical contracting business. The chapter includes information on selecting tools of technology: computers, printers, copiers, business software programs, telephones, answering systems, and related products. You'll learn how to profitably use cellular phones and fax machines to build your electrical contracting business. You'll also learn what the technology of the future has for you and your business.

In this chapter, you've learned how to set business goals, find prospects and clients, name your business, locate it, gather the required licenses, and set up bank accounts. You've also discovered the advantages and disadvantages of the different forms of business, and you've learned about professional associations for electrical contractors, the SBA, SCORE, and other business resources. Yet, you've only begun your journey to success as an electrical contractor.

CHAPTER 3

Equipping your electrical contracting business

TOOLS ARE EXTENSIONS of your hands and your skills. With the correct tools, you can perform nearly any job easily and safely. As an electrical contractor, it's especially important to have the correct tools in your toolbox and to know how to use them. It's also important to have the correct tools in your office. In this chapter, I'll cover tools for both the office and your toolbox.

I won't presume to tell you all of the tools that you should have in your toolbox. First, through your experience you probably have built up a supply of functional tools. Second, your specialty might require very specialized tools that will be found in few contractors' toolboxes. However, let's review the basic tools for the sake of those who are newer to the trade and as a reminder to journeymen.

Electrical contractor tools

In addition to common household tools, such as screwdrivers, saws, hammers, wrenches, chisels, measuring tapes, and electric drills, the following tools should be in your toolbox.

- Circuit tester. A circuit tester can be used to determine if power is flowing through a circuit, as well as if the circuit is properly grounded. The most popular is the neon circuit tester. It's inexpensive and can be used to test and troubleshoot a variety of circuits and appliances. You can use it to check for power at a light switch or outlet, to verify a grounded box, to check power in a panel box, and other vital jobs.

- Continuity tester. The next most important tool is the continuity tester. Working off batteries, it checks for continuity in unenergized circuits. With a continuity tester, you can check a plug-type fuse, test single-pole switches, test three- and four-way switches, and test bulbs, tubes, and fixtures.
- Meters. Depending on the type of electrical work you do, you'll need various voltage testers, ammeters, ohmmeters, wattmeters, and multimeters.
- Pliers. Long-nose pliers are needed to make wire loops, and lineman's pliers are used to pull wire.
- Combination tool. A combination tool crimps and strips wire and also includes wire gauges.
- Fish tape. Use fish tape to pull new electrical wire through walls.
- Plastic electrical tape and twist-on wire connectors. These are needed to secure connections without solder.
- Cable slitter. A cable slitter quickly cuts and removes a cable covering without nicking the wire.
- Utility light. With a cord extension and hanger, a utility light puts illumination where you need it and provides a grounding outlet for a drill or other tool.
- Drill bits. For extending or relocating circuits, a ¾-inch spade bit is needed for running through wood floors and studs; a ½-inch carbide-tipped masonry bit works for masonry. An extension attachment is needed for thick beams.
- Conduit benders. RSC or rigid steel conduit can be bent with a conduit bender made especially for this type of conduit. Thin-walled electrical metallic tubing (EMT) uses a special conduit bender that makes it easy to bend without crimping the conduit.

Contractor office equipment

Chapter 2 reviewed the typical office locations you can use for your electrical contracting business. They include home offices, a vehicle office, a service shop, a shared office, and your own office. Assuming that you've selected the one that's most appropriate to your needs and budget, let's start gathering the office tools and equipment you'll need to manage your business efficiently.

One of the most vital office tools you'll have—and use—is your briefcase. Purchase one that will stand up to the rigors of the job site. Look for hard plastic cases rather than leather. Make sure the hinges will hold up well.

Briefcase

What goes in your portable office? Your daily planner, calculator, bid forms, workbooks, file folders on current projects (if they'll fit), and anything else that will help you be continually productive.

All offices, even a vehicle, require some type of desk or flat surface where you can gather your telephone, records, and other business tools. If in your car, a simple attaché or briefcase can serve as your desk. In fact, many successful small electrical contractors never grow beyond the briefcase stage, managing all of their working jobs out of manila folders carried around in the briefcase. They usually have a secondary storage area—such as a file cabinet in the corner of a bedroom—for inactive jobs and other records.

Desks

The next step up is simply a hollow-core door laid horizontally across two file cabinets. It's practical, inexpensive, and can withstand abuse. It's just not very pretty. A 30-inch door will fit well over standard two-drawer file cabinets. If your budget won't allow two cabinets, buy one and add a couple of legs to the other side.

Depending on how much time you'll be spending in your office, you can eventually graduate to a desk from a business supply store. Such desks sell for $250 and up. How large? If you plan to keep a phone, a fax machine, a computer, files, and trays all on top of your desk, you'll want a larger unit. If your partner, secretary, or office assistant will share some of the duties, you should consider two smaller desks. Many small business people place their desk facing a wall or in a corner so they can attach shelves or mount notes that can be easily read while on the phone.

Most office workers soon learn the value of a good-quality chair, especially if they sit in it more than a couple of hours a day. If you're out at job sites most of the time, you can buy an

Chairs

inexpensive chair. Even a folding chair can serve you until your business is built up. Once your business is successful and you're spending more time in the office, invest in a good-quality chair that will keep you comfortable all day and reduce stress.

Shelves Depending on your specialty, you might want shelves on or near your desk so you can refer to codes, reference books, large phone books, directories, and other materials that you want handy. If cost is a greater concern than attractiveness, consider setting bricks or building blocks a couple of feet apart on the floor, then laying a 1-by across the top, followed by more blocks and 1-bys. However, don't build your block shelves higher than 32 inches unless they're securely anchored.

If you have clients coming to your office and feel that they need to be impressed, consider renting office equipment that will look better than what's described here. This is especially important if you're working with larger jobs where clients aren't familiar with the typical look of a contractor's office: dislocated clutter.

Office supplies You'll also need a variety of office supplies to help you gather, record, correspond, and track your business. These supplies include paper clips, stapler, pens and pencils, a pencil sharpener, file folders and labels, rubber bands, typing paper, calculator tape, stationery (letterheads and envelopes), and postage.

If your office won't include a computer, you should have a typewriter. Look for a good, used electric typewriter and make sure that ribbons are readily available.

Telephones The most important tool for your electrical contractor's office is a telephone. With it, you can talk directly to dozens of prospects or clients each day without leaving your office. Without it, you must drive all over town and hope that your contacts are available when you are. Later, I'll show you how to use your telephone to profitably market your services—even if you don't like talking on the telephone. For now, let's consider selecting your first business phone.

Depending on local phone company requirements, you might need to order a separate business telephone line for your electrical contracting business. The criterion is: if you'll be answering with a business name rather than a personal name, you need a business phone line. If your name is Bob Jones and your firm is "Bob Jones Contracting," you can answer "Bob Jones" and not confuse your prospects and clients. However, if you're "Acme Electrical Contracting" and you answer "Bob Jones," some callers might think that they have the wrong number.

The cost of a business line has decreased during the last few years because of the competition among telephone companies. However, this competition can also make the selection of the best telephone service more difficult. Not so for the small, fledgling contracting business. Your phone bills will not be so large that the typical discount structure will make much difference. Go with your favorite until you've built up your business and better know what your telephone service needs will be. Then you can review the "small business packages" offered by the competing phone companies to see which will save you the most money. Now a word or two about telephone equipment.

Discount stores, drug stores, and many other retail outlets offer standard telephones that can support basic services offered by many telephone companies: call forwarding, call waiting, redial, speed dial, etc. The cost is typically less than $50 per phone. You don't want something fancy; you want something sturdy, with standard features. Again, go with brands you know, and buy from someone who will take the telephone back within a reasonable time if it doesn't work.

Standard telephones

The price goes up for cordless phones, but so does the convenience. Today, you can buy a good-quality cordless telephone for $100 or less. Full-featured models are a little more. The greatest advantage to the cordless phone is its portability. You can carry it throughout your office, wherever

Cordless telephones

you're working, to avoid the quick dash to your desk to answer the phone before the third ring.

However, with every plus, there's a minus or two. In the case of cordless telephones, the minus is that it runs on batteries that need to be recharged. If you keep it with the main unit, it will charge. However, then it won't be handy. So, look for a cordless telephone that can run the longest time away from the main set. Another minus can be overcome: you might forget where you put the gadget. However, many new cordless phones have a "paging" button that can be pressed on the main set, and, if the battery isn't dead, the hand set will beep to tell you where it is.

As with other tools, buy the best quality phone that you can reasonably afford, and purchase it from someone who knows the product. Their product might cost a couple of dollars more than the discount house, but you'll get added value because you bought the most appropriate tool for your budget.

Cellular telephones

Mobile or cellular phones offer the ultimate portability. You can take them in your car, in a briefcase, to a job site, to your home, and still answer calls from your prospects and clients.

How do cellular phones work? They're battery operated and require long-life batteries. Your car battery can support a cellular phone, or you can carry a rechargeable battery pack with you. The signal is carried by wire or satellite link to a transmitter or repeater that covers a wide area. So your conversation is being broadcast much like the signal of an FM radio station. The difference is that anyone with a radio can listen to the FM station. Only you (hopefully) can hear your cellular phone conversation. I say "hopefully" because, with the right equipment, a competitor can listen in on your conversation unless you have special scrambling equipment.

Rather than get into the specifics of cellular phone technology, which changes almost daily, call a local cellular phone service and find out what's new. Prices, too, are changing. To get more customers, cellular services are offering telephones at low initial costs, but you must sign up for at least six months of their service. It's much more expensive than standard line phone service, but it might be a bargain if you're a one-person office that has no one to professionally answer your calls.

Also, if you're brave, ask for a demonstration of a portable cellular workstation. Housed in a briefcase, it's a cellular telephone, laptop computer, modem, fax board, and other goodies. The complete set weighs as much as a bowling ball: 16 pounds. However, it's a whole office for those on the go.

A pager is one of the most valuable—and most annoying—tools an electrical contractor can have. You'll want to purchase or rent one as soon as you've taken on your first or second job. A pager allows other people (office employees, customers, suppliers, field employees) to contact you wherever you are.

Pagers

Which type of pager should you select? That depends on your budget and how you'll use your pager. A tone pager simply alerts you to call a preagreed telephone number, usually that of your office. A voice pager delivers a message—recorded on your office phone—directly to you, wherever you are. A digital display pager will page you and write out the telephone number you should call. An alphanumeric display pager can give you a written message.

Many electrical contractors start by renting a tone pager, then, as business requires, moving up to a voice or display pager. Check your local telephone book's yellow pages under Paging & Signaling Equipment & Systems or similar headings for local suppliers.

Not long ago, an answering machine was an annoying and misused tape recorder that attempted to drive off the people that called you. Today's answering machine is much more accepted, especially in business. It's also easier to use and to buy.

Answering machines

Tape answering machines will use either mini or standard-sized audiotapes to record an outgoing and any incoming message. The good answering machines have a separate tape for each. The better ones don't have time limits for incoming messages. The best ones have features that allow you to hear your messages from any other telephone, can let you know if you have any messages at all, and will allow you to easily change your messages.

Digital answering machines use computer chips to record outgoing messages and, in some cases, incoming calls. The sound quality is often better, but the length of the message might be limited. However, advances in digital sound technology will make next year's models even more useful. Make sure that the system you purchase announces the date and time of the call on the incoming message so you know when they tried to call you.

Unfortunately, many businesses misuse their answering system by putting cryptic announcements and background music on the system; these might confuse or intimidate callers. An effective message should be something like, "Hello, this is ABC Electrical Contractor's answering system. Your call is important to us. Please leave your name and telephone number after the beep and someone will get back to you as soon as possible. Or, if you'd prefer, please call again later. Thank you."

Actually, once you and your clients get comfortable with using an answering machine, you'll find them even more effective than taking live calls. You call a client and leave a list of questions on their machine, then make some other calls. They call your answering machine and leave the answers while your regular phone is busy. Telephone tag becomes obsolete. Also, if necessary, you can review the taped conversation to ensure that you have the accurate information. You can even leave important or confidential messages in private "mailboxes" on your system, which can only be accessed with a code by your manager, your best client, or other important person. It's how business will be conducted in the future.

Fax machines The digital facsimile (fax) machine is actually more than 100 years old in concept. However, it wasn't practical until about a decade ago. Today, there are more than 25 million fax machines in the world, with most of them installed in businesses.

The concept of the fax machine is simple: it "reads" a sheet of paper for light and dark spots, much like a copy machine does. The fax machine then converts these spots into a code that's sent across a telephone line at a speed of nearly 10,000 bits of information per second. Based on some international standards, the fax machine on the other end knows how to read these signals and convert them into light and dark spots that conform to the image that was sent. This image is printed on a piece of paper, and you have a "fax."

The electrical contractor can now send plans, proposals, sales letters, literature, copies of invoices, and other printed material to prospects, clients, and others in just seconds. He or she can also quickly get a written quote from a material supplier anywhere in the country and almost immediately fax a quote or bid to a contractor. A typical one-page fax takes less than 30 seconds to transmit on a Group 3 fax machine. It, too, is dramatically changing the way that businesses conduct business.

Facsimile machines look like a small printer with a tray to hold outgoing paper and a telephone set either attached or nearby. You call the fax number, and your fax machine sends out an inaudible tone that tells the other fax machine that it would like to transmit a facsimile. The receiving machine says, "okay" by sending your machine a high-pitched tone; you manually press your machine's start button and hang up the phone. The fax is being transmitted. Some machines automate the process, and you simply put the copy into the machine and press a button that calls a specific telephone in memory and sends the fax without any help. Smart fellers.

There are dozens of things to know about buying a fax machine for your business. However, most are frills. Most important is that your fax machine is Group 3 compatible. Beyond that, explain to the salesperson what you need your fax machine for, and let him or her show you the newest features and whistles. You can get a basic fax machine for $300–$400, a better one for $400–$800, and your heart's desire for a thousand dollars or more. Or you can rent or lease a fax machine. This is an especially good idea with products like faxes, which quickly become obsolete.

Some fax machines you look at will combine other functions. The fax might have a standard telephone handset that you can use for your primary or secondary business line. Some also include a tape or digital answering machine. In some ways, this makes sense because you have the business phone line feeding into one machine that can serve three purposes: let you answer, take messages, or take faxes. However, like any machine that combines functions, if one goes out or becomes obsolete, they might all go. Compare the cost of a combined unit against the cost of individual units. If there's little difference, go for the separate components.

There's one other option you should consider. In a moment, I'll cover one of the greatest tools to reach small business in a century: the small computer. If you decide to purchase a computer for your electrical contracting business, consider PC fax boards. They're printed circuit boards that are installed inside your computer—even a small one—and allow you to plug in a phone and use it as a fax. There are even models that will serve as your answering machine as well. Fax boards are typically purchased through computer stores.

Computers

Many people are still intimidated by computers, but maybe that's because they haven't discovered how friendly and helpful computers can be. If you do choose to add a computer to your contracting business' office, you'll soon find dozens of ways to profitably put it to work. You can write letters, keep track of your income and outgo, manage your accounts receivable, make collections easier, keep track of your customers and your prospects, schedule jobs, order supplies, learn about your competitors, and much more.

People are often frightened by computers because of all the new terminology that they must decipher: CPUs, bits, bytes, bauds, networks, boards, hard disks, RAM, monitor interlacing, and on and on. Don't worry about it. If you know electricity, you'll easily understand computers and quickly pick up what the terms mean. Here's a simplified introduction to computers.

A CPU is a *central processing unit*. The name gives it away. It's an electronic machine built around a small "chip" called the microprocessor, which processes information for you. It does different work, but you could loosely compare it to the engine in your car.

The CPU is typically called by the same name as the microprocessor chip that is its brain. For example, early PCs (personal computers) used a microprocessor chip called the 8088. So, they were called "88s" or by the IBM brand name for the model, the "XT." The next-generation microprocessor and CPU was the 80286, referred to as the "286" (two eighty-six) or by the IBM brand model, the "AT." Then came the "386," the "486," and, just recently, the "586" microprocessor and CPU. These could be relatively compared to the two-cylinder, four-cylinder, six-cylinder, V8, fuel-injected V8, and other engines— except that each CPU is at least five times faster than the previous model.

In between chips like the 386 and 486 are incremental steps identified by letters like "SX" (a half step) and "DX" (a full step). Don't worry about them for now.

The next number to remember in looking at CPUs is the "clock speed." In our simplified automotive comparison, the clock speed would be like the transmission in that it makes the engine (chip and CPU) go faster. XT chips had a clock speed of about 5 MHz (mega—or million—hertz). Today's 486 and newer microprocessors have clock speeds of 50 MHz and more! What's so amazing to me is that a 486 chip does all that hokus pokus magic stuff in a chip that's about the size of your thumbnail.

So, all you really need to know about buying a PC is that a 486 is faster than a 286 or 386, and a clock speed of 66 MHz is faster than one that's 33 MHz. Especially if you're going to do some drafting or have pictures (graphics) in your system, you'll want the newest and fastest CPU that you can afford. Fortunately, there's not more than a few hundred dollars difference between darn good and great.

Hard disks

So where do you keep all this information? Believe it or not, the hard disk drives in your PC can hold thousands of pages of information on some stacked disks (that look like miniature LP records stacked on a record player). The computer knows where to look for any information you've put into it, and it can give you the data in a small fraction of a second.

A hard disk is measured by the number of "bytes" or computer (not English) words that it can store. Actually, capacity is normally measured in megabytes (Mb). Older PCs were equipped with hard disks of 10, 20, or 40 Mb. Newer PCs can store 80, 120, 200 Mb, or even a gigabyte (Gb) or more. That's one billion bytes. To put that in terms that are more real, a 1 Gb hard disk can theoretically store about a half-million typed pages—quite a large library! Why so much? Because graphics or picture files often require a lot of storage space on the hard disk. Some need as much as a megabyte each.

RAM

A hard disk is a storage area much like a library where millions of pieces of information can be kept. However, a computer also needs a work area—like library tables—where books can be open and used. This place is called the *random access memory* or RAM.

Depending on the size of the programs you'll be using, your PC's RAM should be at least 2 Mb. Older PCs offered between ½ and 1 Mb of RAM, but today's PC typically come with 4 to 16 Mb. The larger this work area is, the more work that can be done simultaneously. Some programs like Microsoft Windows and Novell Netware require at least 2 Mb and really work better if you have 8 Mb of RAM or more. Also, RAM doesn't cost much to upgrade, especially if you do so as you buy your PC.

Diskette drives

So how does all this information get into your PC in the first place? It usually enters on small, portable diskettes that are slipped into your PC's diskette drive and copied to your computer's hard disk. These diskettes, sometimes called "floppies," can store from a third of a megabyte to up to nearly three megabytes of information. Then, once you've written your letter or drawn your plans, you can remove the data by instructing the PC to copy it to a diskette.

In the past ten years since PCs have become popular, a number of diskette "formats" have evolved. A format is what tells the diskette how much information it can store on its surface. Earlier diskettes were 5¼ inches square, and were made of a thin, round plastic disk placed in a bendable (hence "floppy") sleeve and sealed. As programmers learned more about storing information on diskettes, a greater amount of information would fit on the diskette. It started with 360 Kb (kilo—thousand—bytes), and quickly multiplied to 1,200 Kb or 1.2 Mb. Many PCs still use this format.

Another format soon emerged, the 3½-inch diskette with a thin, round plastic diskette housed in a hard plastic case. The first popular format stored 720 Kb or twice that of the larger 5¼-inch diskette of the time. Soon, technology doubled storage on the same size diskette to 1.44 Mb, and the newest format can store up to 2.88 Mb of information on a diskette that will fit into a shirt pocket. Amazing!

As you consider and shop for a PC for your electrical contracting business, you'll also want to know about "ports" in your PC, where you can plug in printers and other equipment. Most PCs today have sufficient ports for most applications. Just let your PC store know what you want to do, and they'll help you select the appropriate PC and "peripherals" or related equipment.

Finally, you'll shop for a *monitor*, similar to a TV screen, where the information you're working on is displayed. A monochrome (black-and-white) monitor is least expensive. Color monitors are easier to read—and more attractive—but also more expensive. Rather than get into a boring description of interlacing and pixels, look for a quality monitor that's easy to read. If you can't see the difference between a $300 monitor and one that costs $1000, don't buy the expensive one.

Printers

Computers are great, but, to share with others, you want a printed copy of your information: business letters, work schedules, plans, income statements. That's where the printer comes in. You can attach a printer to one of your PC's ports and transfer computer data into a readable form. There are many types of printers from which to select. However, I only need to cover the basics of them here so you'll know which ones to look for as you go shopping.

Dot matrix   The dot matrix printer forms letters from a bunch of dots. A 9-pin printer uses 9 tiny pins—3 rows of 3—to form each letter. The 24-pin printer does the same job but uses 24 pins—4 rows of 6. So, the letters formed by a 24-pin printer are easier to read than those formed by a 9-pin printer. Today, most dot matrix printers use 24 pins. Some will even run over each line twice— once backwards—to make the letters easier to read.

Laser   A laser is simply a beam of light that's focused by a mirror. A small laser in your printer actually writes the characters on a piece of paper; some black dust called toner is passed over the paper; the toner sticks to the places where the laser light touched, and then the sheet travels through a heater that fuses the black toner to the paper. Magic! Your words are printed. Some so-called laser printers use LEDs or light-emitting diodes instead of laser beams. Same results.

Bubble jet   Similar to the laser, the bubble jet printer sprays special ink onto the page in patterns cut by heat. Bubble jet printers are typically less expensive than laser printers.

Which type of printer should you buy? That depends on the type of work you'll be doing on your computer. More important, review your needs—and your budget—with your local computer shop. They can help you make a good choice.

Copiers   Copy machines can be very useful to your electrical contracting business, especially if you don't have a PC and a printer. You'll want to conveniently copy outgoing correspondence, plans, proposals, contracts, agreements, drawings, procedures, and other business documents. A good copier can be purchased for less than $500. If you're producing a client newsletter, your own brochures, direct mail pieces, or other marketing documents, your copy machine can be more cost-effective than running down to the copy shop or printer for a few copies every day.

Features you'll want to look for in a copier might include enlargement and reduction, paper trays, collating of multiple copies, and reproduction of photos. You won't need a copier the first day you open your doors, so wait until you have a genuine need before you buy. By then, you'll know what features you require.

If you purchase a medium to large copier, you should consider a service contract, especially if routine maintenance calls are included at a nominal charge. In your busy office, you might forget to perform such maintenance, and it can eventually add up to a major repair. However, be careful of costs; some maintenance programs are more profitable for the copy machine representative than the machines themselves are.

Computer software

Now that you understand the basics of computers, you can better see how computer programs can work for you, and even though computer hardware is discussed here first, you'll probably select the computer programs or software before you choose the hardware to run them on. A *computer program* is a set of instructions written in a language that your computer understands. The program can be as simple as putting your words onto paper or as complex as drafting a plan.

Word processors

Word processors simply process words, letting you type words into the computer, move them around, insert words, take some out, and make any changes you want before you print them to paper. You can use word processors to write letters or other documents to suppliers, clients, prospects, employees, regulatory boards, or anyone else. I've been using computer word processors for ten years, and I'd never go back to manual or even electric typewriters. Word processors let you change your mind.

You don't need a fancy word processing program. If one comes with your computer, use it. If not, you can buy a good one for less than $200 and a great one for less than $500. You only need a great one if you're publishing brochures or other sales documents. Many of the budget word processors also include a built-in function that will help you check spelling. Your high-school English teacher will never know!

Spreadsheets

A *spreadsheet* is to numbers what a word processor is to words. A spreadsheet puts numbers into readable form. It's roughly named after the wide, multicolumn sheets that accountants use to make journal entries. You'll soon find yourself using a spreadsheet software program in many ways.

For example, you can purchase a basic spreadsheet program for about a hundred dollars, and the program will let you enter horizontal "rows" or lines of job expense names (Subcontractor Labor, Materials, etc.) and vertical "columns" of numbers ($428.52, etc.). Most important, you can then tell the program to total any or all of the columns or rows and it will do so in less than a second. If you update a number, it automatically recalculates the total for you.

Fancier and more costly spreadsheets can follow instructions you write, called "macros," to do special calculations automatically. You might want to write a macro that will select all of the invoices more than 60 days old and total them up. Better spreadsheets will also do fancy graphs and pie charts that impress bankers and other financial types.

Databases

A database software program is much like an index card file box. You can write thousands or even millions of pieces of information and store it. However, a database program is even better than a file box because it finds information in the files in a fraction of a second.

The most common application of a database program for electrical contractors is a client file. If you only have a few clients, this might not be necessary. However, as you add clients, prospects, and other business contacts, you might soon need at least a simple database program to keep track of them.

Your database will keep information about your prospect/client's names, addresses, cities and states, zip codes, phone and fax numbers, contact names, annual budget information, lists of projects you've completed for them, information about their businesses, even their hobbies. Then, if you want to find out how many of your clients are located in a specific city and did more than $50,000 in business with you last year, you simply tell your database program to search its files for you. It's that easy.

One note on selecting a database program: there are so-called "relational" databases and "flat-file" databases. Unless you're going to catalog all of your tools, materials, and every bit of information in your business, you probably won't need to spend the extra money for a relational database. Buy a flat file version at a lower price.

Integrated programs

Speaking of relational, you can purchase integrated software programs that combine the three primary programs: word processor, spreadsheet, and database. Ask your local computer store to recommend a good integrated program. Some also include other related programs such as communications software that lets your PC talk to other PCs over the phone using "modems." The cost of a good-quality integrated system is usually much less than the total price for the individual components.

Here's another plus to integrated programs: they talk to each other. That is, your word processor can include financial figures from your spreadsheet in your correspondence, and send it to someone listed in your database. Just as important, an integrated group of programs developed by a single software firm will have similar commands in each program. You won't have to learn three separate programs; you'll learn one larger program. Integrated programs are especially recommended for those who don't want to spend a lot of time selecting and learning numerous software programs.

Other helpful programs

Once you're hooked on computers, you'll buy a PC magazine or two, get on someone's mailing list, and soon be saturated with information about new software programs. The following might help you sort the information out.

CAD is an acronym for computer-aided design. It's a drafting system on your PC that helps you to draw plans quickly and easily. DOS stands for the disk operating system that comes with your computer and translates commands like "copy" into a language that your PC understands.

Windows is a program developed by Microsoft that lets you open a number of overlapping boxes or windows on your computer screen, each with different programs in them. You can be writing a letter when a client calls, and you can quickly switch to a window with information about the client and your current project.

Shell programs make your PC easier to use and perform a number of important maintenance functions. They're called shells because they wrap around the less-friendly DOS program to make it easier for you to copy, delete, prune, and manage files. Some shell programs also include *utilities* or special programs that help you keep your data organized and safe.

Backup programs let you copy all the information on your hard disk onto diskettes as a backup of your system. Backup programs ensure that if something happens to your hard disk and you lose your data, you still haven't lost it. Of course, this means you must back up your hard disk regularly, a process that takes only a few minutes every day and is well worth the time.

Vertical software

The programs I just discussed are called "horizontal" software programs because they're used by nearly all businesses, not just electrical contractors. So, *vertical software* is programs that are written specifically for your trade. Some will be advertised in electrical trade and contracting trade journals. You can find other programs by talking with noncompeting electrical contractors or local association members.

Here are some of the features you can expect to find in computer software programs written for electrical contractors and related businesses:

- *Estimating* helps you develop proposals and bid for clients by entering in the specific requirements of the job and letting the program do all of the calculations and furnish you with a printable estimate (chapter 4).
- *Billing* generates Quotes, Time & Material, Time & Material Not To Exceed, and other types of invoices.

- *Job tracking* keeps track of individual job income and costs in order to report profitability.
- Some *CAD* (computer-aided design) programs are written especially for electrical contractors.
- *Interface* lets you import information from or export to your spreadsheet program with the push of a button.

Some vertical program packages will include their own word processor, spreadsheet, or database programs. Others will allow you to integrate their data into your favorite programs. A few will do both. An excellent source of information on computer software is the *Software Catalog for Home Builders*, published by the National Association of Home Builders (15th and M Streets N.W., Washington, DC 20005).

As an electrical contractor, you have a world of tools and equipment available to you. It's expensive, but it can be very profitable to own. You might or might not use all of the tools that technology offers, but knowing what they are and what they can do for you will help you keep ahead of the pack. You'll be successful longer.

CHAPTER 4

Working with money

MONEY IS A DEVICE for keeping score. You work six hours and someone gives you the amount of money that you both agree that your time and skill is worth. You then take that money and exchange it for food, or clothing, or entertainment at a price that you both agree that the product or service is worth. Money is simply a tool for measuring the value of things—not life.

In this chapter, I'll cover the many ways that you can get the highest value for your services as well as receive the highest value for your money. First, I'll determine how much money you'll need to start your electrical contracting business. Next, I'll consider the many sources for this capital. Then I'll discuss how you can build good credit. Finally, you'll learn how to set your fees and how to present them in the form of estimates and bids. If you've been unsure of starting your own electrical contracting firm because you don't have the money or you lack financial experience, this chapter is especially for you.

How much money do you need?

You've decided to start your own electrical contracting business. However, you're not sure how much money you'll need. Let's develop a capital requirements work-sheet for your new business venture. Let's consider start-up costs and operating costs.

Estimating start-up costs

The first step in estimating capital requirements is determining how much it will cost to start up your business. Answer the following questions:

- How much will it cost to prepare your selected business site as an electrical contractor's office?
- How much will it cost to add the tools and equipment you need to start your business?
- How much will it cost to equip your office with desks, chairs, shelves, and other office equipment?
- How much will it cost to purchase initial office supplies?

- How much will it cost to purchase a start-up inventory of electrical materials and supplies?
- How much will it cost to equip your office with necessary telephone, answering machine, fax, computer, printer, and software?
- How much will it cost to make the necessary utility deposits?
- How much will it cost to obtain the required licenses, permits, and certifications?
- How much will it cost to purchase initial insurance coverage and surety bonds?
- How much will it cost to hire legal and financial professionals to help you set your business up right?
- How much will it cost to purchase initial signs?
- How much will it cost to advertise the opening of your business?
- How much will it cost to cover unanticipated expenses?
- What's the total of the preceding start-up costs?

Estimating operating costs

Once your electrical contracting business is set up and initial start-up costs are covered, you'll be in business. You'll have income and expenses. Your next step in determining capital requirements for your business is to estimate your expenses for an average month. Answer the following questions:

- How much money do you need each month to live comfortably without a significant change in your current lifestyle?
- How much money do you need each month to pay employees (not subcontractors) you plan to hire?
- How much money do you need each month to pay the rent on your home office, vehicle office, service shop, shared office, or your own office?
- How much money do you need each month to pay the utilities (including telephone service) for your office?
- How much money do you need each month to maintain a minimum amount of advertising (yellow pages contracts, service directory listings, etc.)?

- How much money do you need each month to continue insurance premiums for your business?
- How much money do you need each month to replace office supplies used in your business?
- How much money do you need each month to replace electrical materials and supplies used during the month?
- How much money do you need each month to pay required local, state, and federal taxes?
- How much money do you need each month to maintain your equipment and vehicles?
- What's the total of your estimated operating expenses for an average month?

Estimating total capital requirements

A large number of small businesses fail each year—some of them established by otherwise qualified tradespeople. There are a number of reasons for these failures, but one of the main reasons is insufficient funds. Too many entrepreneurs try to start up and operate a business without sufficient capital.

So how much is enough? Obviously, the more the better. However, a reasonable amount to have is enough to cover your start-up expenses and three months of operating expenses. So, add the total of the start-up expenses you've calculated to a total of three months of estimated operating expenses. That's the minimum amount of capital or money you should have before your start your electrical contracting business. If you have the resources, a six-month reserve of estimated operating expenses is much better.

Now let's consider some exceptions to this guideline. If you have a working spouse with a sufficient income to cover household expenses while your business gets on its feet, your capital requirements will be much less than that of a "sole breadwinner" with eight kids. In addition, if you have a number of regular clients lined up who have already made firm commitments to you for work, you won't need as much operating reserves. However, keep in mind that, even if you start work for these clients tomorrow, you might not get paid for 60 or even 90 days. The best advice from those who have been there is, "Build up your reserves before you start and keep your operating expenses at a bare minimum until your business is established."

Few people know their true financial net worth: how much they own minus how much they owe. Before you decide to start your electrical contracting business, you must first determine your financial net worth.

Assets are simply what you own. Maybe you have more financial assets that you might be aware of. First, there are two types of assets: short term and long term. A *short-term asset* is one that can be quickly liquidated or turned into cash. If someone owes you $1000 and promises to pay you next week, that's a short-term asset. If they won't pay you for another five years, that's a *long-term asset*. A short-term asset is usually defined as one that can be turned into cash within one year. So, an asset is important, but also important is its "liquidity" or how quickly it can be turned into cash if necessary.

- How much cash do you have in your checking accounts, savings accounts, in a safe deposit box, or other resources?
- How much money do you have in certificates of deposit, savings certificates, stocks, bonds, securities, and other easily sold short-term assets?
- How much money is owed to you (accounts receivable)?
- What's the market value of real estate that you own (how much could you sell it for)?
- What's the book value of automobiles and other vehicles that you own—even if you have a loan against them?
- What's the cash value of insurance policies in your name?
- What's the value of other assets you own (furniture, jewelry, tools, equipment, etc.)?
- What's the total value of all short-term assets (those you could turn into cash within one year)?
- What's the total value of all long-term assets (those that require more than one year to turn into cash)?
- What's the total value of all short- and long-term assets?

Your liabilities

Your *liabilities* are the money that you owe to others. Some are secured by assets; others are secured by your "signature" or personal pledge to pay. As with assets, there are short-term liabilities and long-term liabilities. A short-term liability is one that will be paid off within a year, such as a credit card. A long-term liability is one that will take more than a year to pay off, such as a car loan.

- How much do you owe on credit cards?
- How much do you owe on installment payments for furniture, appliances, or other household items?
- How much do you owe on your vehicles?
- How much do you owe on local, state, or federal taxes?
- How much do you owe on education loans?
- How much do you owe on a mortgage or note against your home or other real estate?
- Do you have any second mortgages on any real estate?
- How much do you owe on other liabilities?
- What's the total value of all short-term liabilities (those that must be paid off within one year)?
- What's the total value of all long-term liabilities (those that won't be paid off within the next year)?
- What's the total value of all short- and long-term liabilities?

Estimating total net worth

The purpose of this exercise is to discover your total financial *net worth*. That's your assets minus your liabilities. In other words, if you sold everything you owned and paid off everything you owed, how much would you have left?

Don't be discouraged by the results of this exercise. There are a number of things that you can do to improve your financial net worth. In fact, once your business becomes successful your total net worth will grow. You'll own more and more assets while owing less and less people. Even if the total is in negative numbers—you actually owe more than you own—this worksheet will help you learn what to do about it.

Okay. You now know how much you have and how much you need to start your electrical contracting business. However, maybe you've determined that you don't have enough assets to start your business with sufficient funds, or maybe you're determined to put six months' expense reserve in the bank before you start. Here are some sources for additional assets.

By now, you've probably met hundreds of people in your lifetime—maybe thousands. Each is a potential source of assets. You're not begging from them. You're simply asking them if they want to invest money in a potentially profitable enterprise and reap some reward for their investment. Who?

- Relatives.
- Friends.
- Current employers.
- Past employers.
- Your banker.
- Your accountant.
- Your lawyer.
- Your doctor.
- Your prospective clients.
- Your suppliers.
- Members of associations, clubs, and churches to which you belong.
- Friends of friends of friends.

Some of these contacts won't be interested; others might want to participate in the investment but don't want to put in more than a thousand dollars. Still others will become your primary resources. Why would they do so? Because they expect a return on their investment. So, develop a business plan that will help investors understand what you're doing, how much it will cost, what you need, and what they'll get for their risk. In nearly every case, you won't be looking for general partners who advise you on how to run your business—in fact, you don't want that. You probably want investors or limited partners who will invest money but stay out of the day-to-day management.

Where can you get more money?

Who you know

Venture capitalists   There are people in the world who look for small business opportunities in which to invest—at a significant rate of return on their investment. They're called "venture capitalists." You can find them through your banker, financial institutions, your accountant, venture capital directories, investment brokers, and ads in metropolitan newspapers. I'll discuss venture capitalists in greater detail in chapter 7.

Commercial bankers   Bankers are much like you. They have products that they receive from others—money—and they sell it at a profit to someone who needs it. This is not charity. It's good business. However, bankers are notorious for not being risk takers. The caricature that bankers carry umbrellas year-round is not true, but it is based on truth. They're stewardly.

So, your approach to bankers will be conservative. If you want to borrow from them, you must have a complete written description of what you want to do, how you plan to do it, how much it will cost, and what you expect to profit from it. Most important: how will you pay off the loan?

There will be more on bankers and how to work with them later in this chapter. Bankers are important to your business, and your business is important to them.

The SBA   In chapter 2 I covered the Small Business Administration and how it helps businesses start and develop. One of the most noteworthy services they offer is guaranteeing loans made by bankers who would not otherwise loan money to new businesses. Take time to review the SBA loan guarantee program and then talk with an SBA office in your region.

SBICs   The Small Business Investment Act allowed the SBA to license small business investment companies or SBICs. The SBIC supplies equity capital to companies that are unable to raise funds from other sources. The SBIC is privately owned, operated for profit, and chartered under state law. Your regional SBA office can help you find SBICs in your area that might be able to assist you in finding additional assets.

Proprietorships and partnerships can receive long-term loans from an SBIC as long as the loan is secured by real estate or other collateral. Corporations can receive funds from long-term loans or equity financing. Equity financing can be in the form of stock purchased in your company by the SBIC, or loans with stock as equity, or other collateral.

If you incorporate your business, you can sell shares or portions of it to investors. The type of investments they make, the risks involved, how they receive their profits or dividends, and how dividends to them are taxed depend on the type of stock purchased. Talk with your attorney or your accountant about how to sell stock in your state to develop additional capital for your business.

Stock

The ability to get a loan when you need it is as necessary to the operation of your business as the right equipment is. Before a bank or any other lending agency will lend you money, the loan officer must feel satisfied with the answers to these five questions:

Getting a loan

- What sort of person are you, the prospective borrower? In most cases, the character of the borrower comes first. Next is your ability to manage your business.

- What are you going to do with the money? The answer to this question will determine the type of loan and the duration. Money to be used for the purchase of job materials will require quicker repayment than money used to buy fixed assets.

- When and how do you plan to pay it back? Your banker's judgment of your business ability and the type of loan will be a deciding factor in the answer to this question.

- Is the cushion in the loan large enough? In other words, does the amount requested make suitable allowance for unexpected developments? The banker decides this question on the basis of your financial statement, which sets forth the condition of your business and on the collateral pledged.

- What's the outlook for business in general and for your business particularly?

Adequate financial data is a "must." The banker wants to make loans to businesses that are solvent, profitable, and growing. The two basic financial statements used to determine those conditions are the balance sheet and the income statement. The balance sheet is the major yardstick for solvency and the income statement. A continuous series of these two statements over a period of time is the principal device for measuring financial stability and growth potential.

In interviewing loan applicants and in studying their records, the banker is especially interested in the following facts and figures:

- General information. Are the books and records up-to-date and in good condition? What's the condition of the accounts payable? Of notes payable? What are the salaries of the owner-manager and other company officers? Are all taxes being paid currently? What's the order backlog? What's the number of employees? What's the insurance coverage?

- Accounts receivable. Are there indications that some of the accounts receivable have already been pledged to another creditor? What's the accounts receivable turnover? Is the accounts receivable total weakened because many customers are far behind in their payments? Has a large enough reserve been set up to cover questionable accounts? How much do the largest accounts owe, and what percentage of your total accounts does this amount represent?

- Fixed assets. What's the type, age, and condition of the equipment? What are the depreciation policies? What are the details of mortgages or conditional sales contracts? What are the future acquisitions plans?

For many people, additional capital needed to start a business comes from getting a loan from a banker, a venture capitalist, a supplier, or other sources. What types of loans are available? Also, how can you get a loan at the lowest rates? Let's consider these significant questions.

When you set out to borrow money for your firm, it's important to know the kind of money you need from a bank or other lending institution. There are three kinds of money: short term, term money, and equity capital.

Keep in mind that the purpose for which the funds are to be used is an important factor in deciding the kind of money needed. Even so, deciding what kind of money to use is not always easy. It's sometimes complicated by the fact that you might be using some of the various kinds of money at the same time and for identical purposes.

The important distinction between the types of money is the source of repayment. Generally, short-term loans are repaid from the liquidation of current assets that they've financed. Long-term loans are usually repaid from earnings.

You can use short-term bank loans for purposes such as the financing of accounts receivable for, say, 30 to 60 days, or you can use them for purposes that take longer to pay off, such as the purchase of needed equipment. Usually, lenders expect short-term loans to be repaid after their purposes have been served. For example, accounts receivable loans should be paid off when the outstanding accounts have been paid by the borrower's customers.

Banks grant such money either on your general credit reputation with an unsecured loan or on a secured loan. The unsecured loan is the most frequently used form of bank credit for short-term purposes. You don't have to put up collateral because the bank relies on your credit reputation. The secured loan involves a pledge of some or all of your business' assets. The bank requires security as a protection for its depositors against the risks that are involved, even in business situations where the chances of success are good.

Term borrowing provides money you plan to pay back over a fairly long time. Some people break it down into two forms: intermediate (one to five years) and long-term (more than five years). However, for your purpose of matching the kind of money to the needs of your company, think of term borrowing

Types of loans

Short-term bank loans

Term borrowing

as a kind of money that you probably will pay back in periodic installments from earnings.

Equity capital

Some people confuse term borrowing and *equity (or investment) capital*. Yet there's a big difference. You don't have to repay equity money. It's money you get by selling interest in your business. You take people into your company who are willing to risk their money in it. They're interested in potential income rather than an immediate return on their investment.

Let's discuss loans and other types of credit. There are numerous types of loans available, all with their own unique name, depending on the lender. Even so, loans fall into one of the following categories:

Signature loan

A *signature loan* holds nothing in collateral except your promise to pay the lender back on terms that you both agree on. If your money needs are small, you only need the money for a short time, your credit rating is excellent, and you're willing to pay a premium interest rate because you aren't using physical collateral, a signature or character loan is an easy way to borrow money in a hurry.

Term loan

A *term loan* is one that requires good credit and typically some type of collateral, either equipment or real estate. A short-term loan is one of a year or less in length. A long-term loan is paid off in a period longer than a year. Payments can be set up to be monthly, quarterly, annually, or seasonally, depending on security and your business' cash flow.

Collateral loan

A *collateral loan* is one in which some type of asset is put up as collateral; if you don't make payments, you'll lose the asset. So, the lender wants to make sure that the asset is worth more than the value of the loan, usually 50 to 75 percent of asset value. An electrical contractor often doesn't have sufficient collateral—real estate, vehicles, inventory—to secure a collateral loan unless he or she uses personal assets such as a home.

Many a small business has found at least some of its funding in the owner's personal credit card. Tools, equipment, materials, fees, office supplies, office expenses, and other costs can be covered with your personal credit card. However, interest rates on credit cards are extremely high—sometimes double of what you might pay on a collateral loan—but, credit cards can also get you quick cash when you need it. If this is an option for you, talk to your credit card representative about raising your credit limit. It will be much easier to do so while you're employed by someone else instead of self-employed.

Personal credit cards

A *line of credit* is similar to a loan except that you don't borrow it all at once. You get a credit limit, say $50,000, that you can tap anytime you need money for business purposes. The most common is the "revolving" line of credit that you can draw from when business is off and pay back when business is good, providing that you don't exceed your limit. A line of credit is an excellent way for an electrical contractor to work through the ups and downs of seasonal business. With some restrictions, a line of credit can be established using a portion of your home equity as collateral. Using a secured equity earns you a lower interest rate.

Line of credit

A *cosigner loan* should be one of the most popular loans for small businesses, but many business people never consider it. Simply, you find a cosigner or a comaker with good credit or assets who will guarantee the loan with you. If you have a potential investor who believes in your business but doesn't want to put up the cash you need, ask him or her to cosign for a loan with you. Your chances of receiving the loan are much better. Some cosigners will require that you pay them a fee of one to four percent of the balance, or a flat fee; others will do it for your friendship or the hope of future business from you. In any case, consider this as an excellent source of capital for your new contracting business.

Cosigner loan

If you're purchasing a contractor's vehicle, special equipment, or other assets for your business, the supplier might loan or lease the equipment to you. This often requires about 25 percent down, so be ready to come up with some cash of your own.

Equipment loan

Factoring Once you've completed some jobs and billed your clients, you don't have to wait for them to send you the money. You can sell your accounts receivable—at a discount, of course. This is called *factoring*. Or you can use your best accounts receivable as collateral for a loan. There are certainly some pluses and minuses to this method of raising capital, but it's a commonly used option. Talk to your accountant, banker, financial adviser, or another contractor about finding a reputable factoring broker.

Trade credit Depending on your suppliers, you can build working capital for your business by developing *trade credit*. That is, once approved, your electrical materials supplier will give you additional time in which to pay your bill to them. You might start off with 60 days' credit, then earn 90 days and even 120 days before you must pay their bill. There will typically be a finance charge on the balance that's more than 30 days old, but some suppliers will give you low- or no-interest "loans" of materials for this period. Compare prices versus credit terms as you shop for primary and secondary suppliers.

Collateral As previously noted, sometimes your signature is the only security the bank needs when making a loan. At other times, the bank requires additional assurance that the money will be repaid. The kind and amount of security depends on the bank and on the borrower's situation. Of course, a banker will attempt to get as much security as possible, sometimes even more than is required.

If the loan required can't be justified by the borrower's financial statements alone, a pledge of security might bridge the gap. The types of security are the following.

Endorsers, comakers, and guarantors Borrowers often get other people to sign a note in order to bolster the borrower's credit. These endorsers are contingently liable for the note they sign. If the borrower fails to pay up, the bank expects the endorser to make the note good. Sometimes the endorser might be asked to pledge assets or securities, too. A *comaker* is someone who creates an obligation jointly with the borrower. In such cases, the bank can collect directly from either the maker or the comaker. A *guarantor* is someone who guarantees the payment of a note by signing a guaranty commitment. Both private and government lenders often require guarantees from officers of a corporation in order to assure continuity of effective management. Sometimes a manufacturer or supplier will act as guarantor for customers.

The *assigned lease* as security is similar to the guarantee. An assigned lease is used, for example, in some franchise situations. The bank lends the money on a building and takes a mortgage. Then the lease, which the dealer and the parent franchise company work out, is assigned so that the bank automatically receives the rent payments. In this manner, the bank is guaranteed repayment of the loan.

Assignment of leases

If you buy equipment such as a contractor's truck or other construction equipment, you might want to get a *chattel mortgage* loan. You give the bank a lien on the equipment you're buying. The bank also evaluates the present and future market value of the equipment being used to secure the loan. How rapidly will it depreciate? Does the borrower have the necessary fire, theft, property damage, and public liability insurance on the equipment? The banker has to be sure that the borrower protects the equipment used as chattel.

Chattel mortgages

Real estate is another form of collateral for long-term loans. When taking a real estate mortgage, the bank finds out the location of the real estate, its physical condition, its foreclosure value, and the amount of insurance carried on the property. Many electrical contractors use their home as collateral for a real estate loan to begin their business.

Real estate

Many banks lend money on accounts receivable. In effect, you're counting on your customers to pay your note. The bank might take accounts receivable on a notification or a non-notification plan. Under the notification plan, the purchaser of the goods is informed by the bank that his or her account has been assigned to it and must make account payments directly to the bank. Under the non-notification plan, your customers continue to pay you the sums due on their accounts and you

Accounts receivable

pay the bank. Unfortunately, under a notification plan, your customers might assume that your business is financially unsound and reduce future business with you.

Savings account Sometimes you can get a loan by assigning a savings account to the bank. In such cases, the bank gets an assignment from you and keeps your passbook. If you assign an account in another bank as collateral, the lending bank asks the other bank to mark its records to show that the account is held as collateral.

Life insurance Another kind of collateral is life insurance. Banks will lend up to the cash value of a life insurance policy. You have to assign the policy to the bank. If the policy is on the life of an executive of a small corporation, corporate resolutions must be made authorizing the assignment. Most insurance companies allow you to sign the policy back to the original beneficiary when the assignment to the bank ends. Some people like to use life insurance as collateral rather than borrow directly from insurance companies. One reason is that a bank loan is often more convenient to obtain and can usually be obtained at a lower interest rate.

Stocks and bonds If you use stocks and bonds as collateral, they must be marketable. As a protection against market declines and possible expenses of liquidation, banks usually lend no more than 75 percent of the market value of high-grade stock. On federal government or municipal bonds, they might be willing to lend 90 percent or more of their market value. The bank might ask the borrower for additional security or payment whenever the market value of the stocks or bonds drops below the bank's required margin.

How much money should you borrow?

The amount of money you need to borrow depends on the purpose for which you need funds. Figuring the amount of money required for business expansion is relatively easy. However, determining the money you'll need for business start-up is more difficult, as you've learned.

While rule-of-thumb ratios might be helpful as a starting point, a detailed projection of sources and uses of funds over some future period of time—usually for 12 months—is a better approach. In this way, the characteristics of the particular situation can be taken into account. Such a projection is developed through the combination of a predicted budget and a cash forecast.

The budget is based on recent operating experience plus your best judgment of performance during the coming period. The cash forecast is your estimates of cash receipts and disbursements during the budget period. Thus, the budget and the cash forecast together represent your plan for meeting your working capital requirements.

To plan your working capital requirements, it's important to know the cash flow that your business will generate. This involves simply a consideration of all elements of cash receipts and disbursements at the time they occur. These elements are listed in the income statement that has been adapted to show cash flow. They should be projected for each month.

Money is a commodity, bought and sold by lenders. Just like other products, you can often save money by shopping around. Here are some points to consider as you shop for money.

How much should you pay for money?

First, are there any loan fees or other charges required to set up or service the loan? Some lenders will require that a loan fee of one or two percent, or more, be paid in advance. Others will even roll the loan fee into the loan—so you actually pay interest on interest. Others will deduct a monthly service fee from each payment as it's made. This arrangement is not necessarily bad; after all, the lender must get his or her profit from you in some manner. Just make sure that you understand what the actual cost of the loan is before you agree to it. You also need to know actual interest rates as you compare rates between lenders.

Second, consider whether your best option is fixed-rate or variable-rate interest. Fixed-rate interest means that the interest rate charged by the lender is the same throughout the life of the loan. Variable-rate interest can vary during the term of the loan, based on some outside factor. This factor is usually the cost of the money to the lender. The difference between the lender's cost and what he or she charges you is called the "spread." From that spread comes sales costs, office overhead, salaries, and profit. The spread is also based on the amount of risk he or she is taking in loaning the money to you. Higher risk means a higher spread. There are numerous indexes used to establish the "cost" of money. Review all of the options with your lender, ask which one makes the most sense for your needs, and get a second opinion.

Keep in mind that variable-rate interest reduces the amount of risk lenders are taking, especially on long-term loans. They're virtually assured that, unless the money market goes crazy, they'll get their margin of profit from every dollar you pay. Lower risk means lower rates. The point is that you shouldn't disqualify variable-rate loans from consideration. In many cases, they cost less than other loans, and many lenders are more willing to make them.

To make sure that you pay the best interest rate available, don't jump on the first loan offer that comes to you. Shop around and compare. You might eventually decide to take that first offer, but only because you've found nothing better.

However, don't worry about getting the absolute lowest interest rate available. You might want to accept your regular banker's loan terms, even though it's a quarter of a percentage point higher, in order to maintain a mutually profitable relationship. That quarter point might only mean a few dollars to you, but it will reinforce your business relationship with your banker.

Credit

Credit is simply someone else's faith that you'll keep your promise to them. You buy a business truck on credit, and the lender believes that you'll pay him or her what you've borrowed—or that you have assets that the lender can sell to cover what you've borrowed. So, how do you build credit? Easy. You borrow small amounts, pay it back, borrow larger amounts, pay it back, and so on. It also helps to have some assets, like stocks or land, that are already paid off, or in which you have some equity.

A good way to start building your business credit is to use personal assets—signature, real estate equity—as collateral for your business. One enterprising contractor simply applied for a credit card in his business name from the same company that sponsored his long-standing personal credit card. He asked for a small credit limit, used it and paid it off, then asked for an increased credit limit. Meantime, he used the credit card as a reference for a new account with a supplier. Other new business people use equity in their homes or investment land as collateral for credit with banks and suppliers, as discussed earlier.

How much should you charge?

You might consider that this question—how much should I charge?—is one of the most important questions in this book. It really isn't. Many other questions will be just as important to the success of your business. However, this question is often the first one that new electrical contractors ask. So let's get it answered.

Let's consider the three Cs of pricing:

- Cost.
- Competition.
- Consumer.

How much does my service cost me?

Once you've established your start-up costs and your monthly operating costs, as presented earlier in this chapter, you'll have a pretty good idea of how much your service will cost you to furnish to your customers. However, there's one more important factor that you need: your amount of available time.

A month with 20 work days offers you approximately 160 hours of your time that you can sell to customers. You might wind up working more, but 160 is probably all you'll be able to bill to clients. In fact, depending on the size and structure of your business, you might not be able to bill that many. Many one-person businesses require about a quarter of their time to market their services and to manage the business. So, they're down to 120 billable hours per month, unless they do all marketing and management after normal working hours. If the operating costs calculated earlier total $6,000 a month, that amount is divided by 120 billable hours to come up with an hourly fee of $50. With monthly operating expenses of $4,000 and 160 billable hours in a month, the hourly rate becomes $25. Quite a range: $25 to $50 per hour.

How much are my competitors charging?

A few telephone calls should get you the rates charged by your competitors. Of course, you must make sure that you're comparing apples with apples. Your competitor might not have your level of skill in this area, or he or she might have more, or your competitor might be including costs for some specialized equipment that you don't have yet.

Why should you care what your competitors charge? Because your clients will probably get bids from them and from you. You don't necessarily have to match or beat their bids, but you do need to know what their rates are so that you can help the client make a fair comparison.

How much does the customer expect to pay?

This is a toughie. The question isn't how much will the customer pay; it's how much does the customer expect to pay? The difference is expectations. You might get some customers for your service to pay an excessive fee for awhile, but they'll soon move to other sources. What you want to find out is what they think your service is actually worth to them. Most understand that, if they pay you too little, you'll soon be out of business and you won't be there to help them in the future. They might not admit it, but they know it.

How can you know how much the consumer expects to pay for your skills? Ask a few of them. They might tell you what they're used to paying, what they think is a fair price, or maybe what they wish they were paying. Take all of this into consideration. Ask them the question, then let them take a few minutes to explain why they think so. You'll get some valuable insight into what customers expect from you, as well as what you should expect from them. As before, make sure that you're comparing similar skills and similar fees. A customer might expect more skills than you can offer—or maybe fewer.

Establishing your hourly service rate is a simple process of adding overhead and expected profit to the cost of labor. If an employee is paid $16 per hour and has a payroll tax/benefits package worth $4 per hour, add to this your overhead, say $9 an hour, and your expected profit, such as 10 percent of the labor/benefits cost, or $2. You come up with a total of $31 per hour. If you pay your employees for travel time, but the customer doesn't, then you need to add a charge for travel. If it's typically 10 percent of the workday, then add that percent of the labor/benefits package, or $2 in this example, to your hourly service rate. It's now up to $33.00 per hour.

Price versus value

Now you know what your time costs you, what your competitors charge for their time and skills, and what customers expect to pay for your time and skills. So which figure is right? All and none. What you want is a price that will drive away about 20 percent of your prospects as too high, and another 20 percent as too low.

Here's a technique that will make your business more profitable, put your business above your competitors, and keep your customers happy: sell value, not price. How can a fancy restaurant charge five times as much as the diner next door for the exact same ingredients? They sell value. Call it ambiance or image or snobbery or whatever. The fancy restaurant makes the client's purchase an event rather than just a transaction. The fancy restaurant treats the client like a person rather than a number, gives extra service, uses finer dinnerware, and decorates the food to look appetizing.

You'll see the same technique—selling value rather than price—in any competitive business where one firm wants to stand out above the others. Chevies are sold on price; Cadillacs are sold on value—and both are built by General Motors. Value says that, whether the price is large or small, you'll get your money's worth.

So how does an electrical contractor sell value? By offering services that other contractors don't, or by maintaining a clean and orderly image with well-maintained trucks and signage, or by simply turning questions of price into discussions of value.

Extra services   There are many extra services that don't cost much to implement and yet add value to an electrical contractor's service. Depending on the type of electrical work done, some contractors hire a part-time, minimum-wage cleanup person—usually a high-schooler or college student—who cleans up after the electricians and even other contractors at the job site. The cost to the contractor is minimal and is usually factored into his or her hourly rate, but this extra-mile service is a courtesy that few contractors offer. Other electrical contractors add value by offering to produce plans or diagrams or to handle other required paperwork for the general contractor or client.

Value-priced electrical contractors can step ahead of their competition by taking on any jobs that the client might normally have to handle. A contractor who repairs industrial controls or motors might offer a free inspection service on a regular basis to anyone, client or not. This service gives the contractor another chance to sell his or her value to the client or prospect.

Think about what "extra services" you can offer in your specialty that will set you apart from your competitors and help you sell value rather than price.

Professional image   Imagine looking on a grocer's shelf and seeing a can of tomato sauce that's discolored and dented, and the label is torn. You'd probably pass that product by for one that looks neat, fresh, and undamaged. Yet, the contents of each can might be of exactly the same quality. Appearance does make a difference—even in the contracting business. For just a few dollars more, your electrical contracting business can develop a clean, professional appearance that will tell prospects and customers that you offer quality.

First, make sure that your vehicles are all well-painted and reasonably clean, especially if they have your business name written on them. One contractor purchased a spray can of paint that matched his older truck's paint and made sure that any job-site scrapes were quickly and easily covered. Another contractor paid his children a few dollars every Sunday afternoon for the weekly truck wash—and twice a week during the rainy season.

Signage is important. Go to your local library and check the yellow pages in out-of-state phone books for electrical contractor ads. Is there a design or insignia that appeals to you? Modify it to fit your own business and make it your design. Many electrical contractors use a lightning bolt in their design because it says "electricity" and because it's easy for a non-artist to use a straight edge to draw a lightning bolt. Also check with local sign shops for their cost of designing signs for you. You'll want signs on your vehicles, your shop, and your office. The only exception is a home office in a neighborhood that doesn't allow business signs in residential areas.

At a job site, a clean, well-painted truck with an attractive business sign will typically stand out among the shabby and dirty vehicles parked there. It will tell your client and passers-by that you're a quality contractor who cares about your image.

Talk value

The question of price always comes up with a client or prospect. Many contractors dread it and would rather avoid the discussion. Successful contractors encourage the question of price because they want to talk about value. They want the clients to know why they should pay as much or more for the contractor's services.

Price is the cost of something. Value is the worth of something. Why is your service worth something?

- You're knowledgeable; you know about electricity and how to manage it.
- You're efficient; you know how to work smart to get the job done in less time.
- You're honest; you won't knowingly mislead your client or charge for services not performed.
- You're helpful; you want to solve the client's problem, not just perform a job.
- You're fair; you charge a reasonable fee for an important service.
- You're accessible; you respond to questions, you answer telephone calls, you follow up with clients.

Successful electrical contractors don't shun the question of pricing or apologize for high rates. They look forward to the question so they can explain why their service is worth more than that of other electrical contractors. They sell—and give—value.

How do I estimate a job?

An *estimate* is a calculation of your value—the customer's cost—stated in dollars. Clients of your electrical contracting service will require written estimates, so you must learn how to write job estimates that are accurate, fair, and profitable for both you and the client. There are forms and procedures that will help you estimate costs and value. There are also computer programs that automate the estimating process and print out bids for jobs.

Estimating forms

Shown on pages 90 through 96 are some of the estimating forms available through the National Electrical Contractors Association (7315 Wisconsin Ave., Bethesda, MD 20814). Shown on pages 92 and 93 is a take-off sheet. As you read the job's electrical plans, you determine how many of each component you'll need to do the job according to the plan. You might also make notes to recommend any changes to the plan that will make it more functional or cost-effective for your client. Notice that there are no dollar amounts on these take-off sheets—just the number of components required to complete the job.

The full page illustration on page 94 is a typical pricing sheet. Materials that have the same cost and labor requirements are grouped together. The number of units required in each category is then multiplied by the cost of a single unit. This is called the *material extension*.

Next, labor costs for each unit are estimated. If it takes a $30-an-hour electrician three minutes to install an SPST switch, that's $1.50 labor per unit. Multiply this by the number of units to determine the labor extension. Twelve switches will require $18.00 in labor costs. Or you can write the estimated work-hours in each labor column rather than the labor cost. That is, write .05 hours per SPST switch and .6 hours as the labor extension.

A pricing sheet can be your final estimating document for smaller jobs. However, a large job will require an estimate summary sheet. It includes listings for job overhead, labor cost breakdowns, material handling, and other supporting expenses. A pricing sheet takes more time to complete than a summary sheet, but will be worthwhile, especially as you attempt to improve your estimating skills.

For smaller jobs, especially ones that you have experience with, can often be estimated using a formula developed by experience. For many electrical contractors that formula is:

Material costs × 1.666 = Estimate

Another way of stating the same formula is:

Material costs = 60%; Labor costs = 40%

Over time, you might determine that this formula is not completely accurate. It might be that doubling the material costs is more accurate or you might come up with some other ratio. However, many new electrical contractors find that this formula is sufficiently accurate to be profitable for smaller jobs that don't require formal estimating and bidding.

There are also computer software programs that will make your estimating job easier. Contractor estimating and/or billing programs are sold by the following companies:

Estimating and billing programs

Construction Estimating Systems
12819 SE 38th, Suite 113
Bellevue, WA 98006

Estimation, Inc.
805-L Barkwood Court
Linthicum Heights, MD 21090

McCormick Systems
1255 W. Baseline Road, Suite 138
Mesa, AZ 85202

Software Shop Systems, Inc.
P.O. Box 728
Farmington, NJ 07727

TRF Estimating Systems
P.O. Box 728
Coral Springs, FL 33075

Probid Systems, Ltd.
125 Ashwarren Road
Downsview ON M3J 2S6 CANADA

To illustrate what can be done with computer software, let's take a look at one of the systems: TRF. It's actually two systems: an electrical estimating system and a time and material billing system. They operate on IBM-compatible PCs with 640K of RAM and can support a "mouse." Pages 97 through 101 illustrate output reports from the TRF Estimating System.

The electrical estimating system automates bid setup, bid takeoff, preparing assembly information, maintaining parts information, printouts, and more. Menus direct you through steps for creating a new bid, changing an existing bid and numerous other functions. Once done, you can print a bid takeoff summary, allocation by account, bid notes, parts information, a job invoice, a material list, or a bid specifications sheet. The system can store information on nearly 100,000 assemblies and an unlimited number of parts.

In addition, the electrical estimating system can import and store information from two major pricing sources: Trade Service Corp. (Tra-Ser 1500) and National Price Service (Monitor). The system also uses industry-standard NECA Labor Units in its estimates, if desired.

The TRF time and material billing system works with the estimating system to create, print, and post invoices, create and maintain customer records, and update pricing. (Shown on pages 102 through 112.)

Another popular system, offered by McCormick Systems (shown on pages 113 through 116), also automates the jobs of estimating and billing time and materials. This system, too, operates on a single or networked PC and is intended to reduce the amount of time required for the labor-intensive jobs of estimating, bidding, and billing. The McCormick system allows you to review jobs, structure breakout and takeoff, extend, bid, and much more.

The more you can automate the estimating process—while maintaining accuracy—the more bid invitations you can respond to. Also, the more accurate your billing, the faster you'll get paid.

A *bid* is simply a written offer to perform a job at a specified price. A bid might also be called a quote, a price quotation (see full page illustration on page 117), or a proposal (see full page illustration on page 118). A change is made with a change order (see full page illustration on page 119). In each case, once it's accepted and signed, a bid is a legally binding document.

How do I bid a job?

If you learn of an invitation to bid, contact the firm or representative letting the bid and ask for bid instructions. These are rules under which your bid must be submitted. Also ask when the bids will be opened and the job let.

There are numerous other forms available through the NECA (address previously given) and major office supply stores. A bid form should include the names of the contractor and the client, the date, a description of the work, location of the work site, the bid amount, how it should be paid (prior to start, installments, on completion, etc.), and a place for the signatures of both parties.

If you specialize in a segment of electrical contracting that doesn't have preprinted forms, you can modify these or work with your attorney to develop a form that will serve your specific requirements. You might want to incorporate the wording of your bids into a computer word processing program so that you can easily develop and submit a bid in the shortest time.

A *bid record* is simply a written record of bids prepared and submitted. It gives you the opportunity to track your success as a bidder and to determine whether there are specific competitors that are taking too much business from you.

You might be required to post a bid security, typically a certified check or performance bond, to ensure that if you're the successful bidder, you'll perform the bidded service as contracted. If you aren't a successful bidder, your security will be returned to you. Discuss performance bonds with your insurance agent.

Types of bids

Electrical contractors use a variety of bidding types, depending on the requirements of the customer and the marketplace. The following are the most common.

Labor only

The contractor furnishes labor, tools, and equipment, and the customer furnishes materials. The labor charge includes the cost of labor, taxes/benefits, overhead, and a profit.

Time and material

Labor is billed at hourly service rates established for each worker, and material is billed at retail price (sometimes less a discount). Overhead costs are built into the labor rates, and profit comes from the hourly service rates as well as from the sale of materials.

- Fixed price—the total price includes the cost of materials, labor, direct job expenses, prorated overhead costs, and profit.
- Unit price—total price is broken down into components: labor, job expenses, overhead, profit on units of material.
- Cost plus fee—the costs of materials, labor, and job expenses are reimbursed at actual cost, plus a fee to cover overhead and profit.
- Cost plus percentage—the costs of materials, labor, and job expenses are reimbursed at actual cost, plus a percentage to cover overhead and profit.
- Guaranteed maximum—the total lump sum price with the assurance that, if final costs are under the limit, the savings will be split with the contractor.

How will you get paid for your job? That depends on the terms that you offer in the bid or on the requirements of the bidder. Here are some common payment schedules:

- 100 percent due on completion of the work.
- 50 percent at midpoint in the job, and 50 percent on completion.
- 20 percent down with scheduled progress payment throughout the job (20 percent when one-fourth, one-half, three-fourths, and fully done).
- Bill the first of every month for work completed during the previous month.

How many bids will it take to get a job? Of course, that depends on many factors: your local market, economic conditions, your pricing, the perceived value of your bid, and the presentation of your bid. Typically, one out of ten bids will probably come to a job. Based on this 10-percent factor, if you want sales of $500,000 in the coming year, you'd better write good bids for about $5 million. Your factor might be higher or lower, but it's a good rule of thumb.

This chapter revealed how to work with money, how to determine how much capital you need, how to estimate start-up and operating costs, how to discover how much capital you have and where to get more, how much you should pay for money, how much you should charge for services, how to estimate job costs, and how to bid on jobs. The next chapter will help you keep track of the money you do make. It will help you ensure that your electrical contracting business is as profitable as it can be.

FORM 41 - Rev. 1981

National Electrical Contractors
Association, Inc.

PROPOSAL FOR ELECTRICAL WORK

From _____
Electrical Contractor

To _____

Proposal No. _____

Date _____

We hereby propose to furnish all labor and material necessary to provide the Electrical Installation in the _____

_____ located at _____

in accordance with the following specification, and subject to the conditions of contract stated on the reverse side of this sheet.

The price for the work described above will be

payable on the following terms:

This proposal is void if not accepted in writing within _____ days after this date.

No work shall commence until this Proposal is returned to the Contractor signed below by the Customer.

Accepted by _____
Customer

Accepted by _____
Contractor

Date_____

Date_____

Proposal for electrical work. National Electrical Contractors Association.

FORM 40
NATIONAL ELECTRICAL CONTRACTORS
ASSOCIATION, INC.

UNIFORM PROPOSAL

From..
Electrical Contractor

To..

Proposal No...

....

Date...

We hereby propose to furnish all labor and material necessary to install Electric Wiring in the...........................

....located at..

in accordance with the following specifications, and subject to the conditions of contract stated on the reverse side of this sheet.

SCHEDULE OF OUTLETS AND BELL WORK

LOCATION	Ceiling Light Outlets	Bracket Light Outlets	Convenience Outlets Single	Convenience Outlets Duplex	Floor Outlets	Heater Outlets	Range Outlet	S. P. Switches	3-Way Switches	4-Way Switches	Entrance	Special Outlets and Bell Work	Notations
Unit Price for Additions													

Branch Circuit Wiring is to be { Rigid Steel Conduit / Flexible Steel Conduit / Armored Cable / Knob and Tube } work, except exposed work in the basement, which is to be.........................

.... Service wires are to be installed in rigid steel conduit. The service

switch and meter loop are to be located in.. Wall switches are to be the.......................

....type, and receptacles the..type.

The customer has the privilege of cancelling this contract at any time before the work is started, upon payment of 10% of the price stated below. This proposal is void if not accepted in writing within.........................days after this date.

The price for the work described above will be.. Dollars

($.......................) payable on the following terms:

....

....

....

Accepted by..   ....

Customer   Electrical Contractor

Date..   By..

Uniform proposal. National Electrical Contractors Association.

BRANCH CIRCUIT TAKE-OFF

ESTIMATE NO. _____

SHEET NO. _____

JOB _____

OF _____ SHEETS

ESTIMATED BY _____

DATE _____

OUTLET	LIGHTING OUTLETS												SWITCH OUTLETS				
SYMBOL	○	○	○	⊢○		◯		⊂⊃	⊂⊃		⊂⊐	⊂⊐	$	$³	$⁴	$$	$$
DESCRIPTION																	
FLOOR FIRST																	
SECOND																	
THIRD																	
FOURTH																	
BOXES																	
COVERS																	
DEVICES																	

LOCATION	EXPOSED							FRAME OR FURRED SPACE							SLAB				
RUN	╫	╫╫	╫╫╫	╫-╫╫	╫╫-╫╫╫	╫╫╫-╫╫╫	╫╫-╫	╫	-╫╫	╫╫╫	╫╫-╫╫╫	╫╫╫-╫╫╫	╫╫╫╫-╫╫╫	╫╫-╫	╫	╫╫	╫╫╫	╫╫-╫╫
DESCRIPTION																		
FLOOR FIRST																		
SECOND																		
THIRD																		
FOURTH																		
ROTOMETER TOTAL																		
RACEWAY																		
WIRE																		
FIXTURE TYPE																		
WATTS																		
DESCRIPTION																		
FLOOR FIRST																		
SECOND																		
THIRD																		
FOURTH																		
TOTAL FIXTURES																		
LAMPS																		

RECAP. ITEM	CONDUIT.			E.M.T.			FLEX.			CABLE			TYPE				WIRE		
										TYPE						TYPE			
SIZE	1/2"	3/4"	1"	1/2"	3/4"	1"	1/2"	3/4"	1"	2/c ♦	3/c ♦	4/c ♦	♦14	♦12	♦10	♦8	♦14	♦12	♦10
TOTAL																			

Branch circuit take-off. National Electrical Contractors Association.

			RECEPTACLE OUTLETS						OTHER OUTLETS						
	\$\$\$	\$\$\$\$													

									TERMINALS						
									1/2" RIGID	3/4" RIGID	1" RIGID	1/2" E.M.T.	3/4" E.M.T.	1" E.M.T.	1/2" FLEX.	3/4" FLEX.	1" FLEX.	CABLE

FITTINGS
GENERAL TYPE

SPECIFIC TYPE

SIZE

TOTAL FITTINGS

TYPE
#8

Form 4E

PRICING SHEET

JOB

WORK

ESTIMATE NO.

Sheet No.   Of Sheets

	ESTIMATED BY	PRICED BY	EXTENDED BY	CHECKED BY	DATE

	√	MATERIAL	QUANTITY	MATERIAL PRICE	PER	MATERIAL EXTENSION	LABOR UNIT	PER	LABOR EXTENSION
1									
2									
3									
4									
5									
6									
7									
8									
9									
10									
11									
12									
13									
14									
15									
16									
17									
18									
19									
20									
21									
22									
23									
24									
25									
26									
27									
28									
29									
30									
31									
32									
33									
34									

Totals This Sheet Transferred To Recap By-INITIAL ▶   MATERIAL ▶   LABOR ▶

Form 4-E
Reorder From National Electrical Contractors Assoc.

Pricing sheet. National Electrical Contractors Association.

94   Electrical Contractor

FORM S-1b   JOB NO. _____ EXTRA WORK ORDER NO._____

EXTRA WORK ORDER

JOB NAME _____ DATE _____

JOB ADDRESS_____

OWNER OR OCCUPANT_____

AUTHORIZATION AND BILLING INFORMATION

EXTRA WORK Authorized By_____ TITLE_____

BILL TO_____ WHEN _____

ADDRESS _____ BILLING BASIS _____

EXTRA WORK REQUIRED FOR _____

_____

DESCRIPTION OF EXTRA WORK

IMPORTANT: Provide No Other Work Except Upon Written Authorization From The Shop.

GENERAL EXTRA WORK INFORMATION

Work To Start _____ Work To Be Completed By _____

Duplicate Time Cards Required   Yes ☐ No ☐   Duplicate Material Requisitions and Invoice Required   Yes ☐   No ☐

If Duplicates are required, they are to be signed by awarder's representative   Yes ☐   No ☐

Extra Work Completed: Date _____ By _____

Extra Work Accepted: Date _____ By _____

All materials charged to Extra Work: Date_____ By _____

All materials credited to basic job: Date_____ By _____

All Time Cards or Time Record Sheets For Extra Work Turned In: Date _____ By _____

Remarks _____

EXTRA WORK ORDER Written Up By: _____   **Approved By:** _____

Extra work order. National Electrical Contractors Association.

Working with money   95

Form JM-13
Reorder from the
National Electrical Contractors Association, Inc.
© 1983

DELAY REPORT

Job _____

Foreman _____

Date _____ Period Covered _____

Number in Crew: _____ Journeymen _____ Apprentices _____ Other _____

	MANHOURS LOST		
	Number of Hours	X	Number of Workers Affected	Manhours
1. Waiting for materials timely ordered but not received:			
a. From job stockroom	_____	_____	_____
b. From supplier	_____	_____	_____
c. From shop	_____	_____	_____
2. Waiting for materials not timely ordered	_____	_____	_____
3. Waiting for tools:			
a. Timely ordered but not received	_____	_____	_____
b. Not timely ordered	_____	_____	_____
4. Appropriate tools not available	_____	_____	_____
5. Tools not operable	_____	_____	_____
6. Waiting for equipment:			
a. Company owned	_____	_____	_____
b. Rentals	_____	_____	_____
c. Furnished by others	_____	_____	_____
7. Redoing Work:			
a. Because of design errors	_____	_____	_____
b. Because of fabrication errors	_____	_____	_____
c. Because of field errors	_____	_____	_____
8. Changes in scheduled work:			
a. Owner ordered	_____	_____	_____
b. To correct design errors	_____	_____	_____
c. Because of changes in other contractors' work	_____	_____	_____
d. General Contractor demand	_____	_____	_____
e. Other _____	_____	_____	_____
9. Changes in schedule sequence:			
a. Move to other work areas	_____	_____	_____
b. Other delays	_____	_____	_____
10. Waiting for information, instructions, drawings, or changes	_____	_____	_____
11. Interference by other trades' work	_____	_____	_____
12. Overcrowding of work areas	_____	_____	_____
13. Interference by employees or facilities of owner	_____	_____	_____
14. Other _____			

REMARKS: _____

_____

_____

_____

_____

Delay report. National Electrical Contractors Association, with permission.

TIME & MATERIAL BILLING
WORK ORDER FORM
ELECTRICAL

Work/Change Order Number:	
Date:	

Bill To:	Job Name:	Job Number:
Address:	Address:	
City, ST, Zip	City, ST, Zip	

Work Requested By:	Date:	Time:	Dt/Time Promised:

Special Instructions:

Type of Work:	☐ Service Call	☐ Warranty	☐ Contract	☐ Change Order	☐ Other:

Authorization Signature:	Date:	Time In:	Time Out:

Description of Problem / Work:	Work Performed:
	Performed By: Completed: ☐ Yes ☐ No

MISCELLANEOUS ITEMS   LABOR / EQUIPMENT

QUANTITY	DESCRIPTION	WORKMAN / EQUIPMENT	DATE	REGULAR HOURS	OVERTIME HOURS	NOTES

Special Notes:

I hereby acknowledge the satisfactory completion of the above work.

_____   _____   _____
Signature   Printed Name   Date

Time and material billing work order form—page 1. National Electrical Contractors Association, with permission.

BO	QTY	STEEL BOXES
1.1		4"SQ 1-1/2"D BOX 1/2" KO
1.3		4"SQ 1-1/2"D BOX COMB KO
1.4		4"SQ 1-1/2"D BOX 1/2" KO W/BRKT
4.3		4"SQ 2-1/8"D BOX COMB KO
7.3		4-11/16"SQ 1-1/2"D BOX COMB KO
10.3		4-11/16"SQ 2-1/8"D BOX COMB KO
16.1		4"OCT 1-1/2"D BOX 1/2"KO
5.1		HANDY BOX 1 7/8" DEEP
5.2		HANDY BOX EXTENSION
5.3		GEM (WORK) BOX
2.1		BELL BOX 1GANG 3HUB 3/4"
2.4		BELL BOX 2GANG 5HUB 3/4"
NB		**PLASTIC BOXES**
1.1		1GANG 2-1/4"D NM BOX W/NAILS
1.2		1GANG 2-3/4"D NM BOX W/NAILS
16.1		2GANG 2-3/4"D NM BOX W/NAILS
14.1		4"ROUND NM BOX W/NAILS
FS		**FS BOXES**
1.1		1G FS CAST BOX 1/2"KO
3.2		1G FS BLANK COVER
3.3		1G FS DUPLEX REC COVER
3.8		1G FS SINGLE REC COVER
RM		**PLASTER RINGS**
16.1		4"SQ BLANK COVER
1.2		4"SQ 1GANG RING 1/2"D
1.5		4"SQ 1GANG RING 3/4"D
4.5		4"SQ 2GANG RING 1/2"D
4.6		4"SQ 2GANG RING 3/4"D
7.2		4"SQR TO RND RING 1/2"D
7.5		4"SQR TO RND RING 3/4"D
10.1		4"SQR EXTNSN RING
17.1		4-11/16"SQ BLANK COVER
2.2		4-11/16"SQ 1GANG RING 1/2"D
2.3		4-11/16"SQ 1GANG RING 3/4"D
2.5		4-11/16"SQ 2GANG RING 3/4"D
8.1		4-11/16"SQ EXTNSN RING
CM		**CONDUIT**
1.1		1/2" EMT CONDUIT
1.2		3/4" EMT CONDUIT
1.3		1" EMT CONDUIT
1.4		1-1/4" EMT CONDUIT
1.5		1-1/2" EMT CONDUIT
1.6		2" EMT CONDUIT
4.1		1/2" GRC CONDUIT
4.2		3/4" GRC CONDUIT
4.3		1" GRC CONDUIT
4.4		1-1/4" GRC CONDUIT
4.5		1-1/2" GRC CONDUIT
4.6		2" GRC CONDUIT

CM	QTY	CONDUIT
5.1		3/8" FLEX STL CONDUIT
5.2		1/2" FLEX STL CONDUIT
5.3		3/4" FLEX STL CONDUIT
5.4		1" FLEX STL CONDUIT
8.1		3/8" SEALTITE CONDUIT
8.2		1/2" SEALTITE CONDUIT
8.3		3/4" SEALTITE CONDUIT
8.4		1" SEALTITE CONDUIT
3.1		1/2" PVC-40 CONDUIT
3.2		3/4" PVC-40 CONDUIT
3.3		1" PVC-40 CONDUIT
3.4		1-1/4" PVC-40 CONDUIT
3.5		1-1/2" PVC-40 CONDUIT
3.6		2" PVC-40 CONDUIT
EF		**EMT FITTINGS**
13.1		1/2" EMT SS DC COUP
13.2		3/4" EMT SS DC COUP
13.3		1" EMT SS DC COUP
13.4		1-1/4" EMT SS DC COUP
13.5		1-1/2" EMT SS DC COUP
13.6		2" EMT SS DC COUP
16.1		1/2" EMT COMP DC COUP
16.2		3/4" EMT COMP DC COUP
16.3		1" EMT COMP DC COUP
16.4		1-1/4" EMT COMP DC COUP
16.5		1-1/2" EMT COMP DC COUP
18.8		2" EMT COMP DC COUP
1.1		1/2" EMT SS DC CONN
1.2		3/4" EMT SS DC CONN
1.3		1" EMT SS DC CONN
1.4		1-1/4" EMT SS DC CONN
1.5		1-1/2" EMT SS DC CONN
1.6		2" EMT SS DC CONN
7.1		1/2" EMT COMP DC CONN
7.2		3/4" EMT COMP DC CONN
7.3		1" EMT COMP DC CONN
7.4		1-1/4" EMT COMP DC CONN
7.5		1-1/2" EMT COMP DC CONN
7.6		2" EMT COMP DC CONN
15.1		1/2" PLASTIC BUSHING
15.2		3/4" PLASTIC BUSHING
15.3		1" PLASTIC BUSHING
15.4		1-1/4" PLASTIC BUSHING
15.5		1-1/2" PLASTIC BUSHING
15.6		2" PLASTIC BUSHING
3.3		1" EMT ELBOW
3.4		1-1/4" EMT ELBOW
3.5		1-1/2" EMT ELBOW

RF		RIGID FITTINGS
1.1		1/2" LOCKNUT
1.2		3/4" LOCKNUT
1.3		1" LOCKNUT
1.4		1-1/4" LOCKNUT
1.5		1-1/2" LOCKNUT
1.6		2" LOCKNUT
2.1		1/2" GRC COUP
2.2		3/4" GRC COUP
2.3		1" GRC COUP
2.4		1-1/4" GRC COUP
2.5		1-1/2" GRC COUP
2.6		2" GRC COUP
10.2		3/4" METALLIC INSUL. BUSHING
10.3		1" METALLIC INSUL. BUSHING
10.4		1-1/4" METALLIC INSUL. BUSHING
10.5		1-1/2" METALLIC INSUL. BUSHING
10.6		2" METALLIC INSUL. BUSHING
11.1		1/2" MEYERS HUB
11.2		3/4" MEYERS HUB
11.3		1" MEYERS HUB
11.4		1-1/4" MEYERS HUB
11.5		1-1/2" MEYERS HUB
11.6		2" MEYERS HUB
8.1		1/2" ERICKSON COUP
8.2		3/4" ERICKSON COUP
8.3		1" ERICKSON COUP
8.4		1-1/4" ERICKSON COUP
8.5		1-1/2" ERICKSON COUP
8.6		2" ERICKSON COUP
3.1		1/2" GRC ELBOW
3.2		3/4" GRC ELBOW
3.3		1" GRC ELBOW
3.4		1-1/4" GRC ELBOW
3.5		1-1/2" GRC ELBOW
3.6		2" GRC ELBOW
FT		**FLEX FITTINGS**
1.1		3/8" DC SQZ STR FLEX CONN
1.2		1/2" DC SQZ STR FLEX CONN
1.3		3/4" DC SQZ STR FLEX CONN
1.4		1" DC SQZ STR FLEX CONN
4.1		3/8" DC SQZ 90 FLEX CONN
4.2		1/2" DC SQZ 90 FLEX CONN
4.3		3/4" DC SQZ 90 FLEX CONN
4.4		1" DC SQZ 90 FLEX CONN
3.1		3/8" STR SEALTITE CONN
3.2		1/2" STR SEALTITE CONN
3.3		3/4" STR SEALTITE CONN
3.4		1" STR SEALTITE CONN
6.1		3/8" 90 SEALTITE CONN
6.2		1/2" 90 SEALTITE CONN
6.3		3/4" 90 SEALTITE CONN
6.4		1" 90 SEALTITE CONN

Time and material billing work order form—page 2. Trf International, Inc.

PF	QTY	PVC FITTINGS	SS	QTY	CONDUIT SUPPORTS	WI	QTY	WIRE
1.1		1/2" PVC–40 FEMALE ADAPTER	18.1		1/2" EMT NAILER (DRIVE STRAP)	1.1		#14 THHN CU SOLID
1.2		3/4" PVC–40 FEMALE ADAPTER	18.2		3/4" EMT NAILER (DRIVE STRAP)	1.3		#12 THHN CU SOLID
1.3		1" PVC–40 FEMALE ADAPTER	18.3		1" EMT NAILER (DRIVE STRAP)	1.5		#10 THHN CU SOLID
1.4		1–1/4" PVC–40 FEMALE ADAPTER	12.1		1/2" EMT 1HOLE STRAP	4.1		#14 THHN CU STRANDED
1.5		1–1/2" PVC–40 FEMALE ADAPTER	12.2		3/4" EMT 1HOLE STRAP	4.3		#12 THHN CU STRANDED
1.6		2" PVC–40 FEMALE ADAPTER	12.3		1" EMT 1HOLE STRAP	4.5		#10 THHN CU STRANDED
4.1		1/2" PVC–40 MALE ADAPTER	12.4		1–1/4" EMT 1HOLE STRAP	4.7		# 8 THHN CU STRANDED
4.2		3/4" PVC–40 MALE ADAPTER	12.5		1–1/2" EMT 1HOLE STRAP	7.1		# 6 THHN CU STRANDED
4.3		1" PVC–40 MALE ADAPTER	12.6		2" EMT 1HOLE STRAP	7.2		# 4 THHN CU STRANDED
4.4		1–1/4" PVC–40 MALE ADAPTER	15.3		1" EMT 2HOLE STRAP	7.5		# 3 THHN CU STRANDED
4.5		1–1/2" PVC–40 MALE ADAPTER	15.4		1–1/4" EMT 2HOLE STRAP	7.6		# 2 THHN CU STRANDED
4.6		2" PVC–40 MALE ADAPTER	15.5		1–1/2" EMT 2HOLE STRAP	7.8		# 1 THHN CU STRANDED
2.1		1/2" PVC–40 ELBOW	15.6		2" EMT 2HOLE STRAP	7.10		#1/0 THHN CU STRANDED
2.2		3/4" PVC–40 ELBOW	17.1		1/2" EMT STRUT STRAP	7.11		#2/0 THHN CU STRANDED
2.3		1" PVC–40 ELBOW	17.2		3/4" EMT STRUT STRAP	7.12		#3/0 THHN CU STRANDED
2.4		1–1/4" PVC–40 ELBOW	17.3		1" EMT STRUT STRAP	7.13		#4/0 THHN CU STRANDED
2.5		1–1/2" PVC–40 ELBOW	17.4		1–1/4" EMT STRUT STRAP	7.14		#250 THHN CU STRANDED
2.6		2" PVC–40 ELBOW	17.5		1–1/2" EMT STRUT STRAP	7.15		#300 THHN CU STRANDED
10.1		1/2" PVC–40 COUP	17.6		2" EMT STRUT STRAP	7.16		#350 THHN CU STRANDED
10.2		3/4" PVC–40 COUP	1.1		1/2" MINI STRAP W/BOLT	7.17		#400 THHN CU STRANDED
10.3		1" PVC–40 COUP	1.2		3/4" MINI STRAP W/BOLT	7.18		#500 THHN CU STRANDED
10.4		1–1/4" PVC–40 COUP	1.3		1" MINI STRAP W/BOLT	3.1		14/2 ROMEX CU W/GRND
10.5		1–1/2" PVC–40 COUP	1.4		1–1/4" MINI STRAP W/BOLT	3.2		12/2 ROMEX CU W/GRND
10.6		2" PVC–40 COUP	1.5		1–1/2" MINI STRAP W/BOLT	3.3		10/2 ROMEX CU W/GRND
20.1		PVC CEMENT–1PT BRUSH TOP	1.6		2" MINI STRAP W/BOLT	3.4		8/2 ROMEX CU W/GRND
20.2		PVC CEMENT–1QT BRUSH TOP	3.1		1/2" GRC 1HOLE STRAP	3.6		14/3 ROMEX CU W/GRND
			3.2		3/4" GRC 1HOLE STRAP	3.7		12/3 ROMEX CU W/GRND
			3.3		1" GRC 1HOLE STRAP	3.8		10/3 ROMEX CU W/GRND
AM		ANCHORS	6.3		1" GRC 2HOLE STRAP	3.9		8/3 ROMEX CU W/GRND
8.1		1/4" CONCRETE ANCHOR	6.4		1–1/4" GRC 2HOLE STRAP	3.13		14/4 ROMEX CU W/GRND
8.3		3/8" CONCRETE ANCHOR	6.5		1–1/2" GRC 2HOLE STRAP	3.14		12/4 ROMEX CU W/GRND
8.4		1/2" CONCRETE ANCHOR	6.6		2" GRC 2HOLE STRAP	3.15		10/4 ROMEX CU W/GRND
12.1		1/4"x3/4" HEX BOLT	14.1		1/2" GRC STRUT STRAP	6.2		ROMEX BOX CONN 1/2"
12.2		3/8"x3/4" HEX BOLT	14.2		3/4" GRC STRUT STRAP	6.3		ROMEX BOX CONN 3/4"
12.3		1/2"x1" HEX BOLT	14.3		1" GRC STRUT STRAP	6.4		ROMEX BOX CONN 1"
15.1		1/4" WASHER	14.4		1–1/4" GRC STRUT STRAP	13.6		8/3 SE CABLE STYLE U
15.2		3/8" WASHER	14.5		1–1/2" GRC STRUT STRAP	13.8		6/3 SE CABLE STYLE U
15.3		1/2" WASHER	14.6		2" GRC STRUT STRAP	13.10		4/3 SE CABLE STYLE U
15.4		1/4" HEX NUTS	2.2		7/8" STRUT CHANNEL	13.12		3/3 SE CABLE STYLE U
15.5		3/8" HEX NUTS	2.1		1–1/2" STRUT CHANNEL	13.14		2/3 SE CABLE STYLE U
15.6		1/2" HEX NUTS	8.2		1/4" SPRING NUTS	19.1		14/2 UF CABLE CU W/GRND
19.4		3/16"x3" TOGGLE BOLT	8.4		3/8" SPRING NUTS	19.2		12/2 UF CABLE CU W/GRND
19.5		3/16"x4" TOGGLE BOLT	11.4		1/4"x60" THREADED ROD	19.3		10/2 UF CABLE CU W/GRND
19.6		1/4"x3" TOGGLE BOLT	11.8		3/8"x60" THREADED ROD	19.4		8/2 UF CABLE CU W/GRND
19.7		1/4"X4" TOGGLE BOLT	7.1		1/4" BEAM CLAMP	19.6		14/3 UF CABLE CU W/GRND
11.1		#8 PLASTIC ANCHOR W/SCREW	7.3		3/8" BEAM CLAMP	19.7		12/3 UF CABLE CU W/GRND
11.2		#10 PLASTIC ANCHOR W/SCREW				19.8		10/3 UF CABLE CU W/GRND
14.1		METAL STUD SCREW				19.9		8/3 UF CABLE CU W/GRND
14.2		TEK SCREW 10X1						
14.3		TAPCON 1/4X3						

Time and material billing work order form—page 3. TRF International, Inc.

BX	QTY	BX – MC CABLE
1.1		14/2 SOLID BX CABLE
1.2		12/2 SOLID BX CABLE
1.3		10/2 SOLID BX CABLE
4.1		14/3 SOLID BX CABLE
4.2		12/3 SOLID BX CABLE
4.3		10/3 SOLID BX CABLE
4.4		8/3 SOLID BX CABLE
7.1		14/4 SOLID BX CABLE
7.2		12/4 SOLID BX CABLE
7.3		10/4 SOLID BX CABLE
7.4		8/4 SOLID BX CABLE
7.9		14/2 MC CABLE W/GRN GRD
7.10		12/2 MC CABLE W/GRN GRD
7.11		10/2 MC CABLE W/GRN GRD
7.12		14/3 MC CABLE W/GRN GRD
7.13		12/3 MC CABLE W/GRN GRD
7.14		10/3 MC CABLE W/GRN GRD
7.15		14/4 MC CABLE W/GRN GRD
7.16		12/4 MC CABLE W/GRN GRD
7.17		10/4 MC CABLE W/GRN GRD
3.1		BX BOX CONN 3/8"
3.2		BX BOX CONN 1/2"
6.1		14/2,14/3,12/2 BUSHING
6.2		14/4,12/3,6/1,4/1 BUSHING
6.3		12/4,10/2,10/3,2/1 BUSHING
6.4		10/4,8/2,8/3,1/1 BUSHING

WA	QTY	WIRE ACCESSORIES
9.2		3M YELLOW WIRENUTS
9.3		3M RED WIRENUTS
9.4		3M BLUE WIRENUTS
15.4		#14 SPADE TERM
15.5		#14 RING TERM
16.2		#6 SOLDERLESS LUG
16.4		#2 SOLDERLESS LUG
16.6		#1/0 SOLDERLESS LUG
16.7		#2/0 SOLDERLESS LUG
16.10		#250 SOLDERLESS LUG
1.4		#4 SPLIT BOLT
1.5		#2 SPLIT BOLT
1.6		#1/0 SPLIT BOLT
1.8		#3/0 SPLIT BOLT
1.9		#250 SPLIT BOLT
18.1		3M 33+ PLASTIC TAPE
18.2		3M 88 WP PLASTIC TAPE

SL	QTY	SERVICE LABOR
7.1		FOREMAN – ST. TIME
7.2		FOREMAN – OT 1.5
1.1		JOURNEYMAN – ST. TIME
1.2		JOURNEYMAN – OT 1.5
4.1		APPRENTICE – ST. TIME
4.2		APPRENTICE – OT. TIME
10.1		SERVICE TRUCK CHARGE – ST
10.2		SERVICE TRUCK CHARGE – OT

OU	QTY	OUTLETS
1.2		15A RES.DUP.REC 5320–I
2.1		15A INT.SGL.REC 5015–I
1.6		15A INT.DUP.REC 5252–I
1.1		15A SPEC.DUP.REC 5262–I
7.1		15A GFI OUTLET
7.2		20A GFI OUTLET
2.2		20A INT.SGL.REC 5801–I
4.2		20A INT.DUP.REC 5800–I

SW	QTY	SWITCHES
1.2		1P 15A RES SWITCH 1451–I
1.7		3W 15A RES SWITCH 1453–I
7.1		1P 15A SPEC SWITCH 1201–I
7.2		3W 15A SPEC SWITCH 1203–I
7.6		

PM	QTY	PLATES
1.1		1G DUP.REC IV PLASTIC PLT
1.2		2G DUP.REC IV PLASTIC PLT
1.3		2G SW/DUP.REC IV PLASTIC PLT
10.1		1G SWITCH IV PLASTIC PLT
13.1		2G SWITCH IV PLASTIC PLT
2.1		1G SGL.REC SS PLATE
2.2		1G DUP.REC SS PLATE
2.3		2G DUP.REC SS PLATE
5.1		1G SWITCH SS PLATE
5.2		2G SWITCH SS PLATE
18.1		4"SQ 1–SWITCH COVER
18.2		4"SQ 1–SGL.REC COVER
18.3		4"SQ 1–DUP.REC COVER
18.4		4"SQ 2–SWITCH COVER
18.6		4"SQ 1–SW/1–SGL.REC COVER
18.7		4"SQ 1–SW/1–DUP.REC COVER
18.8		4"SQ 2–DUP.REC COVER

SE		SERVICE EQ / EXPENSE
1.1		35' BUCKET TRK PER HOUR
1.2		35' BUCKET TRK PER DAY
1.3		MOTORIZED MANLIFT PER HOUR
1.4		MOTORIZED MANLIFT PER DAY
1.5		SCAFFOLD PLATFORM PER HOUR
1.6		SCAFFOLD PLATFORM PER DAY
1.7		BACKHOE PER HOUR
1.8		BACKHOE PER DAY
1.9		DITCHWITCH PER HOUR
1.10		DITCHWITCH PER DAY
1.11		HYD BENDER PER HOUR
1.12		HYD BENDER PER DAY
2.1		SMALL TOOL CHARGE
3.1		PERMIT EXPENSE
4.1		TRAVEL EXPENSE

SF	QTY	FUSED DISCONNECTS
1		__A 3P 250V GD N1
3		__A 3P 600V HD N1
13		__A 3P 250V GD N3R
8		__A 3P 600V HD N3R

SN	QTY	NF DISCONNECTS
1		__A 3P 250V GD N1
3		__A 3P 600V HD N1
2		__A 3P 250V GD N3R

FU	QTY	FUSES
10.6		30A 250V TD FUSE
10.11		60A 250V TD FUSE
10.15		100A 250V TD FUSE
8.6		600V TD FUSE
8.11		60A 600V TD FUSE
8.15		100A 600V TD FUSE

FX	QTY	FIXTURES
1.1		4' 2LAMP SL STRIP
1.7		8' 2LAMP SL STRIP
5.2		2x4 2LAMP LAYIN ENSAV
5.7		2x4 4LAMP LAYIN ENSAV

BL	QTY	BALLASTS
5.2		40W 2LAMP 120V BALLAST
11.1		72/96W 2LAMP 120V BALLAST
11.3		72/96W/HO 2LAMP 120V BALLAST

LM	QTY	LAMPS
4.1		F40CW LAMP
10.3		F96T12/CW LAMP
10.1		F96T12/CW/HO LAMP

MI	QTY	MISCELLANEOUS
7.14		DUCT SEAL (1LB)
6.1		1QT WIRE PULL SOAP
9.1		DUCT TAPE
11.1		EARTHQUAKE CLIPS

ADDITIONAL ITEMS

Time and material billing work order form—page 4. TRF International, Inc.

INVOICE

```
F   B&J Electric Co.. Inc.
R   1234 Simpson Ave.
O   Suite 505
M   Miami          FL  33089
    Phone 305-111-9988
```

```
B
I   Sun Equipment Company
L   Mr. George Smith
L   2235 South Hampton
T   Miami          FL  33078
O
```

JOB NAME	JOB NO.
Bearing Facility	789

PURCHASE ORDER NO.	CUST. NO.
99-987	SUN001

TERMS	AUTH. BY
2% 10. Net 30	Rob Jones

```
     *** INVOICE TOTALS ***    MATERIAL COSTS: $    154.87
                               LABOR COSTS:         540.00
                               MISC. COSTS:           0.00
                                  TOTAL TAX:           7.74   ( 5% )
                               ====================
                               INVOICE GRAND TOTAL: $  702.61     ***

                 We appreciate your business!!
```
==
```
     DESCRIPTION OF WORK:

     Added isolated ground outlet and circuit in manager's office.
     Tightened connections in panel to eliminate heat problem.

     NOTE:  Panel replacement is suggested due to overload condition!!
```

ITEM DESCRIPTION	QUANTITY	UNIT PRICE	EXTENDED PRICE
Labor (Overtime) on Saturday pre-approved by Rob Jones			
JOURNEYMAN - OT DBL TIME	6.0	$ 90.000	$ 540.00
*** MATERIALS ***			
1/2" EMT CONDUIT	120.0	.245	29.38
1/2" EMT COUP COMP STEEL	15.0	1.255	18.83
1/2" EMT CONN COMP STL	4.0	1.050	4.20
#12 THHN CU STR	400.0	.088	35.04
1/2" EMT 1 HOLE STRAP	40.0	.178	7.10
3/16 X 4 TOGGLE BOLT	40.0	.361	14.45
4" SQ BOX 1-1/2" DEEP 1/2" KO	2.0	1.800	3.60
4IN 1G MUDRING 5/8 RAISED 768	1.0	1.130	1.13
4IN SQ FLAT 1/2KO COVER 753	1.0	.750	.75
20A SINGLE IG OUTLET	1.0	29.280	29.28
SGL OUTLET PLATE SS 302	1.0	1.840	1.84
RED SCOTCHLOKS 3M	6.0	.105	.63
PLUG-IN BRKR 20A SP Q0120	1.0	8.640	8.64

```
              *** End of Invoice Detail ***
```

Sample invoice. TRF International, Inc.

				SALES TAX 6.000%	MATERIAL M/U 1.20	LABOR M/U 1.35	LABOR RATE $15.00

JOE'S SHOE STORE   BID DATE 01-01-90   UNIT PRICE PARAMETERS ====>

ASSM	SYS	LOC	2=DIFFICULTY FACTOR DESCRIPTION	COUNT	EACH LABOR UNIT	EACH LABOR COST	EACH MATERIAL COST	EACH UNIT COST	EACH SELL PRICE
1	1		LIGHTING FIXTURES						
53500	1		2X4 LAYIN FIXTURE 10' P&W	15	1.990	29.85	8.65	38.50	50.67
53701	1		INC FIXTURE <300W WALL/CEIL	1	1.371	20.57	3.97	24.54	32.53
53850	1		HIHAT INC <150W LAYIN 10' PW	4	2.234	33.51	13.70	47.21	61.68
54100	1		EXIT LT LAYIN CEIL 30' P&W	2	3.587	53.81	18.35	72.15	94.65
54125	1		2 HD EM BATTERY PACK 30' PW	1	2.899	43.49	9.67	53.16	70.31
*****	1		System Totals:		50.23	753	235	988	1,299
2	2		SWITCHGEAR						
80034	2		100A MLO 30P 208Y/120V 3PH-4	1	1.750	26.25		26.25	35.44
81736	2		60A 4W SN 208/120 SAFETY SWI	1	.875	13.13		13.13	17.72
			FRN-R 60 RK5 FSETRON FUSE 250V	3	.060	.90	3.56	4.46	5.49
81737	2		100A 4W SN 208/120 SAFETY SW	1	1.125	16.88		16.88	22.78
			FRN-R 100 RK5 FSETRN FUSE 250V	3	.060	.90	8.00	8.90	10.82
*****	2		System Totals:		4.11	62	35	96	125
3	3		FEEDERS						
2249	3		1-1/2" EMT 4#3	150	.120	1.81	2.38	4.19	5.30
			1-1/2" EMT 2 HOLE STRAP	15	.045	.68	.17	.84	1.11
			1-1/2" EMT CONN SS DC	4	.091	1.37	.66	2.02	2.63
			1-1/2" PLASTIC BUSHING	1	.070	1.05	.18	1.23	1.63
			1-1/2" BONDING BUSHING	1	.510	7.65	2.19	9.84	12.96
			1-1/2" EMT 90 ELBOW	2	.175	2.63	2.46	5.09	6.50
6249	3		1-1/2" GRC NIPPLE 4#3	2	.914	13.71	13.83	27.54	35.11
			SPLIBLT SE CNN #2 L/SPCR KS23	8	.190	2.85	3.56	6.41	8.12
			33+ 3/4 X 66FT PLST ELECT TAPE	2	.040	.60	2.33	2.93	3.61
			WIRE LUBE 1 QUART 31-250	1	.001	.02	3.23	3.25	3.90
9104	3		1-1/2" LB W/ COVER & GASKET	1	.666	9.99	22.85	32.84	40.91
*****	3		System Totals:		24.15	362	457	819	1,037

Unit price extension. TRF International, Inc.

JOE'S SHOE STORE	BID DATE 01-01-90				SALES TAX 6.000%	MATERIAL M/U 1.20	LABOR M/U 1.35	LABOR RATE $15.00

			2=DIFFICULTY FACTOR		— LABOR —		— MATERIAL —	
ASSM	SYS	LOC	D E S C R I P T I O N	COUNT	UNIT	HOURS	UNIT	EXTEND
1	1		LIGHTING FIXTURES					
53500	1		2X4 LAYIN FIXTURE 10' P&W	15	1.990	29.85	8.645	129.68
53701	1		INC FIXTURE <300W WALL/CEIL	1	1.371	1.37	3.971	3.97
53850	1		HIHAT INC <150W LAYIN 10' PW	4	2.234	8.93	13.697	54.79
54100	1		EXIT LT LAYIN CEIL 30' P&W	2	3.587	7.17	18.346	36.69
54125	1		2 HD EM BATTERY PACK 30' PW	1	2.899	2.89	9.674	9.67
*****	1		System Totals:			50.23		234.81
2	2		SWITCHGEAR					
80034	2		100A MLO 30P 208Y/120V 3PH-4	1	1.750	1.75		
81736	2		60A 4W SN 208/120 SAFETY SWI	1	.875	.87		
			FRN-R 60 RK5 FSEIRON FUSE 250V	3	.060	.18	3.561	10.68
81737	2		100A 4W SN 208/120 SAFETY SW	1	1.125	1.12		
			FRN-R 100 RK5 FSEIRN FUSE 250V	3	.060	.18	8.003	24.00
*****	2		System Totals:			4.11		34.69
3	3		FEEDERS					
2249	3		1-1/2" EMT 4#3	150	.120	18.09	2.381	357.29
			1-1/2" EMT 2 HOLE STRAP	15	.045	.67	.166	2.50
			1-1/2" EMT CONN SS DC	4	.091	.36	.655	2.62
			1-1/2" PLASTIC BUSHING	1	.070	.07	.178	.17
			1-1/2" BONDING BUSHING	1	.510	.51	2.190	2.19
			1-1/2" EMT 90 ELBOW	2	.175	.35	2.461	4.92
6249	3		1-1/2" GRC NIPPLE 4#3	2	.914	1.82	13.833	27.66
			SPLITBLT SE CONN #2 L/SPCR KS23	8	.190	1.52	3.561	28.49
			33+ 3/4 X 66FT PLST ELECT TAPE	2	.040	.08	2.332	4.66
			WIRE LUBE 1 QUART 31-250	1	.001		3.233	3.23
9104	3		1-1/2" LB W/ COVER & GASKET	1	.666	.66	22.854	22.85
*****	3		System Totals:			24.15		456.62

Assembly extension. TRF International, Inc.

| | | | | | | SALES TAX 6.000% | MATERIAL M/U 1.20 | LABOR M/U 1.35 | LABOR RATE $15.00 |

JOE'S SHOE STORE   BID DATE
                       01-01-90

				LABOR		MATERIAL	
ASSM SYS LOC	2=DIFFICULTY FACTOR D E S C R I P T I O N	COUNT	UNIT	HOURS		UNIT	EXTEND
1 1	LIGHTING FIXTURES						
53500 1	2X4 LAYIN FIXTURE 10' P&W	15					
	#12 THHN CU SOLID	330	.006	1.98		.049	16.43
	1/2" EMT CONDUIT	150	.040	6.00		.168	25.33
	1/2" EMT CONN SS DC	30	.056	1.68		.081	2.44
	1/2" EMT COUP SS DC	15	.040	.60		.088	1.32
	1/2" EMT 1 HOLE STRAP	15	.036	.54		.051	.77
	4" SQ BOX 1-1/2" DEEP 1/2" KO	15	.175	2.62		.528	7.93
	4IN SQ FLAT 1/2KO COVER 753	15	.060	.90		.312	4.68
	YELLOW SCOTCHLOKS 3M	30	.040	1.20		.054	1.62
	RED SCOTCHLOKS 3M	30	.040	1.20		.072	2.16
	3/16 X 4 TOGGLE BOLT	15	.065	.97		.223	3.35
	3/8" X 6' FIXTURE WHIP	15	.125	1.87		3.180	47.70
	EARTHQUAKE CLIPS	60	.020	1.20		.265	15.90
	2X4 3 LAMP LAYIN FIXTURE	15	.605	9.07			
53701 1	INC FIXTURE <300W WALL/CEIL	1					
	#12 THHN CU SOLID	22	.006	.13		.049	1.09
	1/2" EMT CONDUIT	10	.040	.40		.168	1.68
	1/2" EMT CONN SS DC	2	.056	.11		.081	.16
	1/2" EMT COUP SS DC	1	.040	.04		.088	.08
	4" SQ BOX 1-1/2" DEEP 1/2" KO	1	.175	.17		.528	.52
	4IN SQ TO RND RING 5/8 756	1	.060	.06		.395	.39
	METAL STUD SCREW	2	.001			.005	.01
	SURF INC FIXTURE < 300 WATTS	1	.450	.45			
53850 1	HIHAT INC <150W LAYIN 10' PW	4					
	#12 THHN CU SOLID	88	.006	.52		.049	4.38
	1/2" EMT CONDUIT	40	.040	1.60		.168	6.75
	T-BAR BOX HANGER 512	8	.170	1.36		3.055	24.44
	1/2" EMT CONN SS DC	8	.056	.44		.081	.65
	1/2" EMT COUP SS DC	4	.040	.16		.088	.35
	1/2" EMT 1 HOLE STRAP	4	.036	.14		.051	.20
	4" SQ BOX 1-1/2" DEEP 1/2" KO	4	.175	.70		.528	2.11
	4IN SQ FLAT 1/2KO COVER 753	4	.060	.24		.312	1.24
	YELLOW SCOTCHLOKS 3M	8	.040	.32		.054	.43
	RED SCOTCHLOKS 3M	8	.040	.32		.072	.57
	3/16 X 4 TOGGLE BOLT	4	.065	.26		.223	.89
	3/8" X 6' FIXTURE WHIP	4	.125	.50		3.180	12.72

Exploded assembly extension. TRF International, Inc.

JOE'S SHOE STORE		BID DATE 01-01-90			SALES TAX 6.000%	MATERIAL M/U 1.20	LABOR M/U 1.35	LABOR RATE $15.00

ASSM	SYS	LOC	2=DIFFICULTY FACTOR DESCRIPTION	COUNT	— LABOR — UNIT	HOURS	— MATERIAL — UNIT	EXTEND
			#12 THHN CU SOLID	626	.006	3.75	.049	31.16
			1/2" EMT CONDUIT	290	.040	11.60	.168	48.98
		512	T-BAR BOX HANGER	10	.170	1.70	3.055	30.55
			1/2" EMT CONN SS DC	46	.056	2.57	.081	3.75
			1/2" EMT COUP SS DC	29	.040	1.16	.088	2.57
			1/2" EMT 1 HOLE STRAP	28	.036	1.00	.051	1.45
			3-1/2X1-1/2 OCT BX 1/2 KO 110	2	.350	.70	.993	1.98
			4" SQ BOX 1-1/2" DEEP 1/2" KO	23	.175	4.02	.528	12.16
		753	4IN SQ FLAT 1/2KO COVER	21	.060	1.26	.312	6.56
		756	4IN SQ TO RND RING 5/8	2	.060	.12	.395	.79
			YELLOW SCOTCHLOKS 3M	42	.040	1.68	.054	2.27
			RED SCOTCHLOKS 3M	42	.040	1.68	.072	3.02
			3/16 X 4 TOGGLE BOLT	21	.065	1.36	.223	4.70
			METAL STUD SCREW	4	.001		.005	.02
			3/8" X 6' FIXTURE WHIP	21	.125	2.62	3.180	66.78
			EARTHQUAKE CLIPS	68	.020	1.36	.265	18.02
			2X4 3 LAMP LAYIN FIXTURE	15	.605	9.07		
			SURF INC FIXTURE < 300 WATTS	1	.450	.45		
			INCANDESCENT HIHAT < 150 WATTS	4	.589	2.35		
			EXIT LIGHT CLG/WALL MOUNTED	2	.490	.98		
			EMERGENCY 2 HEAD LIGHT	1	.750	.75		
*****	1		Lighting Fixture Totals:			50.23		234.81
80034	2		100A MLO 30P 208Y/120V 3PH-4	1	1.750	1.75		
81736	2		60A 4W SN 208/120 SAFETY SWI	1	.875	.87		
81737	2		100A 4W SN 208/120 SAFETY SW	1	1.125	1.12		
			FRN-R 60 RK5 FSETRON FUSE 250V	3	.060	.18	3.561	10.68
			FRN-R 100 RK5 FSETRN FUSE 250V	3	.060	.18	8.003	24.00
*****	2		Switchgear Totals:			4.11		34.69

Parts extension—sorted by system. TRF International, Inc.

JOE'S SHOE STORE   BID DATE
                        01-01-90

| | | | | | SALES TAX 6.000% | MATERIAL M/U 1.20 | LABOR M/U 1.35 | LABOR RATE $15.00 |

2=DIFFICULTY FACTOR

PART NUMBER	DESCRIPTION	COUNT	UNIT	LABOR HOURS	% TTL	MATERIAL UNIT	EXTEND
Cost Code:	**12 - BRANCH ROUGH**						
12001002001	1/2" EMT CONDUIT	870	.040	34.80	24.8	.168	146.96
12001002002	3/4" EMT CONDUIT	20	.047	.94	.7	.244	4.89
14005002321	1/2" SEALTITE TYPE UA	3	.055	.16	.1	.600	1.80
14005002361	1" SEALTITE TYPE UA	3	.100	.30	.2	1.221	3.66
1500CN06241	1/2" PVC FEMALE ADAPTER	2	.120	.24	.2	.106	.21
2210CD67751	T-BAR BOX HANGER 512	10	.170	1.70	1.2	3.055	30.55
2230RC01404	1" PLASTIC BUSHING	2	.047	.09	.1	.113	.22
23007013511	1/2" EMT CONN SS DC	95	.056	5.34	3.8	.081	7.79
23007013512	3/4" EMT CONN SS DC	4	.056	.22	.2	.138	.55
23007013581	1/2" EMT COUP SS DC	85	.040	3.40	2.4	.088	7.53
23007013583	1" EMT COUP SS DC	4	.040	.16	.1	.275	1.10
24107014682	1/2" SEALTITE STR CONN	1	.110	.11	.1	.764	.76
24107014684	1" SEALTITE STR CONN	1	.170	.17	.1	1.794	1.79
24107014782	1/2" SEALTITE 90 CONN	1	.150	.15	.1	1.066	1.06
24107014784	1" SEALTITE 90 CONN	1	.180	.18	.1	4.452	4.45
2710MB30204	BELL BOX 1G 3HUB 3/4 KO	1	.450	.45	.3	4.621	4.62
2710RC00110	3-1/2X1-1/2 OCT BX 1/2 KO 110	2	.350	.70	.5	.993	1.98
2710RC00189	4" SQ BOX 1-1/2" DEEP 1/2" KO	47	.175	8.22	5.9	.528	24.85
2710RC00192	4" SQ BOX 1-1/2"D 1/2"&3/4" KO	2	.175	.35	.2	.618	1.23
2710RC00753	4IN SQ FLAT 1/2KO COVER 753	27	.060	1.62	1.2	.312	8.43
2710RC00756	4IN SQ TO RND RING 5/8 756	2	.060	.12	.1	.395	.79
2710RC00768	4IN 1G MUDRING 5/8 RAISED 768	7	.067	.47	.3	.688	4.82
2710RC00769	4IN 2G MUDRING 5/8 RAISED 769	1	.067	.06		1.002	1.00
2710RC00772	4IN 1G MUDRING 1/2 RAISED 772	12	.067	.81	.6	.384	4.61
	Subtotal: BRANCH ROUGH			60.79	43.3%		265.74
Cost Code:	**14 - BRANCH WIRE**						
01110022400	#12 THHN CU SOLID	2183	.006	13.10	9.3	.049	108.72
0720CC05682	2CND THRMST TWSTD L/JKT CAROL	6	.004	.02		.041	.24
0720CC05685	5CND THRMST TWSTD L/JKT CAROL	21	.004	.08	.1	.090	1.90
	Subtotal: BRANCH WIRE			13.21	9.4%		110.87

Parts extension—sorted by job cost code. TRF International, Inc.

					LABOR		MATERIAL	
JOE'S SHOE STORE	BID DATE 01-01-90				SALES TAX 6.000%	MATERIAL M/U 1.20	LABOR M/U 1.35	LABOR RATE $15.00

	2=DIFFICULTY FACTOR			LABOR		MATERIAL	
PART NUMBER	D E S C R I P T I O N	COUNT	UNIT	HOURS	% TTL	UNIT	EXTEND

Category: — SPECIAL TAKE-OFF ITEMS

Part Number	Description	Count	Unit	Hours	% TTL	Unit	Extend
80034	100A MLO 30P 208Y/120V 3PH-4	1	1.750	1.75	1.2		
81736	60A 4W SN 208/120 SAFETY SWI	1	.875	.87	.6		
81737	100A 4W SN 208/120 SAFETY SW	1	1.125	1.12	.8		
	Subtotal: SPECIAL TAKE-OFF ITEMS			3.75	2.7%		

Category: 111 — *COPPER WIRE

Part Number	Description	Count	Unit	Hours	% TTL	Unit	Extend
01110021750	#3 THW CU STR	632	.007	4.42	3.1	.413	261.25
01110022400	#12 THHN CU SOLID	2183	.006	13.10	9.3	.049	108.72
01110023100	#8 THHN CU STR	5	.009	.04		.173	.86
01110023150	#6 THHN CU STR	141	.011	1.55	1.1	.270	38.20
	Subtotal: *COPPER WIRE			19.12	13.6%		409.04

Category: 720 — * THERMOSTAT WIRE

Part Number	Description	Count	Unit	Hours	% TTL	Unit	Extend
0720CC05682	2CND THRMST TWSTD L/JKT CAROL	6	.004	.02		.041	.24
0720CC05685	5CND THRMST TWSTD L/JKT CAROL	21	.004	.08	.1	.090	1.90
	Subtotal: * THERMOSTAT WIRE			.10	.1%		2.14

Category: 1200 — *EMT CONDUIT

Part Number	Description	Count	Unit	Hours	% TTL	Unit	Extend
12001002001	1/2" EMT CONDUIT	870	.040	34.80	24.8	.168	146.96
12001002002	3/4" EMT CONDUIT	20	.047	.94	.7	.244	4.89
12001002003	1" EMT CONDUIT	40	.060	2.40	1.7	.374	14.98
12001002005	1-1/2" EMT CONDUIT	150	.080	12.00	8.5	.625	93.83
	Subtotal: *EMT CONDUIT			50.14	35.7%		260.67

Parts extension—sorted by commodity code. TRF International, Inc.

JOE'S SHOE STORE	BID DATE 01-01-90			SALES TAX 6.000%	MATERIAL M/U 1.20	LABOR M/U 1.35	LABOR RATE $15.00

MAN HOURS:	140.51	LABOR COST: LABOR MARGIN:	2,108 738

*** Q U O T E   M A T E R I A L S   ***

ACT	COST	TAX	M/UP	PRICE
M 70 LIGHTING FIXTURES				
	850.00	51.00	1.15	1,036.15
M 96 SWITCHGEAR				
	650.00	39.00	1.20	826.80

MATERIAL COST:	2,676
MATERIAL MARGIN:	490

LABOR + MATERIAL COST:	4,784
LABOR + MATERIAL MARGIN:	1,228

CONSTRUCTION PRICE:	6,012

**** J O B   E X P E N S E S   ****

	COST	TAX	M/UP	PRICE
PERMIT	150.00		1.00	150.00

JOB EXPENSE NET COST:	150
JOB EXPENSE MARGIN:	

TOTAL BID PRICE:	6,162

Brief takeoff recap. TRF International, Inc.

RECAP BY SYSTEM

BID NAME: JOE'S SHOE STORE	SQUARE FOOTAGE: 1,500
BID NUMBER: 1	TAKE-OFF MATERIAL SALES TAX: 6.000%
BID DATE: 01-01-90	TAKE-OFF MATERIAL MARKUP: 20%
ESTIMATOR: SJ	HOURLY LABOR RATE: $15.00
JOB ADDRESS:	LABOR MARKUP: 35%
CUSTOMER:	LABOR DIFFICULTY: LEVEL 2

SYSTEM	SYSTEM NAME	COSTS TAXED	% OF TOTAL	COST PER SQ. FT.	LABOR HOURS	% OF TOTAL	HOUR PER SQ. FT.
**** BID TAKE-OFF ITEMS ****							
1	LIGHTING FIXTURES	234.81	8.3	.1565	50.23	35.7	.0335
2	SWITCHGEAR	34.69	1.2	.0231	4.11	2.9	.0027
3	FEEDERS	456.62	16.2	.3044	24.15	17.2	.0161
4	BRANCH ROUGH, TRIM, AND EQ H	359.77	12.7	.2399	62.01	44.1	.0413
	SUBTOTAL - BID TAKE-OFF ITEMS:	1,085.89	38.4	.7239	140.50	100.0	.0937
**** QUOTED MATERIALS ****							
	LIGHTING FIXTURES	901.00	31.9	.6007			
	SWITCHGEAR	689.00	24.4	.4593			
	SUBTOTAL - QUOTED MATERIALS:	1,590.00	56.3	1.0600			
*** EXPENSE ITEMS ****							
	PERMIT	150.00	5.3	.1000			
	SUBTOTAL - EXPENSE ITEMS:	150.00	5.3	.1000			
	GRAND TOTALS:	2,825.89	100.0	1.8839	140.50	100.0	.0937

Recap by system. TRF International, Inc.

JOE'S SHOE STORE   BID DATE   SALES   MATERIAL LABOR   LABOR
                         01-01-90   TAX   M/U   M/U   RATE
                                                     6.000%   1.20   1.35 $15.00

JOB COST CODE	— LABOR —		— MATERIAL —			
	HOURS	COST	NET COST	TAX	GROSS	M/UP
12 BRANCH ROUGH	60.79	911.96	250.70	15.04	265.74	1.20
14 BRANCH WIRE	13.21	198.16	104.60	6.28	110.88	1.20
35 EXPLOSION PROOF FITTINGS	.66	9.99	21.56	1.29	22.85	1.20
40 FEEDER ROUGH	18.64	279.72	135.71	8.14	143.85	1.20
42 FEEDER WIRE	6.02	90.30	283.32	17.00	300.32	1.20
46 FIXTURE WHIPS 6' 3/8" GREENFIELD	2.62	39.38	63.00	3.78	66.78	1.20
50 FUSES	.36	5.40	32.73	1.96	34.69	1.20
55 LIGHTING FIXTURE ACCESSORIES	1.36	20.40	17.00	1.02	18.02	1.20
70 LIGHTING FIXTURES	13.61	204.17				
94 SUPPORTS	7.31	109.74	19.34	1.16	20.50	1.20
96 SWITCHGEAR	3.75	56.25				
104 TRIM	4.52	67.85	52.50	3.15	55.65	1.20
110 WIRE FITTINGS	7.62	114.32	43.98	2.64	46.62	1.20
TOTAL WORKSHEET ITEMS:	140.50	2,107.64	1,024.44	61.46	1,085.90	1.20

QUOTED ITEMS

	NET COST	TAX	GROSS	M/UP
70 LIGHTING FIXTURES	850.00	51.00	901.00	1.15
96 SWITCHGEAR	650.00	39.00	689.00	1.20
TOTAL QUOTED ITEMS:	1,500.00	90.00	1,590.00	1.17

JOB EXPENSE ITEMS   — EXPENSES —

	NET COST	TAX	COST	M/UP
318 PERMIT	150.00		150.00	1.00
TOTAL JOB EXPENSES:	150.00		150.00	1.00

	NET COST	TAX		
TOTAL RAW COST:	4,782.08	151.46	4,933.54	
TOTAL MARGIN:			1,227.79	1.25
GRAND TOTAL:			6,161.33	

Job cost code recap. TRF International, Inc.

SQUARE FOOTAGE RECAP

BID NAME: JOE'S SHOE STORE
BID NUMBER: 1
BID DATE: 01-01-90
ESTIMATOR: SJ
JOB ADDRESS:
CUSTOMER:

SQUARE FOOTAGE: 1,500
TAKE-OFF MATERIAL SALES TAX: 6.000%
TAKE-OFF MATERIAL MARKUP: 20%
HOURLY LABOR RATE: $15.00
LABOR MARKUP: 35%
LABOR DIFFICULTY: LEVEL 2

	COST W/O SALES TAX	SALES TAX	MARGIN	SELLING PRICE	% OF SELL	COST PER SQ. FT.	SELL PER SQ. FT.
LABOR	2,107.61	.00	737.66	2,845.27	46.2	1.41	1.90
MATERIAL	1,024.44	61.47	217.18	1,303.09	21.1	.72	.87
QUOTED	1,500.00	90.00	272.95	1,862.95	30.2	1.06	1.24
EXPENSE	150.00	.00	.00	150.00	2.4	.10	.10
TOTALS	4,782.05	151.47	1,227.79	6,161.31		3.29	4.11

****

* * * MATERIAL TO LABOR RATIOS * * *

(A) TOTAL LABOR HOURS: 140.51
(B) TOTAL LABOR COST: 2,107.64

(C) TAKE-OFF MATERIAL COST: 1,085.91
(D) QUOTED MATERIAL COST: 1,590.00
(E) TOTAL MATERIAL COST: 2,675.91

	MATERIAL	–	LABOR	RATIO (M to L)
TAKE-OFF MATERIAL COST (C) TO LABOR COST (B):	34.00%	–	66.00%	.52 to 1
QUOTED MATERIAL COST (D) TO LABOR COST (B):	43.00%	–	57.00%	.75 to 1
TOTAL MATERIAL COST (E) TO LABOR COST (B):	55.94%	–	44.06%	1.27 to 1

Square footage recap. TRF International, Inc.

* * * VENDOR QUOTE WORKSHEET * * *

	DCI NUMBER	DESCRIPTION	QUANTITY	UNIT COST	EXTENDED
1	98010021750	#3 THW CU STR	632		
2	98010022400	#12 THHN CU SOLID	2,184		
3	98010023100	#8 THHN CU STR	5		
4	98010023150	#6 THHN CU STR	141		
		*COPPER WIRE [0111] TOTAL:			
5	78189105682	2CND THRMST TWSTD L/JKT CAROL	6		
6	78189105685	5CND THRMST TWSTD L/JKT CAROL	21		
		* THERMOSTAT WIRE [0720] TOTAL:			
7	98001002001	1/2" EMT CONDUIT	870		
8	98001002002	3/4" EMT CONDUIT	20		
9	98001002003	1" EMT CONDUIT	40		
10	98001002005	1-1/2" EMT CONDUIT	150		
		*EMT CONDUIT [1200] TOTAL:			
11	98005002321	1/2" SEALTITE TYPE UA	3		
12	98005002361	1" SEALTITE TYPE UA	3		
		* SEALTITE CONDUIT [1400] TOTAL:			
13	78188206241	1/2" PVC FEMALE ADAPTER	2		
		*PVC CONDUIT & FITTINGS [1500] TOTAL:			
14	98002000528	GALV NPPLE 1-1/2X6IN COND.PIPE	2		
		*GRC ELLS & NIPPLES [2110] TOTAL:			
15	98007012005	1-1/2" LOCKNUT	8		
16	98007012149	1-1/2" BONDING BUSHING	3		
17	78285667751	T-BAR BOX HANGER	512 10		
		*GRC CONDUIT FITTINGS [2210] TOTAL:			

Material list—vendor quote work-sheet. TRF International, Inc.

ELECTRICAL WORK ORDER   No.

Name/Company: _____ Phone _____ Date _____

Billing Address: _____

Job Location: _____

Description: _____

Code: Q - T&M - NTE _____

TALLY
Material .... $ _____
Labor .... $ _____
Truck .... $ _____
Other .... $ _____
TOTAL .... $ _____

CODE	MATERIAL	QTY	CODE	MATERIAL	QTY	CODE	MATERIAL	QTY	CODE	MATERIAL	QTY
	EMT		535	3/4 GRC			GRC LOCK/BUSHING		856	3/4 PVC 45	
505	1/2 EMT		536	1 GRC		1368	1/2 Locknut		857	1 PVC 45	
506	3/4 EMT			GRC		1369	3/4 Locknut			PVC 45	
507	1 EMT			GRC		1370	1 Locknut			PVC 45	
	EMT			GRC			Locknut			PVC 45	
	EMT			GRC ELBOWS			Locknut		829	1/2 PVC 90	
	EMT		1044	1 GRC 90			Locknut		830	3/4 PVC 90	
	EMT ELBOWS			GRC 90		1394	1/2 Bushing		831	1 PVC 90	
1602	1 EMT 90			GRC 90		1395	3/4 Bushing			PVC 90	
	EMT 90			GRC 90		1396	1 Bushing			PVC 90	
	EMT 90			GRC COUPLINGS			Bushing			PVC 90	
	EMT 90		1028	1/2 GRC Coup			Bushing			PVC COUPLING	
	EMT SS FITTINGS		1029	3/4 GRC Coup			Bushing		637	1/2 PVC Coup	
1623	1/2 EMT SS Conn		1030	1 GRC Coup		1421	1/2 G Bushing		638	3/4 PVC Coup	
1624	3/4 EMT SS Conn			GRC Coup		1422	3/4 G Bushing		639	1 PVC Coup	
1625	1 EMT SS Conn			GRC Coup		1423	1 G Bushing			PVC Coup	
	EMT SS Conn			GRC Coup			G Bushing			PVC Coup	
	EMT SS Conn			GRC CLOSE NIPPLE			G Bushing			PVC TERMINATORS	
1712	1/2 EMT SS Coup		1175	1/2 GRC C Nipple			G Bushing		692	1/2 PVC Term	
1713	3/4 EMT SS Coup		1187	3/4 GRC C Nipple			OFFSET NIPPLE		693	3/4 PVC Term	
1714	1 EMT SS Coup		1198	1 GRC C Nipple		1360	1/2 Offset Nipple		694	1 PVC Term	
	EMT SS Coup			GRC C Nipple		1361	3/4 Offset Nipple			PVC Term	
	EMT SS Coup			GRC C Nipple		1362	1 Offset Nipple			PVC Term	
	EMT SS Coup			GRC C Nipple			Offset Nipple			PVC Term	
	EMT RT FITTINGS			GRC NIPPLE			Offset Nipple		720	1/2 PVC FA	
1634	1/2 EMT RT Conn		1181	1/2 X 4 Nipple			Offset Nipple		721	3/4 PVC FA	
1635	3/4 EMT RT Conn		1192	3/4 X 4 Nipple			RIGID FITTINGS		722	1 PVC FA	
1636	1 EMT RT Conn		1203	1 X 4 Nipple		1481	1/2 GRC TL Conn			PVC FA	
	EMT RT Conn			Nipple		1482	3/4 GRC TL Conn			PVC FA	
	EMT RT Conn			Nipple		1483	1 GRC TL Conn			PVC FA	
	EMT RT Conn			Nipple			GRC TL Conn		754	1/2 PVC Condulet	
1723	1/2 EMT RT Coup			Nipple			GRC TL Conn		755	3/4 PVC Condulet	
1724	3/4 EMT RT Coup			GRC STRAPS		1492	1/2 GRC TL Coup		756	1 PVC Condulet	
1725	1 EMT RT Coup		1585	1/2 GRC Strap		1493	3/4 GRC TL Coup			PVC Condulet	
	EMT RT Coup		1586	3/4 GRC Strap		1494	1 GRC TL Coup			PVC Condulet	
	EMT RT Coup		1587	1 GRC Strap			GRC TL Coup			CONDULETS	
	EMT RT Coup			GRC Strap			GRC TL Coup		1093	1/2 SLB	
	EMT STRAPS			GRC Strap			GRC TL Coup		1094	3/4 SLB	
1771	1/2 EMT Strap			GRC Strap		1900	Reducing Bush		1095	1 SLB	
1772	3/4 EMT Strap		1596	1/2 GRC J Nail		1892	KO Seal			SLB	
1773	1 EMT Strap		1597	3/4 GRC J Nail			PVC (Conduit)			SLB	
	EMT Strap			KINDORF		562	1/2 PVC			SLB	
	EMT Strap		2251	1 1/2 Kindorf Strut		563	3/4 PVC		1115	1/2 Condulet	
	EMT Strap			Kindorf Strut		564	1 PVC		1116	3/4 Condulet	
1778	1/2 EMT J Nail		2201	1/2 Kindorf Stp			PVC		1117	1 Condulet	
1779	3/4 EMT J Nail		2202	3/4 Kindorf Stp			PVC			Condulet	
1780	1 EMT J Nail		2203	1 Kindorf Stp			PVC			Condulet	
	GRC (Conduit)			Kindorf Stp			PVC ELBOW			Condulet	
534	1/2 GRC			Kindorf Stp		855	1/2 PVC 45			Condulet	

Electrical work order—page 1. McCormick Systems, Inc.

STEEL FLEX

CODE	MATERIAL	QTY
	STEEL FLEX	
588	1/2 Steel Flex	
589	3/4 Steel Flex	
590	1 Steel Flex	
	Steel Flex	
	Steel Flex	
	Steel Flex	
1790	1/2 Stl Flex Conn	
1791	3/4 Stl Flex Conn	
1792	1 Stl Flex Conn	
	Stl Flex Conn	
	Stl Flex Conn	
1809	1/2 Stl 90 F/Conn	
1810	3/4 Stl 90 F/Conn	
1811	1 Stl 90 F/Conn	
	Stl 90 F/Conn	
	Stl 90 F/Conn	
	LT FLEX	
612	1/2 LT Flex	
613	3/4 LT Flex	
614	1 FT Flex	
	FT Flex	
	FT Flex	
	FT Flex	
1907	1/2 LT Flex Conn	
1908	3/4 LT Flex Conn	
1909	1 LT Flex Conn	
	LT Flex Conn	
	LT Flex Conn	
1929	1/2 LT 90 F/Conn	
1930	3/4 LT 90 F/Conn	
1931	1 LT 90 F/Conn	
	LT 90 F/Conn	
	LT 90 F/Conn	
	LT 90 F/Conn	
	ENT CONDUIT	
517	1/2 Plastic Flex	
518	3/4 Plastic Flex	
	Plastic Flex	
968	1/2 Plastic Conn	
969	3/4 Plastic Conn	
	Plastic Conn	
972	1/2 Plastic Coup	
973	3/4 Plastic Coup	
	Plastic Coup	
	SERVICE HEAD	
1517	1/2 Service Head	

CODE	MATERIAL	QTY
1518	3/4 Service Head	
1519	1 Service Head	
	Service Head	
	Service Head	
1529	1 1/4 Flashing	
3961	#6 Bail	
3962	#2 Bail	
	WIRE	
170	#8 Bare cu	
171	#6 Bare cu	
172	#4 Bare cu	
173	#2 Bare cu	
174	#1 Bare cu	
175	1/0 Bare cu	
	Bare cu	
	Bare cu	
29	#14 THHN CU Wire	
30	#12 THHN CU Wire	
31	#10 THHN CU Wire	
35	#8 THHN CU Wire	
36	#6 THHN CU Wire	
37	#4 THHN CU Wire	
	THHN CU Wire	
	THHN CU Wire	
	THHN CU Wire	
13	#2 THW CU Wire	
14	#1 THW CU Wire	
15	1/0 THW CU Wire	
16	2/0 THW CU Wire	
17	3/0 THW CU Wire	
18	4/0 THW CU Wire	
19	250 THW CU Wire	
	THW CU Wire	
	THW CU Wire	
	THW CU Wire	
83	#2 THW AL Wire	
84	#1 THW AL Wire	
85	1/0 THW AL Wire	
86	2/0 THW AL Wire	
87	3/0 THW AL Wire	
88	4/0 THW AL Wire	
89	250 THW AL Wire	
	THW AL Wire	
	THW AL Wire	
	THW AL Wire	
194	#6 USE AL Wire	
195	#4 USE AL Wire	
196	#2 USE AL Wire	
	USE AL Wire	

CODE	MATERIAL	QTY
	USE AL Wire	
	USE AL Wire	
473	18/2 Stat Wire	
	Stat Wire	
	Stat Wire	
312	14/2 W/G NM	
313	12/2 W/G NM	
314	10/2 W/G NM	
317	14/3 W/G NM	
318	12/3 W/G NM	
319	10/3 W/G NM	
343	12/2 W/G UF	
348	12/3 W/G UF	
344	10/2 W/G UF	
349	10/3 W/G UF	
3291	Staple	
357	#4 SEU al	
361	#1 SEU al	
	SEU al	
	SEU al	
373	#6 SER al	
374	#4 SER al	
376	#1 SER al	
	SER al	
	SER al	
450	Triplex	
	SO CORD	
438	14/3 SO Cord	
	SO Cord	
	SO Cord	
	SO Cord	
	WIRE TERMINATORS	
1841	1/2 2 Screw Term	
1842	3/4 2 Screw Term	
1843	1 2 Screw Term	
	2 Screw Term	
	2 Screw Term	
	WIRE TERMINATORS	
3288	Yellow Wirenut	
3286	Red Wirenut	
3284	Blue Wirenut	
3285	Gray Wirenut	
3277	#6 Lug	
3278	#2 Lug	
3280	#2/0 Lug	
	Lug	
	Lug	
3296	Tape, Black	
3294	Tape, 2200	

CODE	MATERIAL	QTY
	Tape,	
	Tape,	
	Tape,	
	PLASTIC BOXES	
2175	1g Plastic Box	
2177	2g Plastic Box	
2178	3g Plastic Box	
2174	4/S Plastic Box	
	Plastic Box	
	Plastic Box	
	Plastic Box	
2179	3/0 Nail-on	
2180	4/0 Nail-on	
	METAL BOXES	
2023	Handy Box	
2028	1g Blank	
2029	1g Blank W/KO	
2032	1g Device Cover	
1973	3/0 Box	
2048	3/0 Blank	
1977	4/0 Box	
2049	4/0 Blank	
1989	4/S Box	
1990	4/S Bracket Box	
1992	4/S Ext Box	
2051	4/S Blank	
2062	4/S 1g Mud Ring	
2066	4/S 2g Mud Ring	
2128	4/S RS Cover	
2008	5/S Box	
2053	5/S Blank	
2005	1g Bell Box	
	Box	
	Box	
	Box	
	Box	
	Box	
	Box	
2167	Ground Clip	
2166	Ground Screw	
	J BOX / GUTTER	
2639	6X6X4 NEMA1 JB	
2655	8X8X4 NEMA1 JB	
2675	12X12X4 NEMA1 JB	
2638	6X6X4 NEMA3 JB	
2654	8X8X4 NEMA3 JB	
2676	12X12X4 NEMA3 JB	
2678	12X12X6 NEMA3 JB	
	NEMA JB	
	NEMA JB	

Electrical work order—page 2. McCormick Systems, Inc.

CODE	MATERIAL	QTY
	NEMA JB	
2548	4X4X12 Gutter	
2550	4X4X24 Gutter	
2551	4X4X36 Gutter	
2552	4X4X48 Gutter	
2553	4X4X60 Gutter	
	Gutter	
	Gutter	
	Gutter	
	ANCHORS	
3399	10X3/4 Pan	
3401	10X1 1/4 Pan	
3403	10/2 Pan	
3459	6/32X1 1/4	
3465	8/32X1 1/4	
3578	1/8X3 Toggle	
3582	3/16X3 Toggle	
3588	1/4X4 Toggle	
3305	1/4 Concrete	
3306	3/8 Concrete	
3307	1/2 Concrete	
	Anchor	
	Anchor	
	Anchor	
	DISCONNECT	
4068	30A 3p 250vN1 SW	
4069	60A 3p 250vN1 SW	
4070	100A 3p 250vN1 SW	
4071	200A 3p 250vN1 SW	
4106	30A 3p 250vN3 SW	
4107	60A 3p 250vN3 SW	
4108	100A 3p 250vN3 SW	
4109	200A 3p 250vN3 SW	
	p 250vN SW	
	p 250vN SW	
	p 250vN SW	
4098	30A 3p 600vN1 SW	
4099	60A 3p 600vN1 SW	
4100	100A 3p 600vN1 SW	
4101	200A 3p 600vN1 SW	
4110	30A 3p 600vN3 SW	
4111	60A 3p 600vN3 SW	
4112	100A 3p 600vN3 SW	
4113	200A 3p 600vN3 SW	
	p 600vN SW	
	p 600vN SW	
	p 600vN SW	
4059	Blank Hub	
1445	Sml Myers Hub	
1449	Lge Myers Hub	

CODE	MATERIAL	QTY
	PANELS	
	Panel	
	Panel	
	Panel	
	Panel	
	BREAKERS	
	Breaker	
	Breaker	
	Breaker	
	Breaker	
	Breaker	
	METER BASES	
	Meter Base	
	Meter Base	
	CT CAN	
	CT Can	
	CT Can	
	FUSES	
3249	15-30a FRN Fuse	
3251	40-60a FRN Fuse	
3252	70-100a FRN Fuse	
3253	110-200a FRN Fuse	
	a FRN Fuse	
	a FRN Fuse	
	a FRN Fuse	
3258	15-30a FRS Fuse	
3251	40-60a FRS Fuse	
3252	70-100a FRS Fuse	
3261	110-200a FRS Fuse	
	a FRS Fuse	
	a FRS Fuse	
	a FRS Fuse	
	TRIM	
2836	1p Switch	
2838	3w Switch	
2817	4w Switch	
2823	2p Switch	
2796	1p Spec Switch	
2802	3w Spec Switch	
2805	4w Spec Switch	
	Switch	
	Switch	
	Switch	
2776	600w Dimmer	
2867	Single Recp	
2864	Duplex Recp	
2861	30a Recp	
2860	50a Recp	
	Recp	
	Recp	

CODE	MATERIAL	QTY
	Recp	
2974	1g Plate	
2975	2g Plate	
2976	3g Plate	
2977	4g Plate	
2848	WP Plate	
	Plate	
	Plate	
	Plate	
	FLOR FIXTURES	
3814	C-240 Fixture	
3819	C-296 Fixture	
3826	2t Florscent	
3828	4t Florscent	
	Florscent	
	Florscent	
	Florscent	
	INCD FIXTURES	
	Inc Fix	
	Inc Fix	
	Inc Fix	
	Inc Fix	
	Inc Fix	
	LAMPS/BALLASTS	
	Lamp	
	Lamp	
	Lamp	
	Lamp	
	Ballast	
	Ballast	
	Ballast	
	Ballast	
	HEAT	
	Heat	
	Heat	
	Heat	
	Heat	
	Heat	
	Heat	
	Heat	
MISC		

CODE	MATERIAL		QTY
	ASSEMBLIES		
2452	Recp	Com	
2453	Switch	Com	
2454	Tel	Com	
2457	Troffer	Com	
2458	Slimline	Com	
2461	1 1/4" Feeder	EMT	
2462	2" Feeder	EMT	
2465	Recp	House	
2466	Switch	House	
2467	Range	House	
2468	Dryer	House	
2469	Water Heater	House	
2472	Fixture	House	
2476	200A O/H Ser Change		
2477	200A U/G Ser Change		
	LABOR		
4554	Helper		
4555	App		
4556	Journyman		
4557	Foreman		
	Other		
	Other		

Electrical work order—page 3. McCormick Systems, Inc.

DESCRIPTION OF WORK DONE:

Customer
Signature_____

COMMENTS:

ADDITIONS AND/OR DELETIONS:

HINDERANCE TO JOB PROGRESS BY WHOM:

STATUS REPORT:

TRUCK		
TRUCK #	DATE	HOURS

SPECIAL EQUIPMENT	
ITEM	TIME

TRAVEL		
EMPLOYEE	DATE	MILES

© McCormick Systems

Electrical work order—page 4. McCormick Systems, Inc.

YOUR COMPANY NAME HERE
123 Main Street
ANYTOWN, STATE, ZIP CODE

(123) 456-7890

PRICE QUOTATION

Please refer to this number on all correspondence ➤ **1001**

TODAY'S DATE	YOUR ORDER DATE
PROPOSED SHIPPING DATE	
TERMS	
F.O.B. POINT	DELIVERY
	☐ POSTAGE PRE PAID
SHIPPED VIA	☐ C.O.D.
SALES REPRESENTATIVE	

HERE IS OUR QUOTATION ON THE GOODS NAMED.
SUBJECT TO THE FOLLOWING CONDITIONS:

CONDITIONS: The prices and terms on this quotation are not subject to verbal changes or other agreements unless approved in writing by the Home Office of the Seller. All quotations and agreements are contingent upon strikes, accidents, fires, availability of materials and all other causes beyond our control. Prices are based on costs and conditions existing on date of quotation and are subject to change by the Seller before final acceptance. Typographical and stenographic errors subject to correction. Purchaser agrees to accept either overage or shortage not in excess of ten percent to be charged for pro-rata. Purchaser assumes liability for patent and copyright infringement when goods are made to Purchaser's specifications. When quotation specifies material to be furnished by the purchaser, ample allowance must me made for reasonable spoilage and material must be of suitable quality to facilitate efficient production. Conditions not specifically stated herein shall be governed by established trade customs. Terms inconsistent with those stated herein which may appear on Purchaser's formal order will not be binding on the Seller.

QUANTITY	DESCRIPTION	UNIT PRICE	TOTAL AMOUNT

THIS QUOTE WILL REMAIN VALID FOR _____ DAYS   BY

FORM 702 3

Price quotation form. McBee Systems, Division of Romo Corporation, reproduced with permission.

• P R O P O S A L •

YOUR COMPANY NAME HERE
123 Main Street
ANYTOWN, STATE, ZIP CODE
(123) 456-7890

Mr. John Williamson   Date: May 12,
Williamson and Associates
Main Street   Job: Promotional
New York, New York   Brochure

Dear Mr. Williamson:

We hereby submit specifications and estimates for the
design and printing of your twenty-four(24) page self-
promotional brochure.

All design and layouts, mechanicals, typesetting, photostats,
photography, photography supervision, color separations,
and four-color printing of your 24 page brochure.

Photography will include eighteen(18) color chromes using
minor props for enhancement.

We will submit three(3) cover designs and two(2) full
24 page layouts for the inside.

All copy to be supplied by Williamson and Associates.

Printing will be on 80 lb. Coated Cover stock with four color
on both sides. Saddle stitch binding. 10,000 Quantity.
All color separations will be approved by Williamson and
Associates before final press run.

Design and Layouts, Mechanicals, Typesetting, Photostats, Eighteen(18) Photography Shots, Photography Supervision, and Press Run Coordination	$3,000.00
Printing 10,000 Quantity	6,400.00
Total	$9,400.00

WE PROPOSE to furnish labor and material—complete in accordance with the above specifications, and subject to conditions found on both sides of this agreement, for the sum of

Nine Thousand Four Hundred and 00/100 _____ dollars ($ $9,400.00).

Payment to be made as follows: _____ due upon completion of job

ACCEPTED: The above prices, specifications and conditions are satisfactory and are hereby approved. You are authorized to proceed work as specified. Payment will be made as outlined above. (Please see reverse side).

Respectfully submitted.

YOUR COMPANY NAME ALSO PRINTED HERE

Acceptance Date: _____

By: _____   By: _____

By: _____   Note: This proposal may be withdrawn by us if not approved within _____ days.

FORM 709-3

Proposal form. McBee Systems, Division of Romo Corporation, reproduced with permission.

CHANGE ORDER

┌ **YOUR COMPANY NAME HERE** ┐
123 Main Street
ANYTOWN, STATE. ZIP CODE

└   ┘

(123) 456-7890

NUMBER _____

PHONE	DATE OF ORDER
JOB NAME LOCATION	
JOB NUMBER	JOB PHONE
EXISTING CONTRACT NO	DATE OF CONTRACT

WE hereby agree to make the change(s) specified below

WE AGREE hereby to make all the designated change(s) specified above at this price ◆		
DATE OF CHANGE(S)	**PREVIOUS CONTRACT AMOUNT**	
AUTHORIZED SIGNATURE (CONTRACTOR)	**REVISED CONTRACT TOTAL** ◆	

ACCEPTED - the above prices and specifications of this Change Order are satisfactory and are hereby accepted. All work to be performed under the same terms and conditions as specified in the original contract unless otherwise stipulated.

DATE OF ACCEPTANCE

SIGNATURE (OWNER)

McBee · 1055 EAST STATE ST. · ATHENS, OHIO 45701

NOTE. This Change Order becomes part of and in conformance with the existing contract.

Change order form. McBee Systems, Division of Romo Corporation, reproduced with permission.

CHAPTER 5

Easy record keeping

W<small>HY KEEP RECORDS?</small> Many reasons. For the individual just starting an electrical contracting business, an adequate record-keeping system helps increase the chances of survival and reduces the probability of early failure. With a good record-keeping system, established electrical contractors can enhance their chances of staying in business and earning increased profits.

How do good accounting records decrease the chances of failure and increase the likelihood of remaining in business and making a profit? Here are some of the things that good business records can tell you:

- How much business am I doing?
- How much credit am I extending?
- How much is tied up in receivables?
- How much of my receivables are more than 60, 90, or 120 days overdue?
- How are my collections?
- What are my losses from credit sales?
- Who owes me money?
- Who is delinquent?
- Should I continue extending credit to delinquent accounts?
- How soon can I anticipate realizing a return on my accounts receivable?
- How much cash do I have on hand?
- How much cash do I have in the bank?
- Does this amount agree with what records tell me I should have, or is there a shortage?
- How much is my investment in materials?
- How often do I turn over my inventory?
- Have I allowed my inventory to become obsolete?
- How much do I owe my suppliers and other creditors?

- Have I received all of my outstanding credits for returned materials?
- How much gross profit or margin did I earn?
- What were my expenses, including those not requiring cash outlays?
- What's my weekly payroll?
- Do I have adequate payroll records to meet the requirements of Workers' Compensation, Wage Hour Laws, Social Security, Unemployment Insurance, and Withholding Taxes?
- How much net profit did I earn?
- How much income taxes will I owe?
- What's my capital?
- Are my sales, expenses, profits, and capital showing improvements, or did I do better than this last year?
- How do I stand as compared with two periods ago?
- Is my business' position about the same, improving, or deteriorating?
- On what services am I making a profit, breaking even, or losing money?
- Am I taking full advantage of cash discounts for prompt payments?
- How do my discounts taken compare with my discounts given?
- How do the financial facts of my electrical contracting business compare with those of similar businesses?

Get the point? Your business requires a good record-keeping system to help you work smarter rather than harder.

Keeping accurate and up-to-date business records is, for many people, the most difficult and uninteresting aspect of operating a business. If this area of business management is one that you believe will be hard for you, plan now how you'll handle this task. Don't wait until tax time or until you're totally confused. Take a course at a local community college, ask a volunteer SCORE representative (see chapter 2), or hire an accountant to advise you on setting up and maintaining your record-keeping system.

Your records will be used to prepare tax returns, make business decisions, and apply for loans. Set aside a special time each day to update your records. It will pay off in the long run with more deductions and fewer headaches.

Requirements of a good system

So, what do you need for a good record-keeping or accounting system. A good record-keeping system should be:

- Simple to use.
- Easy to understand.
- Reliable.
- Accurate.
- Consistent.
- Timely.

There are several published systems and software systems that provide simplified records, usually in a single record book. These systems cover the primary records required for all businesses; some are modified specifically for the electrical contracting business. Check your local office supply store, your contracting association, or advertisements in electrical contracting trade journals for more information on specialized record books.

Your records should tell you these three facts:

- How much cash you owe.
- How much cash is owed to you.
- How much cash you have on hand.

To keep track of everything, you should have four basic journals:

- A *check register* (as shown at the top of following page) shows each check disbursed, the date of the disbursement, number of the check, to whom it was made out (payee), the amount of money disbursed, and for what purpose.
- *Cash receipts* show the amount of money received, from whom, and for what.

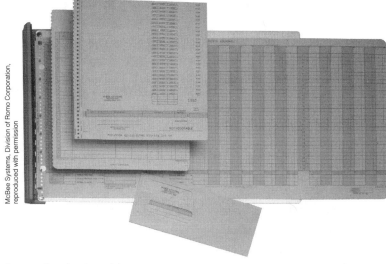

One-write check writing system.

- A *sales journal* (as shown at the top of following page) shows the business transaction, date, for whom it was performed, the amount of the invoice, how much for labor, how much for materials, and any applicable sales tax.
- A voucher register records bills, money owed, the date of the bill, to whom it's owed, the amount, and the service.

Some businesses combine all of these journals into a single journal. In fact, there are many good "one-write" systems that allow you to make a single entry for each transaction. I'll cover those under "Record-keeping systems" in a moment.

Single entry versus double entry

There are basically two ways to record transactions in your business: with a single entry or with a double entry. The primary advantage to single-entry record keeping is that it's easy. As the name implies, you make a single entry that records the source of each income or destination of each expense. Each entry is either a plus or a minus to the amount of cash that you have. Receipt of a check on an outstanding account is a plus.

Portable register.

Payment of a supplies order is a minus. As long as you have a limited number of transactions, single-entry accounting is adequate.

However, as your business grows in complexity, you'll want a check-and-balance system that ensures that records are accurate. Double-entry accounting requires that you make two offsetting entries that balance each other. A check received on an outstanding account is a debit to cash, and a credit to accounts receivable. Payment for a supplies order is a debit to supplies and a credit to cash.

Every account has two sides: a left or debit side and a right or credit side. The posted debits must always equal the posted credits. Some types of accounts are called debit accounts because their balance is typically a debit. Asset accounts (cash, accounts receivable) are debit accounts. Liability accounts (accounts payable, notes payable) usually carry a credit balance. Income carries a credit balance, while expenses carry a debit balance.

Everything else within double-entry bookkeeping is based on the previously stated rules. Here are some examples of common double entries:

- Cash income = debit cash and credit income.
- Accrued income = debit accounts receivable and credit income.
- Cash expense = debit the expense account and credit cash.
- Accrued expense = debit the expense account and credit accounts payable.
- Prepaid expense = debit prepaid expenses and credit cash.

If, at the end of the month, the debits don't equal the credits, check for debits erroneously posted as credits, credits erroneously posted as debits, transposition of numbers ($123 to $132), and incorrect math.

Assets, liabilities, and net worth

Throughout this chapter and in your business, you'll hear about assets, liabilities, and net worth. Before moving deeper into record keeping, let's define these terms. *Assets* include not only cash, inventory, land, building, equipment, machinery, furniture, and the like, but also money due from individuals or other businesses (known as accounts or notes receivable).

Liabilities are funds acquired for a business through loans or the sale of property or services to the business on credit. Creditors don't acquire ownership in your business, but promissory notes to be paid at a designated future date (known as accounts or notes payable). *Net worth* (or shareholders' equity or capital) is money put into a business by its owners for use by the business in acquiring assets.

The formula for this structure is:

Assets = Liabilities + Net Worth

That is, the total funds invested in assets of the business is equal to the funds supplied to the business by its creditors, plus the funds supplied to the business by its owners. If a business owes more money to creditors than it possesses in value of assets owned, then the net worth or owner's equity of the business will be a negative number. This accounting formula can also be expressed as:

Assets – Liabilities = Net Worth

Bank account

As covered in chapter 4, be sure to establish a separate bank account for your business—even before your first sale. Then you'll have a complete and distinct record of your income and expenditures for tax purposes, and you won't have to remember which expenses were business and which were personal.

Cash or accrual?

Many small businesses are operated primarily on a cash basis. The customer buys products with cash; the merchant buys inventory with cash. As businesses become larger and more complicated, many keep records on the *accrual basis*. The dividing line between cash basis and accrual basis might depend on whether or not credit is given to customers, as well as the amount of inventory required.

Accrual basis is a method of recording income and expenses in which each item is reported as earned or incurred, without regard as to when actual payments are received or made. Charge sales are credited at once to sales and charged to accounts receivable. When the bills are collected, the credit is to accounts receivable. Accruals should also be made for expense items payable in the future, such as annual or semiannual interest on loans.

If you're comfortable with accounting, accrual can be the most accurate basis for records. However, the *cash basis* is easiest to understand. As long as you don't prepay many of your expenses, a cash basis is fine for your new electrical contracting business.

Journals

All businesses need some form of journal or book where all business transactions can be recorded. Information for each transaction or journal entry is derived from original source documents: check stubs, invoices, statements, credit vouchers, purchase orders, expense records and receipts, etc.

General ledgers are kept to record transactions and balances of individual accounts: assets, liabilities, capital, income, and expenses. The full page illustration on page 128 illustrates a chart of accounts for a typical electrical contractor. Your firm's chart of accounts might be somewhat different, depending on its size, services, and business structure.

At the end of each fiscal year or accounting period, accounts are balanced and closed. Income and expense account balances are transferred to the summary of revenue and expenses and are used in the income statement. The remaining asset, liability, and capital accounts provide figures for the balance sheet.

How many accounts should your business have? Not so many as to make analysis confusing. Break down sales into enough categories to show a clear picture of the sources of your business income. Use different expense accounts covering frequent or substantial expenditures, but avoid minor distinctions that will tend to confuse rather than qualify. Use the miscellaneous expense category for small, unrelated items.

Income not yet paid to you is called *accounts receivable*. Here are a few rules that can help you keep accounts receivable current. First, be sure bills are prepared immediately after the service is performed. Also, make sure that the statement is mailed to the correct person and address, with sufficient information on the statement to fully identify the source and purpose of the charge. Note that some businesses will simply set aside any bills that they question.

Accounts receivable

At the end of each month, "age" your accounts receivable. That is, list accounts and enter the amounts that are current, unpaid for 30 days, and those unpaid for 60 days or more. Most accounts receivable computer programs will produce reports on aged receivables. Then you can call each account in the 60+ days column and find out why the bill is unpaid. Keep an especially close watch on larger accounts.

To ensure that you get paid promptly, pay close attention to customers' complaints about bills. If a complaint is justified,

ABC ELECTRICAL CONTRACTORS
Chart of Accounts

INCOME
Contract Sales
Miscellaneous Income
Sales Adjustments
Discounts Received
Interest Income

EXPENSES
JOB COSTS
Job Labor
Subcontractor Fees
Sales Commissions
Primary Materials
Secondary Materials
Shipping
Sales Tax
Misc. Job Costs

OVERHEAD
Administrative Salaries
Administrative Payroll Taxes and Insurance
Administrative Benefits Package
Advertising and Promotion
Bad Debts and Collection Costs
Bank Charges
Business Insurance
Depreciation-Office Equipment
Depreciation-Tools and Equipment
Depreciation-Vehicles
Discounts Allowed
Donations
Entertainment
Equipment
Interest
Job Payroll Taxes and Insurance
Leases
Licenses and Fees
Office Rent
Office Expenses
Office Utilities
Postage
Professional Dues
Professional Services
Telephone
Tools
Travel Expenses
Unapplied Labor
Vehicle Maintenance and Repair
Vehicle Fuels

A chart of accounts for a typical electrical contractor.

offer an adjustment and reach an agreement with the customer. Then get a date from the customer as to when you can expect to receive the payment.

As you get a new customer who asks for credit, use a simple form listing name, address, telephone number, employment, bank, and credit references. Such credit application forms are available at many office supply and stationery stores. Make sure that the customer is worthy of credit before you grant it.

Quarterly and yearly reports of individual payroll payments must be made to federal and state governments. After the end of the calendar year, each individual employee must receive a W-2 form showing total withholding payments made for the employee during the previous year.

Each payday, a payroll summary should be made, showing the names, employee number, rate of pay, hours worked, overtime hours, total pay, and amount of deductions for FICA (Social Security), Medicare, state and federal withholding taxes, deductions for insurance, pension, savings, and child support, as required.

To ensure that you maintain adequate records for this task, keep an employee card for each employee of your firm. The employee card or computer file should show the full legal name, Social Security number, address, telephone number, name of next of kin and their address, marital status, number of exemptions claimed, and current rate of pay. A federal W-4 form completed and signed by the employee should also be attached to the employee card or record.

Also maintain a running total of earnings, pay and deductions for each individual employee. In addition, if your business employees are union members, you might have additional deductions for union dues, pensions, and other fees.

To begin your payroll system, contact the Internal Revenue Service (Washington, DC 20224) and request the Employer's Tax Guide (Circular E) and get a nine-digit Employer Identification Number. The IRS will then send you deposit slips

Managing payroll records

(Form 8109) with your new ID number printed on them. Use these deposit slips each time you pay your payroll taxes. Payroll taxes are paid within a month of the ending of a quarter—that is, January 31, April 30, July 31, and October 31. As your business grows, you might be required to pay payroll taxes more frequently. By then, your accountant will help you determine need and the process.

Petty cash fund

Most business expenses will be paid by business check, credit card, or placed on account with the seller. However, there might be some small expenses that will be paid by an employee or with cash that requires reimbursement. Because the amount is typically small, the fund from which the reimbursement comes is usually known as *petty cash*.

A petty cash fund should be set up to be used for payments of small amounts not covered by invoices. A check should be drawn for, say, $50. The check is cashed and the fund placed in a box or drawer. When small cash payments are made for such items as postage, freight, or bus fares, the items are listed on a printed form or even a slip of paper. When the fund is nearly exhausted, the items are summarized and a check drawn to cover the exact amount spent. The check is cashed and the fund replenished. At all times, the cash in the drawer plus the listed expenditures should equal the established amount of the petty cash fund. (A sample petty cash register is included in this book's appendix.)

Equipment records

Keep an accurate and up-to-date list of permanent equipment used in your electrical contracting business. Especially keep track of equipment that's useful for a year or longer and of appreciable value. Equipment records should show date purchased, name of supplier, description of item, check number of payment(s), and amount of purchase, including tax. If you own a number of items, keep a separate list for vehicles, tools, related work equipment, and office furniture and fixtures. From these records you'll develop depreciation and provide supporting information for fixed-asset accounts.

A note about depreciation. A charge to expenses should be made to cover depreciation of fixed assets other than land.

Fixed assets are any item you purchase to use in your business for a year or longer. Examples are buildings, vehicles, tools, equipment, furniture, and office fixtures. Smaller businesses will usually charge depreciation at the end of their fiscal year, but if your business grows and you have major fixed assets, you or your accountant might decide to calculate depreciation monthly.

Insurance helps to safeguard your business against losses from fire, illness, injury, and other hazards. You can't operate without insurance. Talk with an insurance representative about your business needs.

Insurance records

Your electrical contracting business will have several types of insurance. Each policy should be listed, showing the type of insurance coverage (automotive, fire, theft, bonding, etc.), name of the insurance company and agent, expiration date, and premiums (monthly and annual). Keep a file with all of your insurance policies in them, or keep separate files for the types of policies. In addition to fire, theft, and hazard insurance, some of the most common types of business insurance are:

- Liability coverage to protect you in case a service you perform leads to an injury of the user.
- Auto liability insurance for any vehicle that you use in your business in any way.
- Medical payments insurance to reimburse anyone who is injured while at your place of business.
- Worker's compensation to cover people who work for you in case of on-the-job injury.
- Business interruption insurance to cover you in case your business is damaged by fire or some other hazard that requires you to totally or partially suspend operation.
- Disability income protection to provide you with income if you become disabled.
- Business life insurance to provide funds for transition when you die.

Be sure to keep all of your insurance records and policies in a safe place—either with your accountant or in a safe deposit box at your bank. If you keep them in your office for convenience sake, give your policy numbers and insurance company names to your accountant or lawyer or put them in your safe deposit box.

Outside accounting service

Many new electrical contractors have the right skills for plying their trade, yet they fail because of poor financial management. Sometimes the best decision is to hire the services of a public accounting firm. An accountant can design records, set up ways for maintaining them, draw off vital information, and help relate that information to a profitable operation.

Daily bits of information will flow into your electrical contracting business. As customers are served, pieces of information are generated about sales, cash, equipment, purchase expenses, payroll, accounts payable, and, if credit is offered to customers, accounts receivable.

To capture these facts and figures, a system is necessary. If you don't feel comfortable yet with setting up and managing such a system, don't be shy about hiring an accounting service. An accountant can help design a system for recording the information that you need to control finances and make profitable decisions.

Once a system of records has been set up, the question is: Who should keep the books? The accounting service who has set up the books can keep them. However, if you have a general understanding of record keeping, you can do them yourself and save some money. Use your accountant for checking and analyzing your records. Once your business has grown, you might consider hiring someone to keep your records and perform other office functions, or maybe your spouse can assist you.

In addition to record keeping, an accountant can advise you on financial management. He or she can assist you with cash flow requirements, budget forecasts, borrowing, business organization, and taxes.

On cash flow requirements, an accountant can help you work out the amount of cash needed to operate your firm during a specific period—for example, three months, six months, the next year. He or she considers how much cash you'll need to carry customer accounts receivable, to buy equipment and supplies, to pay current bills, and to repay loans. In addition, an accountant can determine how much cash will come from collection of accounts receivable and how much will have to be borrowed or pulled from an existing line of credit. While working out the cash requirements, your accountant might notice and call your attention to danger spots such as accounts that are past due.

When you borrow, your accountant can assemble financial information such as a profit and loss or income statement and a balance sheet. The purpose of such data is to show the lender the financial position of your business and its ability to repay the loan. Using this information, your accountant can advise you on whether you need a short-term or long-term loan. The financial data that your accountant compiles will include:

- Assets that you'll offer for collateral.
- Your current debt obligations.
- A summary of how you'll use the money you borrow.
- A schedule of how you intend to repay the borrowed money.

If you've never borrowed before, your accountant might help you by introducing you to a banker who knows and respects the accountant's reputation. This alone might be worth the cost of hiring an accountant to advise and help you.

Taxes are another area in which an accountant can provide advice and assistance. Normally, a record-keeping system that provides the information you need for making profitable decisions will suffice for tax purposes. However, if you purchase a lot of equipment that requires special depreciation, if you have employees that require payroll taxes, and if you have extensive bad debts, a good accountant can help you identify the problems, suggest a method of keeping good records, and help you minimize your tax obligation. Chapter 8 offers guidelines for selecting a good accountant.

Financial information you need

As the owner of an electrical contracting firm, you need accurate information on a regular basis to ensure that your business is running smoothly. As a single-person firm, you might have all the information you need in your head. However, as your firm grows you'll need some information daily, other information weekly, and still other data on a monthly basis. Let's take a look at what you'll need and when.

Daily report

In order to manage your electrical contracting firm, you'll want the following information on a daily basis:

- Cash on hand.
- Bank balance.
- Daily summary of sales and cash receipts.
- Daily summary of monies paid out by cash or check.
- Correction of any errors from previous reports.

You can either prepare this information yourself, have your office employee prepare it for you, or rely on your accountant. While daily records will not show you trends, they will help you get a feel for the level of business that you're doing. Also, you'll be able to spot problems before they occur.

Weekly report

Once a week, you or someone you employ should prepare a weekly report on your firm. While still not sufficient for long-term planning, weekly figures will help you make small corrections in the course your business is taking. Weekly, you'll want:

- Accounts Receivable Report listing accounts that require a call because they're more than 60 days overdue.
- Accounts Payable Report listing what your business owes, to whom, and if a discount is offered for early payment.
- Payroll Report, including information on each employee, the number of hours worked during the week, rate of pay, total wages, deductions, net pay, and related information.
- Taxes and reports required to be sent to city, state, and federal governments.

Your weekly reports should be prepared by the end of business Friday so you can review them during the weekend or early Monday morning.

Once a month, you'll want to review a number of pieces of information that have accumulated through your daily and weekly reports but were too small to analyze clearly. Now that they're part of a full month, information about cash flow, accounts receivable, and other parts of your business make more sense—and you can more easily act on them. Here are some of the reports and information you'll want to see every month:

- General ledger, including all journal entries.
- Income statement showing income for the prior month, expenses incurred in obtaining the income, overhead, and the profit or loss received.
- Balance sheet showing the assets, liabilities, and capital or current worth of the business.
- Reconciled bank statement that shows what checks were deposited and which were applied by payees against your business checking account; this statement also verifies that the cash balance is accurate.
- Petty cash fund report to ensure that paid-out slips plus cash equals the beginning petty cash balance.
- Tax payment report showing that all federal tax deposits, withheld income, FICA taxes, state and other taxes have been paid.
- Aged receivables report showing the age and balance of each account (30, 60, 90 days past due, etc.).

There are numerous commercial record-keeping systems available through local office suppliers, stationers, and contractor's supply firms. Here are a few systems that are specifically for contractors:

Binex Automated Business System for Building Contractors (Binex Automated Business Systems, 3102 "O" St., Sacramento, CA 95816).

Blackbourn Systems for Contractors' Job Analysis (Blackbourn Systems Inc., 1821 University Ave., St. Paul, MN 55104).

Blue Book for Building Contractors (Columbia Bookkeeping Systems Inc., 2 Central Square, Grafton, MA 01519).

Marcoin System and Business Services for Building Contractors (Marcoin Inc., 1924 Cliff Valley Way NE, Atlanta, GA 30329).

McBee Systems for Building Contractors (McBee Systems, 151 Cortlandt St., Belleville, NJ 07109).

Practical Bookkeeping and Accounting Systems for Contractors (Frank R. Walker Co., 5030 N. Harlem Ave., Chicago, IL 60656).

Safeguard Business Systems for Building Contractors (Safeguard Business Systems Inc., 470 Maryland Drive, Fort Washington, PA 19034).

Shaw/Walker for Building Contractors (Shaw/Walker, 57 E. Willow St., Millburn, NJ 07041).

Simplified Master System-Contractor (Simplified Business Services Inc., 233 E. Lancaster Ave., Ardmore, PA 19003).

Financial reports you need

A major reason for business failure is the lack of financial planning. As this chapter illustrates, good records can help you in this financial planning, and the two most important documents to business financial planning are your balance sheet and your income statement.

Your balance sheet

Your *balance sheet* is a summary of the status of your business—its assets, liabilities, and net worth—at an instant in time. By reviewing your balance sheet along with your income statement and your cash flow statement, you'll be able to make informed financial and business planning decisions.

The balance sheet is drawn up using the totals from individual accounts kept in your general ledger. Your balance sheet shows what you have left when you pay all your creditors. Remember: assets less liabilities equals capital or net worth. The assets and liabilities sections must balance—hence the name "balance sheet." It can be produced quarterly, semiannually, or at the end of each calendar or fiscal year. If your record keeping is manual, you'll be less likely to develop a frequently updated balance sheet. Many accounting software programs can give you a current balance sheet in just a couple of minutes.

While your accountant will be most helpful in drawing up your balance sheet, it's you who must understand it. *Current assets* are anything of value that you own, such as cash, inventory, or property that you can convert into cash within a year. *Fixed assets* are things such as land and equipment. *Liabilities* are debts the business must pay. They might be current, such as amounts owed to suppliers or your accountant, or they might be long term, such as a note owed to the bank. *Capital*, also called equity or net worth, is the excess of your assets over your liabilities.

Your *income statement* is a detailed, month-by-month tally of the income from sales and the expenses incurred to generate the sales. It's a good assessment tool because it shows the effect of your decisions on profits. It's a good planning tool because you can estimate the impact of decisions on profit before you make them.

Your income statement

Your income statement includes four kinds of information:

- Sales information lists the total revenues generated by the sale of your service to clients.
- Direct expenses include the cost of labor and materials to perform your service.
- Indirect expenses are the costs you have even if your service is not sold, including salaries, rent, utilities, insurance, depreciation, office supplies, taxes, and professional fees.
- Profit is shown as pretax income (important to the IRS) and after-tax or net income (important to you and your loan officer).

Your cash flow statement

Your business must have a healthy cash flow to survive. *Cash flow* is the amount of money available in your business at any given time. To keep tabs on cash flow, forecast the funds you expect to disburse and receive during a specific time. Then you can predict deficiencies or surplus in cash and decide how best to respond.

A cash flow projection serves one other very useful purpose in addition to planning. As the actual information becomes available to you, compare it to the monthly cash flow estimates you previously made to see how accurately you're estimating. As you do this, you'll be giving yourself on-the-spot business training in making more accurate estimates and plans for the coming months. As your ability to estimate improves, your financial control of the business will increase. Cash flow is such an important aspect of your business' success that I cover it in great detail in chapter 12, "Growing your electrical contractor business."

Handling cash

If your electrical contracting business is a "one-person band," you'll have no problem with one of the greatest enemies of business: employee theft. However, as your business grows and you hire others to handle some of your tasks, you'll need to manage them to ensure that employee theft doesn't become a problem.

Here are some ideas for handling cash and checks within your business:

- The person who handles your cash receipts shouldn't be the person who makes bank deposits. Cash is too easily misappropriated. Don't tempt an employee by letting him or her handle both of these duties.
- Deposit your daily cash receipts in the bank each day.
- Set up and use a petty cash fund and voucher system for small cash outlays.
- For the same reason, the person who writes the checks shouldn't also sign them or have the authority to sign them. Whenever checks are signed, the signer should view the bill being paid and then write the check number on the bill.

- Use only prenumbered checks and maintain records of all canceled or voided checks.
- The monthly bank reconciliation should be done by the owner or an outside accountant.

Remember that human error is more common than dishonesty, but both can damage your business.

Like it or not, the government is your business partner, and as your partner, the government receives a portion of your profits—even before you do. However, government can also help you make a profit through the Small Business Administration, Department of Commerce, state corporate divisions, and numerous services.

The government is your partner

The Federal Internal Revenue Service will collect income taxes, corporate taxes, FICA and other taxes from you. To find out more about your tax obligations, contact your regional IRS office for the following publications:

- Your Federal Income Tax (Publication 17).
- Tax Guide for Small Business (Publication 334).
- Employer's Tax Guide (Circular E).
- Self-Employment Tax (Publication 533).
- Tax Information on Retirement Plans for the Self-Employed (Publication 560).
- Tax Withholding and Estimating Tax (Publication 510).
- Business Use of Your Home (Publication 587).

In addition, there are a number of federal and state forms you'll need for good record keeping and accurate taxation:

- Application for Employer Identification Number (Form SS-4), if you have employees.
- Employer's Annual Unemployment Tax Return (Form 940).
- Employer's Quarterly Federal Tax Return (Form 941).
- Employee's Withholding Allowance Certificate (W-4) for each employee.

- Employer's Wage and Tax Statement (W-2) for each employee.
- Reconciliation/Transmittal of Income and Tax Statements (W-3).

Financial planning

There's one simple reason to understand and explore financial planning in your business—to avoid failure. Eighty percent of new businesses fail primarily because of the lack of good financial planning.

Financial planning affects how and on what terms you'll be able to attract the funding you need to establish, maintain, and expand your business. Financial planning determines the human and physical resources you'll be able to acquire to operate your business. It will be a major factor in whether or not you'll be able to make your hard work profitable.

The balance sheet and the income statement are essential to your business, but they're only the starting point for successful financial management. The next step is called *ratio analysis*. Ratio analysis enables you to spot trends in a business and to compare its performance and condition with the average performance of similar businesses in the same industry. To do this, compare your ratios with the average of other electrical contractors as well as with your own ratios over several years. Ratio analysis can be the most important early warning indicator for solving business problems while they're still manageable.

One note before we get into ratios: members of trade associations often will share their balance sheet, income statement, and management ratios with other members through studies and reports published by the association. It's just one more good reason to join one of the local or national electrical contracting trade associations.

For example, one business association issues a summary of income and expenses for members. The most recent summary presents the following approximate percentages for typical electrical contractors:

- Prime cost:
  a. Material—36%
  b. Direct labor wages—21%
  c. Labor adder—7%
  d. Other direct job expense—2%
  e. Subcontract expense—4%
- Total prime cost—70%
- Total overhead expense—25%
- Operating profit—5%
- Interest expense—1%
- Net profit before taxes—4%
- Income taxes—1%
- Net profit after taxes—3%

These percentages can help you in determining whether your contracting business is being operated as efficiently as other firms in your industry.

Balance sheet ratio analysis

Important balance sheet ratios measure liquidity (a business' ability to pay its bills as they come due) and leverage (measuring the business' dependency on creditors for funding). Liquidity ratios indicate the ease of turning assets into cash. They include the current ratio, quick ratio, and working capital.

Current ratio

The current ratio is one of the best-known measurements of financial strength. Current ratio is figured like this:

$$\text{Current ratio} = \frac{\text{Total current assets}}{\text{Total current liabilities}}$$

The main question this ratio answers is: Does your business have enough current assets to meet the payment schedule of its current debts with a margin of safety? A generally acceptable current ratio is 2 to 1. That is, twice as many current assets as current liabilities.

Let's say that you—or your lender—decide that your current ratio is too low. What can you do about it?

- Pay some debts.
- Combine some of your debts into a long-term debt.
- Convert noncurrent assets into current assets.
- Put profits back into the business.
- Increase your current assets with new equity (bring some more cash into the business).

The ideal current ratio for electrical contractors is 2:1.

Quick ratio The quick ratio is sometimes called the *acid test ratio* and is one of the best measurements of liquidity. Quick ratio is figured like this:

$$\text{Quick ratio} = \frac{\text{Cash + securities + receivables}}{\text{Total current liabilities}}$$

The quick ratio is a much more exact measure than the current ratio. By excluding inventories (typically small in electrical contracting businesses), the quick ratio concentrates on the really liquid assets with value that's fairly certain. The quick ratio helps answer the question: If all sales revenues should disappear, could my business meet its current obligations with the readily convertible, "quick" funds in hand?

A quick ratio of 1:1 is considered satisfactory unless the majority of your quick assets are in accounts receivable, and the pattern of collection lags behind the schedule for paying current liabilities.

Working capital Working capital is more a measure of cash flow than a ratio. The result of the following calculation must be a positive number:

Working capital = Total current assets – Total current liabilities

Bankers look at net working capital over time to determine a company's ability to weather financial crises. Bank loans are often tied to minimum working capital requirements.

A general rule about these three liquidity ratios is that the higher they are, the better, especially if your business is relying heavily on creditor money or financed assets. As a related indicator, the ideal ratio of gross revenue to working capital is 10:1.

The leverage or debt/worth ratio indicates the business' reliance on debt financing (loans) rather than owner's equity. Here's how to figure leverage ratio:

$$\text{Leverage ratio} = \frac{\text{Total liabilities}}{\text{Net worth}}$$

Generally, the higher this ratio, the more risky a creditor will consider your loan. The ideal ratio is 1:1.

Here are two commonly used ratios derived from your income statement, or similar report: gross margin ratio and net profit margin ratio.

The gross margin ratio is valuable to contractors who stock and resell their inventory rather than just sell their services. The ratio is the percentage of sales dollars left after subtracting the cost of goods sold from net sales. The gross margin ratio measures the percentage of sales dollars remaining to pay the company's overhead. Comparing your business' ratio to those of other electrical contractors will reveal the relative strengths or weaknesses in your business. Here's how to calculate the gross margin ratio:

$$\text{Gross margin} = \frac{\text{Gross profit}}{\text{Net sales}}$$

Note that gross profit is calculated by deducting the cost of goods sold from net sales.

The net profit margin ratio is a percentage of sales dollars left after subtracting the cost of goods sold and all expenses, except income taxes. This ratio provides a good opportunity to compare your company's "return on sales" with the performance of other companies in the industry. It's calculated before income tax because tax rates and tax liabilities vary from company to company, for a variety of reasons. The net profit margin ratio is calculated like this:

$$\text{Net profit margin ratio} = \frac{\text{Net profit before tax}}{\text{Net sales}}$$

The net profit for a typical electrical contractor's business ranges from 3.5 percent of sales for firms doing more than $6 million in annual sales to about 4.5 percent for firms with sales of less than $1 million.

Management ratios

Other important ratios, often referred to as management ratios, are also taken from information on the balance sheet and the income statement. These ratios can help you better manage your business.

Inventory turnover ratio

If your contracting business requires the resale of inventory, the inventory turnover ratio reveals how well your inventory is being managed. It's important because the more times inventory can be turned over in a given period, the greater the profit. Here's how to calculate the inventory turnover ratio:

$$\text{Inventory turnover ratio} = \frac{\text{Net sales}}{\text{Average inventory at cost}}$$

Accounts receivable turnover ratio

This ratio shows you how well accounts receivable are being collected. If receivables aren't collected reliably and on time, you should reconsider your credit policies. If receivables are too slow to convert to cash, your business might not be adequately "liquid." The accounts receivable ratio is figured like this:

$$\frac{\text{Net credit sales/year}}{\text{365 days/year}} = \text{Daily credit sales}$$

Then:

$$\text{Accounts receivable turnover (in days)} = \frac{\text{Accounts receivable}}{\text{Daily credit}}$$

The return on investment (ROI) is perhaps the most important ratio of all. It's a percentage of return on money invested in the business by its owners. In short, this ratio tells you whether or not all the effort you put into the business has been worthwhile. If the ROI is less than the rate of return on a risk-free investment (certificate of deposit or a bank savings account), the owner should consider selling the business and putting the money in a savings account. Here's how to calculate ROI:

$$\text{Return on investment} = \frac{\text{Net profit before taxes}}{\text{Net worth}}$$

A goal for many successful businesses is a 25 percent ROI, depending on equity, market position, and risk.

Return on investment ratio

As mentioned earlier, electrical contracting trade associations can often supply you with "typical" current, quick, working capital, leverage, gross margin, net profit margin, inventory turnover, accounts receivable, and return on investment ratios. In addition, you can check your local or regional library for the following books on ratios: *Key Business Ratios*, Dun & Bradstreet, Inc.; *Almanac of Business and Industrial Financial Ratios* by Leo Troy (Prentice Hall); *Annual Statement Studies* by Robert Morris Associates. Your accountant or tax preparer might also be able to furnish you with these ratios in your specialty.

Sources of ratios

In the next chapter, you'll learn two of the most important aspects of managing your electrical contracting business: how to get customers, and how to keep them.

Getting & keeping customers

IN CHAPTER 2 of this book, you learned the importance of clients or customers in your electrical contracting business. It's obvious that, without customers, you have no business. So, the question is: How can you get customers for your business?

This chapter will give you the answers. You'll learn what you need to know about marketing, advertising, prospecting, and client relationships. You'll find out what works for other electrical contractors, and you'll determine what works best for you.

Identifying your customers

In chapter 1, I discussed defining your market. Your "market" is simply the group of prospects who would most benefit from your services. The first step in defining your market is defining who you are to them. In chapter 1, you only defined your market in broad terms such as, "I'm an electrical contractor who specializes in one-person jobs that can be performed with minimal tools." Let's get more specific.

Because there are dozens of types of electrical contractors—and hundreds of potential markets—I'll use broad examples. However, you'll quickly get the idea and be able to apply it to your specialty.

In the previous example of a one-person electrical contractor with minimal tools, your customers would be those with jobs that don't require a large labor force or numerous tools. The most common application of this market definition is the small contractor who works out of his or her home and trade vehicle and offers residential electrical services as a subcontractor to general contractors, and as a contractor to homeowners remodeling their residence or small businesses that need electrical work. Depending on your trade area, you might have to either perform all of these types of jobs or, preferably, specialize in one or two.

Let's say that, based on your study of the local market, you determine that the best opportunity for you and your skills is to specialize in electrical work remodeling stores for new businesses moving into an older part of your town. You look around and decide that there's enough work in your community to keep you busy for quite awhile, yet not so much as to attract lots of competition.

In this example, who are your customers? Your customers are those who own these older buildings, as well as those who lease the buildings from the owners. So, either way, your customer or initial contact is the building owners. From them you can get leads as to which of their lessees need electrical work in their new stores.

So, how do you find out who owns what buildings in this older part of town? Your city hall or county courthouse is the best place to start. Get or draw a detailed map of the area you expect to serve, slip the map into a notebook, and begin making notes on the ownership of each retail storefront in the area. Tax records will typically show ownership, zoning, valuation, and other information. From your local building permits office, you can add information on the date of construction, age of the building or store, and other specifics. Write it all down in your notebook.

Now it's time to approach your prospects. Through the rest of this chapter, you'll learn how to market to your prospects and turn them into customers. In my example, you'd begin building a notebook, card file, or computer database on the owners and lessees of retail buildings in your selected market. You'd then focus your attention on them with one goal: get them to recognize their need for your services and your qualifications to serve them.

Obviously, how you approach your prospects as an industrial electrical contractor will be somewhat different, yet the principles will be the same. You'll first determine whether there's sufficient opportunity for you to build your business and whether potential competitors are already adequately serving this market. Then you'll focus your attention and your marketing on those who can best use your services. An industrial electrical contractor will learn as much as possible about industries in his or her region or specialty, find out whether the market is now over- or underserved, and what specific electrical contracting needs these industries have. Depending on your specialty, you can also subscribe to local or regional contracting, business, and government publications that will keep you informed of construction, jobs let for bidding, and planned jobs.

Who are your customers? They're those recommended to you by other satisfied customers, those who have been influenced by your advertising, or those who have been solicited by your sales force. They're former customers, newcomers to the area, customers who need immediate emergency help, and your competitors' dissatisfied customers. They're businesses who have never before required electrical services, as well as those who have decided to change contractors because of price, quality, or service. Customers are your most valuable asset.

One more idea: some start-up electrical contractors begin their business by serving customers that can't be served by their current or ex-employer. By working with them, you reduce the amount of marketing you must do to develop customers. These start-up contractors then pay a marketing fee or a finders fee to these sources. It's another reason to maintain a good relationship with all of your past and current employers.

How to market your services

Marketing is a science. It's not a perfect science, where the answer to a question is always the same. It's a science based on data, information, knowledge, and wisdom. Data is easy to get and build into information. From this information comes knowledge and, eventually, wisdom. Wisdom is what makes your business profitable. Marketing builds your business.

The purpose of marketing is to get more customers. That's it. If you're new to business, the purpose is to get your first customers. If you've established a substantial business, the purpose is to keep those customers that you have. In this chapter, you'll learn how to get and keep customers through marketing.

There are dozens of ways that you can market your services to prospects and customers. These methods include the many forms of advertising, as well as literature, direct mail, and telephone marketing.

Advertising

The purpose of advertising is to tell your potential customers why they'll benefit from using your services. The best way to do so is to let your other customers tell your prospects how much they could gain from your service. That's called word-of-mouth advertising, and it's the most valuable type of advertising there is. Unfortunately, it's also the slowest to develop. Your first satisfied client might, in conversations, mention your good service once or twice a month. After hearing that a number of times, and when they're looking for your service, that prospect might call you for your service. By that time, you might be out of business due to lack of work.

Impressions

Every time your prospect sees or hears your name, you make what's called an "impression." It might be something small like seeing your truck's sign on the freeway or seeing your sponsorship sign on a baseball field, or it might be a listing in the yellow pages or a mutual acquaintance making a positive (or negative) comment about your last job. Each makes an impression.

Each impression is cumulative. After numerous impressions, large and small, your prospect might bring your name into the "possible source" part of his or her brain. Then, when a legitimate need for your service arises, the prospect considers you as a supplier. Think about it. How many times did you see or hear about "Ford" or "Jello" or "Mr. Coffee" or "Hawaii" before you even considered trying them. Probably dozens or even hundreds of impressions were made. Also consider that any negative feelings about these products are impressions too. The point is that you'll need to positively impress your prospects many times and in many ways before they can be upgraded to a customer.

Testimonials Of course, you can speed the process along by developing testimonials. When you have a client who expresses satisfaction with your service, ask him or her to write you a testimonial letter. The letter, on business stationery, will describe how professional your service is and how well you respond to the needs of customers.

Unfortunately, only a small percentage of those who say they'll write a testimonial letter actually do so. However, the problem isn't sincerity, it's time. Most customers just don't have the time to write such a letter, especially one that will be valuable to your business. So, some electrical contractors will hire a writer (check the local phone book for "Writers" or "Resume Services") to interview the client and actually write the letter for the customer. You foot the bill. A well-written testimonial from a respected business person will be worth literally thousands of dollars in new business to you. You'll copy it and include it in with your brochure, quote from it in advertisements, and pass it out to prospects. It will be your best form of advertising.

To encourage satisfied customers and their testimonials, some contractors establish and promote a policy of "satisfaction guaranteed." The profits lost are usually replaced by the profits gained through this policy. It's a helpful persuasion tool when trying to close a sale.

Free advertising There are numerous ways to advertise your new electrical contracting service at little or no cost. Exactly which methods you use will depend somewhat on your specialization. Once you have your business card printed, take a stack of them with you wherever you go. Pass them out to anyone who might be or might know a prospect. As you stop for lunch, put your business card on the restaurant's bulletin board. Do the same if you stop at a local market for anything: put your card on their bulletin board. All it costs is the price of a business card.

Many electrical contractors overlook one of the best sources of free advertising: publicity. As you start your business, write a short article (called a "press release") and give copies to your local newspaper, radio stations, shoppers, and other media.

Include information about your business, such as owners, experience, affiliations, background, expertise, purpose of the business, location, to whom the business sells its services, and how to contact the business. If your market is across an industry rather than across a geographic area, send this press release to magazines in this trade, called "trade journals."

A single sheet of paper, printed on both sides and folded, can become your first brochure describing your services and your qualifications. The cost is very small, especially if you have the skills to write and produce it yourself. You can pass your brochure out at chambers of commerce meetings, at local trades meetings, anywhere where you'd pass out your business card. Your brochure doesn't have to be slick and expensive, but a few dollars spent on a neat and accurate brochure will bring you many hundreds of dollars in new business. That's a good return on your investment.

While business signs aren't free of charge, they offer a second "free" benefit beyond their main purpose of informing. They repeat their message whenever they're seen. So, you want signs that are frequently seen. One excellent reason for selecting a delivery van rather than a pickup truck as your contractors vehicle is that a van offers more space on its side for a large sign. Using a picture, a graphic image, or a "logo" in your sign helps viewers to better identify and remember what you do. Some enterprising contractors park their work vehicles over the weekend at locations that offer high visibility: shopping centers, prominent job sites, at park-and-ride lots near major freeway off-ramps. Make sure, though, that your vehicle is securely locked.

Other contractors buy or make their own standing sign that they place at the job site, with permission. "Another quality project by Jones Electrical Contracting." Regular passers-by might see the sign daily, and each time they see it, it's another "impression" or point for your business. Even if they aren't a potential client, the impression might be passed on verbally to someone who is. "I sure see a lot of signs for Jones Electrical Contracting. They must be good."

Traditional advertising

When most people think of advertising, they think of billboards, large newspaper ads, catchy radio ads, and the like. Should electrical contractors use this type of advertising to develop their business? In most cases, no. Why? Because the cost is typically too high for the results. Let's say that you purchase a quarter-page ad in your local daily newspaper and it's seen by 100,000 people for a price of just $500. That's just a half-cent-per-impression or reader. Pretty cheap. However, of those 100,000 people, only 50 are true prospects for your service. Then the price goes to $10 per impression. You could take each one to Burger King for about the same price. You'd be better off to spend $50 for an article that appears in the paper's business section, or mailing your brochures and a personalized letter to each of those 50 prospects.

Yellow pages advertising

There's one exception to this recommendation that you shouldn't use traditional advertising: ads in the phone book. In fact, depending on your specialty, an ad in the yellow pages might be one of your best sources of new business.

In most locations, if you purchase a required business telephone line, you'll get a listing in one category of your local telephone book. In some areas, this is optional. The listing might be as simple as:

ABC Electrical Contractors, 123 Main St.—555-1234

Or the firm name can be in capital letters such as:

ABC ELECTRICAL CONTRACTORS
123 Main St.—555-1234

Or you can include information on your specialty, and even an alternate telephone number, like this:

ABC ELECTRICAL CONTRACTORS
Residential Remodeling Is Our Specialty
123 Main St.—555-1234
If no answer—555-2345

Many businesses upgrade their listing with a space ad. A space ad is simply an advertisement that takes up more space than a line or two and is usually surrounded by a box.

To determine the size and cost of an appropriate space ad, check your local and nearby telephone book's yellow pages under headings for Electrical Contractors and related topics. Look for your competitors (as defined earlier in this book). When a potential client looks in their yellow pages, which ads stand out the best? Which have the greatest eye-appeal? Which are easiest to read? Remember that you don't need the largest ad in the phone book; you need the one that's the most cost-effective for you.

The last few pages in your yellow pages section frequently have information on how to select a space ad. You'll learn terms like "double half," "double quarter," and "triple quarter" as well as "columns." It's actually quite easy to follow. Most larger telephone books have four vertical columns per page; community phone books in rural areas are half-size, with only two columns per page. So, a "triple quarter" is three columns wide and a quarter page long; a "double half" is two columns wide and a half-page long.

At the end of the yellow pages section, there will often be a toll-free telephone number for ordering a space ad or listing, or you might find the number in the front of the phone book under Business Telephone Service or a similar title. Also ask about cost and availability of color in your ad. The firm that produces your telephone book will help you design and write your ad— with input from you. Then they'll supply a "layout" of the ad and a contract for you to sign. Most contracts for yellow page listings or space ads are for one year and can be paid in monthly installments.

Depending on your specialty, you might be able to get someone to help pay for your yellow pages ad. If you stock and sell or use a specific brand of electrical supplies or equipment, the manufacturer or wholesaler might pay some of your advertising cost for prominently displaying their name in your advertisement. This is called cooperative advertising, or simply "co-op." Talk to your supplier about available "co-op ad money."

One more thing about yellow pages ads: make sure you include any state or local licensing information. Some will include the phrase "Licensed—Bonded—Insured," while others will include a state license board number such as "Contractor's Board #12345." Some electrical contractors will also include information about affiliations, including the NECA logo or listings of other association memberships.

How to find prospects

A *prospect* is a prospective customer, someone who could potentially use your service but hasn't done so yet. They might not have heard of your service, or they might not know enough about your service to determine its value, or they simply haven't been asked.

Who is a prospect for your electrical contracting service? Of course, that depends on what service you perform for customers. If you're an electrical contractor who specializes in installing and repairing neon business signs, your prospects are anyone who might purchase or who already owns/rents a neon sign. To turn these prospects into customers, you must first think like they think, only faster. For example, electrical sign repair contractors can check the local permit records to determine the age, value, and ongoing support for electrical signs in their area. They would look for the initial installation date and compare this against the typical age of such signs; they might make an on-site examination for condition. They would also check for stickers on the sign that identify the manufacturer, the installer, and any inspection dates. They might determine that the sign is of sufficient age that the owner might become a customer, or that the firm who previously maintained the sign has since gone out of business. In any case, the sign's owner will be a good prospect.

The U.S. Census Bureau is an excellent source of statistical data for market surveys. Based on the every-ten-year census, the Bureau divides large cities into census tracts of about 5,000 residents within Standard Metropolitan Statistical Areas (SMSAs). Data on these tracts cover income, housing, and related information that can be valuable to you. The Bureau also publishes a monthly report called "Housing Units Authorized by Building Permit and Public Contract." For this and other market information, contact the Office of Business Liaison, U.S. Department of Commerce, Washington, DC 20230. The Bureau of the Census offers construction statistics, housing data, and special demographic studies among its services.

If your customers include the federal government, you can subscribe to the "Commerce Business Daily," a daily list of U.S. Government procurement invitations, contract awards, subcontracting leads, and other opportunities. It's available by subscription from the Government Printing Office or at larger public libraries.

Another source of information on construction projects in major cities is the "Dodge Report." Published by the F.W. Dodge Division of McGraw-Hill Information Systems, the "Dodge Report" includes detailed information on construction projects in specific geographic areas that are let out for bidding. There are more than 60 building categories, from small remodeling jobs to large commercial complexes. The service is expensive, but the cost can be recouped in just one or two additional jobs per year.

In my example, any sign owner would be a prospective customer. None should be overlooked. By digging through local records and making a physical inspection of local lots, the contractor is "qualifying" the prospect or determining the chances for turning the prospect into a customer. If the sign is fairly new and is maintained by another local contractor with regular inspections, the chances of turning the owner into a customer are smaller, but still within possibility. A prospect can be further qualified by interviewing the owner in person or by telephone.

Qualifying prospects

Qualifying or determining the needs of prospects, of course, depends on your specialty. If you work primarily as a subcontractor to general contractors who specialize in contracts, you'll have a different set of qualifications to look for: years in business, size of projects, electrical contractors currently used, name of the person who decides which bids are accepted, etc.

Keeping track

How should you keep track of your prospects? There are many ways, depending on how many prospects there are and how you plan to market to them. Some contractors simply use 3-×-5-inch file cards available at any stationery store. A sample card will include both basic information—name, owner, address, telephone number, business, etc.—as well as qualifying information and notes from prospecting contacts. For example:

3/17: Found out that owner is selling out to Frank Smith, who might want to upgrade signage.

3/21: Smith says he wants proposal on signage maintenance contract and minor changes to sign face.

Other new contractors use their business notebook, described earlier, to list out prospecting information and contacts.

If you're using a computer to automate your business records, there are diverse "contact management" software programs that will help you keep track of prospects. These programs range in price from about $100 for a simple system to $500 or more for a specialized prospecting system that can even help you write personalized sales letters. For example, a good contact management program will give you standard "fields" or areas where you can type the firm name, contact name(s), address, telephone and fax numbers, the names of mutual friends or associations, information about contacts; a field can even serve as a simple order entry form. If you're making regular telephone calls to prospects, the program might help you schedule call-backs, maintain records of conversations, and help you write personalized proposals that can be quickly printed for mailing or even faxed to your prospect while they're still thinking about you.

Working with contracts

You are an "electrical contractor." That means you "contract" or agree to provide electrical services to customers. The agreement is usually in the form of a written contract. There are numerous stock contracts available from industrial associations. You should also have your attorney write up a contract form that you can use for the majority of your business agreements with customers. To help you in working with contracts, here's a list of the clauses included in the typical electrical services contract:

- Performance time: This clause outlines the construction or project schedule and describes any penalties for missing deadlines.
- Scheduling: This vital clause requires that all parties be notified if there's a change to the construction or project schedule.
- Approvals: This clause ensures that required approvals are submitted and returned so as not to interrupt the work flow.
- Changes: A clause should be included to cover how changes to the original contract and work order can be authorized and approved. This is usually done with a change order.
- Design errors: In case there's an error in the design of the electrical system, who is responsible for its correction and—most important—who pays for the error?
- Payment: A most important clause in your contract. It must detail when and how payment is to be expected and include the requirements for payment. In addition, it should ensure that, if you're working for a general contractor, there's prompt pass-through of payment from the customer.
- Disputes: In case of a dispute between your firm and the customer, how are problems resolved? What if the contractor and customer are in dispute? How will this affect your part of the contract and payment? Make sure you have a clause in your contracts to cover this concern.
- Indemnity: If you or your workers are negligent, you'll be liable for the damage. However, what liability is involved if another sub, the contractor, or the customer is negligent?
- Insurance: Make sure that there's a clause clearly detailing insurance requirements for all parties.
- Retainage: Some contracts allow the customer to retain a specified amount of the payment for a period of time to allow for final inspection or late materials bills. Make sure that the specific terms are clearly spelled out. In many cases, your profit is tied up in the retainage.
- Claims: This clause spells out who can file claims against whom, if required. That is, if you're a subcontractor, is your claim against the contractor or the customer?

- Damages: If there are damages, who is responsible, and for what? A clause covering damage responsibility should be included in your contracts with customers or contractors.
- Waivers: Some contracts waive any claims the contractor or subcontractor has against the customer once final payment is issued. In some cases, this clause should be amended. Discuss it with your attorney.
- Termination of work: This clause includes the terms of terminating any contractor who doesn't meet contractual requirements.
- Contract administration: Who is the administrator of the contract?

Keeping customers

One of the most satisfying aspects of becoming a successful electrical contractor is helping your customers solve problems. They might need cost-effective residential wiring, or attractive signage, or an electrically safe mobile home, or lighting in a new barn. In each case, they have a problem that requires a solution that you offer.

The more customers you can help, the more those customers will help you succeed. As you've learned, the best advertising is word-of-mouth, where your satisfied customers tell your prospects about the value you give. That's the real key to keeping customers: keep them happy. Of course, keeping your customers happy doesn't mean that you always have to agree with them or that they're always right—but they are always your customer, and they always deserve your respect and best efforts.

In the next few pages of this chapter, let's discuss how you can ensure your business' success by keeping and increasing your number and quality of customers. Remember that, to many businesses, you're a customer. Your bank, your utility companies, your grocery and hardware stores, and other businesses want to keep you as their customer. How do they do it? Are they successful? What would it take for you to switch to the services of a competing business? What's the most important services these businesses give you? How do they make you feel as a customer? The golden rule of business is: treat your customers as you want your suppliers to treat you.

Your customers must be satisfied with the value of your service, or they'll no longer be your customers. You might have some customers who are temporarily dissatisfied, but they'll soon get satisfaction either from you or from one of your competitors. If you don't have any significant competitors, customer dissatisfaction might breed them. The point is that your electrical contracting business can't afford dissatisfied customers.

Customer satisfaction

So, how do you continue to make sure that your customers are satisfied with your service? You listen to them. You watch how they pay their bills; you call them up for a friendly chat to learn what business problems they're facing; you ask other customers if they've heard of anyone who is dissatisfied with your services. Here are some of the questions that smart contractors periodically ask their customers:

- Is everything going well with our project?
- Have you seen anything that we can do better?
- Are any of my employees doing an exceptional or an inadequate job for you?
- How can I get more great customers like you?

Why should you take time to ask these questions of customers? Because, if you don't, someone else will, and you might soon lose your valuable customers. Remember that it's much less expensive to keep a customer than to find a new one.

A repeat customer is simply one who hires you for more than one job. If the customer is satisfied and needs your services again, you have a good chance of getting a repeat customer. You didn't have to go out and spend additional money on advertising, or work extra hours to promote your business. Your quality of business promotes itself.

Repeat customers

The best way to get repeat business is to ask for it. As you call up your clients to determine their satisfaction, also ask them:

- Do you have any other jobs coming up?
- Would you like us to bid on them?
- What services do you expect to need from us in the coming year?
- Are there any related electrical services that we could implement for you in the future?

You can also build repeat business by continually trying to sell your services to current customers. It's more productive to get more business from current customers than to find new ones. Here's how some successful electrical contractors build repeat business:

- Write a monthly newsletter to all customers; include information on the industry (summarized from trade journals) as well as a listing of the jobs you're currently working and the services you offer.
- Perform extra services that other local electrical contractors don't do for their customers, like designs and plans, or special permits.
- Serve as a consultant at no charge to clients; for example, review electrical plans and make recommendations with no obligation.

Referral customers

Earning referrals is one of the most powerful types of business promotion. A referral is simply having one of your satisfied customers sell your services to prospective buyers. The word of a trusted business person is much more believable to prospects than the word of an unknown business person or salesperson.

So, how do you get your customers to refer prospects to you? You ask them to do so. In fact, it should be an automatic question that you ask: Do you know anyone who might need our services? Ask right after you close a sale, as you start a job, as you complete a job, and—especially—whenever anyone compliments an aspect of your work. For example, if a customer says, "I really appreciate the way you finished the rewiring job on the Jones home so quickly." You might reply, "I'm glad to hear that. Do you know anyone who might also need our services?"

Once a customer has referred others to you, the referring customer might feel a stronger obligation to continue using your services. That will not only help you grow your business, but it will also help you keep the customers you have.

One of the most important, and overlooked, aspects of keeping customers satisfied is making sure you understand what they expect from you. Until you know, you won't be able to satisfy their needs. Here are some questions to ask about your customers:

Defining expectations

- What are your customers' expectations?
- Do customers expect immediate response to calls, or do most customers need your services "sometime in the next 30 days?"
- Do customers expect "instant credit" from you, or do they usually pay all or some of the costs in advance?
- Do customers expect you to be on call 24 hours a day or only during normal business hours?
- Do customers expect to talk to "the boss" when they call, or can an office person handle most calls?
- Do your customers expect discounts for off-season jobs or for paying cash in advance?
- Do your customers expect to pay you in payments or within 30, 60, or 90 days of completion?
- Do your customers expect bids that are priced "cost-plus," by the hour, by the job, or by another pricing structure?

So, how can you know what your customers expect? Simply ask them. Spend some time in person or on the phone with your customers—large and small—talking about what they expect from you.

In fact, you can develop prospects into customers by telling them you're conducting a survey for your new electrical contracting business and you'd like to learn what the expectations of potential customers are. Finally, you can also ask, "Is your current electrical contractor meeting your expectations?"

I'm certain that you, as a customer, are the same way. You have distinct expectations when you buy from someone. If the business is a restaurant, you expect fast food at a low cost from a take-out restaurant, and you expect quality food served well from a fine restaurant. From an electrical supplier you want materials that are cost-effective while meeting all requirements. You might also want fast service or a broad inventory from which to choose. In fact, you might use one supplier for fast delivery of common materials and another for specialized materials.

Of course, the next question to ask yourself—and your customers and prospects—is, "Are these expectations realistic?" That is, you might want to pay less than wholesale price for hard-to-get materials, but that isn't a realistic expectation. Or a customer might say that he or she "expects" you to be available 24 hours a day for questions about the job when you know that, during business hours, responding to questions within an hour is a realistic expectation.

Of course, if you find sufficient customers who express the same unmet expectation—such as easy credit—you might consider this as an expectation that you can meet. By teaming up with an easy-finance broker you might be able to get discounted cash for your jobs from the broker, while offering quick credit to your customers.

Defining requirements

An expectation is something that a customer would like to happen. A requirement is something that a customer demands to happen. A customer might expect that a job be done as quickly as possible, but require that it be completed by a specific date.

So what does this have to do with a successful electrical contractor's getting and keeping customers? Plenty. In fact, unless you, as a supplier, clearly define and understand your customer's requirements, you won't keep your customer very long. What you're selling to your customer is your clear understanding of what's required to do a job. In most cases, you'll know the job's requirements even more than your customer will. The customer might hire you to install an industrial controls system and even give you the plans to do so, but you must understand and furnish the specific requirements for the job to be a success.

How can you clearly define your customers' requirements? Again, by asking. By interviewing your prospect or customer, you can determine what's required as well as what's expected to complete the job. Of course, plans will define many of the requirements. However, you must probe past the plans to make sure that they accurately express the customer's requirements. You might find that the plans, even when implemented, will not give the client what he or she requires or expects. It's your job, as a professional, to help the customer redefine the requirements and review his or her expectations. By doing so, you'll help ensure the job's success, as well as your own.

Getting and keeping customers will bring you greater income. In the next chapter, you'll learn how to increase your chances of success as an electrical contractor by increasing efficiency, reducing costs, and reducing risks.

CHAPTER 1

Reducing costs

INCREASING INCOME in your business is only half of the profit picture. The other half is reducing costs and risks. That's what this chapter is about. It answers the question vital to any successful business: How can I efficiently reduce operating costs and risks?

In the coming pages, you'll learn about analyzing expenses, locating reducible expenses, reducing overhead, earning discounts, hiring accountants, scheduling work, doing inspections, using depreciation, collecting payments, controlling cash flow, and many other ways to turn income into profit.

How you use this chapter depends somewhat on your specialty. If you carry little inventory, discounts on supplies might not mean much to you. However, if your electrical contracting business urgently depends on expensive equipment and other capital assets, accurate depreciation can mean the difference between profit and loss. So, review all of the following cost-reducers for ideas that will help your electrical contracting business meet its financial goals.

Cost reduction

The object of reducing costs in your electrical contracting business is to increase profits. Increasing profits through cost reduction must be based on the concept of an organized, planned program. Unless adequate records are maintained through an efficient and accurate accounting system, there can be no basis for analyzing costs.

Cost reduction is not simply attempting to slash any and all expenses without order. The owner-manager must understand the nature of expenses and how expenses interrelate with sales, inventories, overhead, gross profits, and net profits. Nor does cost reduction mean only the reduction of specific expenses. You can achieve greater profits through more efficient use of your expense dollar. Some of the ways you do this are by increasing the average sale per customer, by getting a larger return for your promotion and sales dollar, and by improving your internal methods and procedures.

For example, one small electrical contractor was quite pleased when, in a single year, sales went from $200 thousand to $1 million. However, at the end of the year, records showed that net profit the prior year—with lower sales—was actually higher than it was with increased sales. Why? Because the expenses of doing business grew faster than income.

Your goal should be to pay the right price for prosperity. Determining that price for your operation goes beyond knowing what your expenses are. Reducing expenses to increase profit requires that you obtain the most efficient use of your expense dollars.

Analyzing your expenses

Checking job records, you might determine that one of your employees is significantly less efficient than other employees performing the same tasks. You can then reduce expenses by increasing this employee's efficiency through training. By watching this employee perform his or her job, you can determine where the inefficiencies are and help him or her to overcome them. If done with consideration for the person, he or she will appreciate it, and so will your profit line.

An understanding of the worth of each expense item comes from experience and an analysis of records. Adequate job and expense records tell what's happening, and their analysis provides facts that can help you set realistic cost and profit goals.

Sometimes you can't cut an expense item. However, you can get more from it and thus increase your profits. In analyzing your expenses, you should use percentages rather than actual dollar amounts. For example, if you increase sales and keep the dollar amount of an expense the same, you've decreased that expense as a percentage of sales. When you decrease your cost percentage, you increase your percentage of profit.

On the other hand, if your sales volume remains the same, you can increase the percentage of profit by reducing a specific item of expense. Your goal, of course, is to do both: to decrease specific expenses and increase their productive worth at the same time.

Before you can determine whether cutting expenses will increase profits, you need information about your operation. This information can be obtained only if you have an adequate record-keeping system, as described in chapter 3. Such records will provide the figures to prepare an income statement, a budget, break-even calculations, and evaluations of your operating ratios compared with those of similar types of business.

Break-even A useful method for making expense comparisons is a break-even analysis, which tells you the point at which gross profit equals expenses. In a business year, the break-even point is the time at which your sales volume has become sufficient to enable your overall operation to start showing a profit. The two condensed income statement examples illustrate this point (see below). In Statement A, the sales volume is at the break-even point, and no profit is made. In Statement B, for the same business, sales volume is beyond the break-even point, and a profit is shown. In the two statements, the percentage factors are the same, except for fixed expenses, total expenses, and operating profit.

Condensed income statements

| | A | | B | |
	Break-even amount	Percent of sales	Profit amount	Percent of sales
Sales	$500,000	100	$600,000	100
Cost of sales	300,000	60	360,000	60
Gross profit	200,000	40	240,000	40
Operating expenses				
Fixed	150,000	30	150,000	25
Variable	50,000	10	60,000	10
Total	200,000	40	210,000	35
Operating profit	$NONE	0	$ 30,000	5

As shown in the example, once your sales volume reaches the break-even point, your fixed expenses are covered. Beyond the break-even point, every dollar of sales should earn you an equivalent additional profit percentage.

It's important to remember that once sales pass the break-even point, the fixed expenses percentage goes down as the sales volume goes up. Also, the operating profit percentage increases at the same rate as the percentage rate for fixed expenses decreases—provided that variable expenses are kept in line. In the table on the preceding page, fixed expenses in statement B decreased by 5 percent, and operating profit increased by 5 percent.

Locating reducible expenses

Your income statement also provides a summary of expense information and is the focal point in locating expenses that can be cut. For this reason, the information should be as current as possible. As a report of what has already been spent, an income statement alerts you to expense items that should be watched in the present business period. If you get an income statement only at the end of the year, you should consider having one prepared more often. At the end of each quarter is usually sufficient for smaller firms. Larger contractors should receive the information on a monthly basis.

Regardless of the frequency, the best option is to prepare two income statements. One statement should report the sales, expenses, profit/loss of your operations cumulatively for the current business year to date. The other statement should report on the same items for the last complete month or quarter. Each of the statements should also carry the following information:

- This year's figures and each item as a percentage of sales.
- Last year's figures and the percentages.
- The difference between last year and this year—over or under.
- Budgeted figures and the respective percentages.
- The difference between this year and the budgeted figures— over or under.

- Average percentages for similar businesses (available from trade associations and the U.S. Department of Labor).
- The difference between your annual percentages and the industry ratios—over or under.

This information allows you to locate expense variations in three ways:

- By comparing this year to last year.
- By comparing expenses to your own budgeted figures.
- By comparing your percentages to the operating ratios for similar businesses.

The important basis for comparison is the percentage figure. It represents a common denominator for all three methods. When you've indicated the percentage variations, you should then study the dollar amounts to determine what kind of corrective action is needed.

Because your cost cutting will come largely from variable expenses, you should make sure that they're flagged on your income statements. *Variable expenses* are those that fluctuate with the increase or decrease of sales volume. Some variable expenses are overtime, subcontractors, advertising, sales salaries, commissions, and payroll taxes. *Fixed expenses* are those that stay the same, regardless of sales volume. Among them are your salary, salaries for permanent employees, depreciation, rent, and utilities.

When you've located a problem expense area, the next step obviously is to reduce that cost so as to increase your profit. A key to the effectiveness of your cost-cutting action is the worth of the various expenditures. As long as you know the worth of your expenditures, you can profit by making small improvements in expenses. Keep an open eye and an open mind. It's better to do a spot analysis once a month than to wait several months and then do a detailed study.

Take action as soon as possible. You can refine your cost-cutting action as you go along. Be persistent. Sometimes results are slower than you might like, but keep in mind that only persistent analysis of your records and constant action can help keep expenses from eating up profit.

Business overhead is simply the costs of keeping your doors open. If your electrical contracting business is located in your home, overhead costs are probably small. However, if you have a shop, an office, and office personnel, your overhead is greater. It's also large if you have high debt to banks, suppliers, and backers.

The suggestion made earlier in this book was to start out small and let your growing business force you into larger quarters. Depending on your electrical contracting specialty, start with an office in a corner of your home and/or your work truck. Then, as business grows, take on greater obligations for additional overhead. If you build a perception of quality in your customer's mind, you won't have to maintain impressive offices or shops. Few customers will decide not to do business with you because your office is in your home or a small shop, and that's nothing you really need to advertise.

You can also reduce overhead by carefully watching the costs of supplies. Printed stationery is an excellent way to promote the quality of your business, but you don't need printed notepads unless the customer will see them. For the price of low-cost ink pens, you can often get notepads that include your business name and phone number. However, don't buy so many that they wind up costing more than quality ink pens because you've changed your address or phone number. Buy supplies in quantity if you can, but don't buy more than you'll use in three to six months, unless you're certain that they won't become out-of-date.

Personnel is one place where the profits of a small electrical contracting business can quickly be eaten away. Don't hire an office manager or secretary until you absolutely must. It's more profitable to do the required filing and office functions yourself after normal business hours or on weekends, or you can ask the help of a wife or older child who could be put on the payroll as soon as your business can afford it.

Reducing overhead

Some small electrical contractors use temporary help or outside services rather than get into hiring employees and all the taxes and records that come with it. They have records kept by a bookkeeping or accounting service; office cleaning is done by a janitorial service; telephones are answered by an answering service; correspondence is performed by a secretarial service. Electrical jobs that the owner can't handle are subcontracted out to other electrical contractors. These contractors know that the complexity of regulations and taxation is endlessly multiplied when the first employee is hired—so they avoid hiring anyone until their success requires them to do so.

Earning discounts

Every business person wants to take advantage of discounts. If your gross profit is 5 percent of sales, a 10 percent discount on materials can dramatically increase overall profits. So, how do you ensure that you're getting the best price for the materials and equipment you buy? Ask!

Let's say that you order job materials through a specific electrical parts house in your area. Do you know what discounts are available to you for cash in advance? Do you know what discounts can be earned by ordering all of your materials through a single supplier? Can you receive materials at no charge because ordering a few more of a component will lower your per-unit charge enough to pay for the extra materials? Can you receive higher discounts from the supplier's competitor for all the materials you buy from them? How about if you buy only materials in which a supplier specializes? Here are a few ways you can ensure that you're earning the greatest available discounts:

- Pool your purchases with other friendly competitors in order to earn greater quantity discounts.
- Order through a single clerk, especially one that works on commission, and always ask for "best pricing" and available discounts.
- Ask, "Are there any discounts or price breaks that I should be aware of?"

- If necessary, sign a contract with a single supplier to give them all of your business if you can get an additional 3 or 5 percent discount—as long as their standard prices are equal to or less than other suppliers.
- Ask if members of any local or national trade associations earn additional discounts.
- Find out if your supplier allows a discount for cash and carry.
- Even if you have a favorite supplier, always continue to shop around for better pricing, discounts, and terms.

Keep in mind, though, that some suppliers charge a little more because they offer services that are worth the difference in price. For example, a cross-town supplier can give you immediate delivery of hard-to-find materials that you often need but can't afford to stock in quantity. The loss of a 5 percent discount might be small compared to the cost of stocking these components or having to stop what you're doing to pick them up. Remember, you don't want the lowest price; you want the one that's most profitable to you in the long term. Of course, that means you don't want "cheap"; you want quality at the best price. That's also what your customers want!

Also be aware of the commission salesperson who says, "Take a few hundred more units and I'll give you another 4 percent discount." If you use a hundred units a week, this might be a good deal. However, if it will take you six months or more to use, a 4 percent return on your cash invested is not a good discount.

Hiring an accountant

Believe it or not, hiring an accountant can help you reduce your business costs. Not only will hiring an accounting service mean that you don't have to hire an employee to manage your records, but a good accountant can also help you find ways to reduce your costs of doing business.

Of course, with any investment, you can't show a profit unless what you receive is more than what you pay. So, only hire an accounting service for those functions that you can't do yourself or as an auditor to your records. Also, as you interview accountants, look for one with experience in your specific trade; such an accountant can offer you valuable ideas on how to save money in your business. When do you need to hire an accountant or accounting service for your electrical contracting business? Anytime.

As soon as you start The best way to start off on the right road is to get a quality map. An accountant can help you draw such a map, based on his or her knowledge and experience as well as the experience of others. This "map" might show the potholes that contractors typically find on their road to success: cash flow, record keeping, taxation, etc. Just as important, an accountant can help you smooth out the road by offering techniques for increasing the inflow of cash during the crucial first few months of business, by setting up an easy-to-use record-keeping system, and by marking your calendar with important dates when tax forms must be submitted.

As you grow An accountant can help you as your business picks up speed. He or she can help you make informed decisions about hiring employees, hiring subcontractors, investing excess cash, purchasing capital assets, collecting bad debts, signing large contracts, purchasing supplies and materials, improving balance sheet ratios, applying for loans, and preparing tax forms.

As you change your business structure Your accountant can also be a valuable adviser when you're considering taking on a partner, forming a limited partnership, or incorporating your contracting business. The accountant will help you prepare required balance sheets and income statements, hire an independent auditor, and outline the tax advantages and disadvantages involved. A good accountant is like a navigator; you're at the helm steering the appropriate course, but your accountant/navigator is the one who tells you where the shallow water is and how to stay in the shipping lane.

Scheduling your work How does scheduling your work have anything to do with reducing the costs of doing business? In many ways. By prioritizing your jobs into most-important, less-important, and least-important, you can make sure that you're always doing what's most valuable to your business. A "most-important" job is one with the shortest deadline, the quickest payout, the most important customer, the greatest opportunity for your electrical contracting firm.

Of course, this doesn't mean that any of your customers are less important than any others. All have equal potential for helping your business succeed, either through jobs they hire you to complete or through other customers they bring you. However, the cash customer who must have a remodeled home finished for the inspector on Friday has a greater need for your services than does the customer who needs you to bid on a house he's building in six months. So, you "prioritize" your work based on the customer's needs as well as your own.

Where many successful electrical contractors can reduce costs through scheduling is by managing each job to balance both the customer's need and the contractor's need. How do they do so?

- First take care of the jobs that require inspections or sign-offs the soonest.
- If possible, group similar jobs together during the same time period (new construction, motor rewiring, sign installation, etc.) to reduce tool-gathering, materials-purchasing, and research.
- As practical, group jobs regionally (valley jobs, dock jobs, industrial park jobs, etc.) to reduce travel time between jobs.
- As available, give highest priority to jobs that provide your business with the greatest cash flow (cash, net 15 days, etc.) rather than slow-paying jobs (insurance jobs, net 90 days, etc.).
- If workable, give highest priority to those jobs that improve your relations with customers (special favors, rechecking a job, offering no-charge advice or assistance, etc.).

One more point that will help you reduce costs as you schedule work: plan for problems. We all know that problems will arise—insufficient materials, inaccurate plans, broken tools, inclement weather—so assume that they'll happen and plan for them as part of every job. How? By making sure that you have sufficient materials as well as a quick source for more, that electrical specs have been checked in advance for accuracy, and that backups are available for your most crucial tools. Of course, you can't carry "good weather" around with you as a backup, but you can have inside jobs that can be done if outside weather gets severe. By doing so, you can ensure that you'll have profitable work to do instead of unprofitable downtime.

Depreciation

Depreciation is simply a method of spreading out the expense of a purchase over time. In order to "depreciate" or slowly charge off the cost, the purchase must be of a fixed asset (other than land) that you use in your business, and it must meet other requirements. Depreciable assets include those purchased to be used in your business for more than a year: buildings, vehicles, equipment, tools, furniture, and fixtures.

Most small businesses don't have enough fixed assets to worry about depreciation more than once a year, typically as the year's books are being closed. So what do you need to know about depreciation? First, keep in mind that nothing is certain while Congress is in session. Any rules of depreciation that are current as this book is written might be invalid as Congress and the IRS make changes to tax law. So, check with your accountant about setting up a depreciation system for your business, based on current rules and guidelines. Here's what's current as this book is written:

Modified Accelerated Cost Recovery System (MACRS) Depreciation allows all fixed assets placed in service after 1986 to be assigned a "recovery period" over which the expense can be spread. The length of the recovery period depends on the type of fixed asset. The current schedule allows for 3-, 5-, 7-, 10-, 15-, 20-, 27.5-, and 31.5-year recovery periods. Under the MACRS rules, the entire cost of an item is recovered. There's no "salvage value" at the end of the recovery period, as there was with prior depreciation methods.

To make things somewhat more confusing, there are three methods of depreciation allowed, depending on the type of asset and its recovery period. Shorter recovery periods (10 years or less) use the "200 percent declining balance" method, and 15- and 20-year recovery periods use the "150 percent declining balance" method. Longer periods are used only for real estate and use the "straight-line" method.

Not to get too deep into depreciation, but to help you understand ways of reducing business costs, here are definitions for the three depreciation methods: The *straight line method* is quite simple. A $10,000 fixed asset with a 5-year recovery rate is depreciated at $2,000 (⅕ or 20 percent) per year. The *declining balance method* accelerates the amount of depreciation taken in the early years and reduces the amount taken in the later years. The *200 percent declining* (or double declining) balance approach would depreciate the $10,000 asset by $4,000 (⅖ or 40 percent) the first year, then $2,400 the second year ($10,000 – $4,000 = $6,000 × 40 percent), $1,440 the third year ($6,000 – $2,400 = $3,600 × 40 percent), $864 the fourth year ($3,600 – $1,440 = $2,160 × 40 percent), and $518.40 the final year ($2,160 – $864 = $1,296 × 40 percent). In the example, the 150 percent declining balance method depreciates 30 percent (150 percent of ⅕) of the remaining balance per year.

Depending on your cash flow and tax liability, you could elect to "expense" the purchase of a fixed asset (up to $10,000) during the year in which it's purchased. In the example of a $10,000 purchase, you'd write off the entire $10,000 as an expense during the year it was purchased. No depreciation is necessary. The only requirement is that your business must show a profit. That is, the expense must not force your business into a loss for the year. Many small businesses who have few fixed assets, who typically show a profit, and who don't want to mess with depreciation, will expense the purchase of fixed assets that are less than $10,000, or any lower limit that they set for themselves.

Every time you have to purchase on credit, you add interest costs to your business. If you had more cash, you'd be able to save more on interest expense. For this and other reasons, you can reduce your costs by increasing cash flow.

Reducing costs by increasing cash flow

The *cash flow statement* identifies when cash is expected to be received and when it must be spent to pay bills and debts. It shows how much cash will be needed to pay expenses and when it will be needed. It also allows the owner/contractor to identify where the necessary cash will come from. For example, will the funds needed for the purchase of new tools come from the collection of accounts receivable, or must it be borrowed?

The cash flow statement, based on estimates of sales and expenses, indicates when money will be flowing into and out of the business. It enables you to plan for shortfalls in cash resources so that short-term working capital loans—or a line of credit—can be arranged in advance. That allows you to schedule purchases and payments so you can borrow as little as possible. Because not all sales are cash sales, you must be able to forecast when accounts receivable will be cash in the bank as well as when regular and seasonal expenses must be paid.

The cash flow statement can also be used as a budget, helping you increase your control of the business through comparing actual receipts and payments against forecasted amounts. This comparison helps you identify areas where you can manage your finances even better.

By closely watching the timing of cash receipts and payments, cash on hand, and loan balances, you can readily identify potential shortages in collecting receivables, unrealistic trade credit, or loan repayment schedules. You can also identify surplus cash that can be invested for a greater return on your investment. In addition, the cash flow statement will help you convince your banker why you need a specific loan and how you expect to pay it off.

A cash flow statement or budget can be prepared for any period of time. However, a one-year budget matching the fiscal year of your business is the most useful. Many successful contractors prepare their cash flow statements on a monthly basis for the next year. It should be revised no less than quarterly to reflect actual performance in the previous three months of operations to verify projections.

Table 7-2 illustrates a typical cash flow statement. It includes sales budgets, selling expenses, direct labor expenses, and other vital components. The result of all this budgeting is the cash budget. In addition, the following are some ideas for increasing cash flow implemented by successful electrical contractors.

Typical cash flow statement

	Jan.	Feb.	Mar.	Apr.	May	Jun.	Jul.	Aug.	Sep.	Oct.	Nov.	Dec
Expected available cash												
Cash balance												
Expected receipts												
Job A												
Job B												
Job C												
Bank loans												
Total expected cash												
Expected cash requirements												
Job A												
Job B												
Job C												
Equipment payments												
Taxes												
Insurance (including surety bond payments)												
Overhead												
Loan repayments												
Total cash required												
Cash balance												
Total loans due to bank												

Construction progress payments

Many larger jobs will be paid for in payments based on the amount of the job completed. Even if the agreement you have with your general contractor doesn't require construction progress payments, you should be aware of how they work. If the general contractor doesn't complete specified jobs, he or she might not be paid on time, and neither will you.

Paying bills   Another way of increasing cash flow is by reviewing every invoice you receive to ensure its accuracy before paying it. Some invoices inadvertently include misdirected charges. Others incorporate service charges that are unearned. A few dishonest people make a living by sending bogus invoices to thousands of businesses each month, hoping that a few will pay them without reviewing them.

Set aside a time each week when you review all invoices received against your records. As you incur any charges, write them in a notebook or slip a note into a box so each one can be verified. If you have a staff that prepares your bills for payment, you'll need more complete records so that they or you can verify each invoice or statement received against your records.

Some businesses use a rubber stamp for invoices and require a checkoff for charge created, invoice checked, and invoice paid. Larger firms use formal "purchase orders" that are required for every charge created, other than those that use petty cash.

One more point: as you call accounts payable and ask them questions regarding their invoices, you'll find that many will attempt to be even more accurate. They know that you review your invoices. They might be perfectly honest, but still make honest mistakes—unless they know that you'll probably call them to ask about any questionable charges. This is especially true if you tell them that you'll set the invoice aside for later payment if you find any questionable charges.

Owning a business is a form of legalized gambling. The next chapter will help you reduce the risks of business and help you to beat the odds.

Reducing risk

IN THE PAST FEW CHAPTERS, you've learned how to increase sales and reduce expenses for your electrical contracting business. However, even as your business grows and profits, you can still lose money. How?

- An employee is injured on the job and sues you.
- An employee runs off with money stolen from your business.
- A fire or flood wipes out your office, tools, machinery, and important records.
- A partner in your business files bankruptcy, and the courts attach your business.
- The local economy goes sour and you can't find any profitable jobs for six months or more.
- A general contractor for which you work files bankruptcy or is subject to a large lien and you don't get paid what's owed to you.
- A business partner is involved in a divorce settlement and business assets must be sold to meet a court order.
- The IRS comes after you for a large tax bill that they think you owe them, and they take over your bank account until everything is resolved.

The list goes on. There are many ways that an otherwise profitable business can quickly be thrown into a situation where the business' future is in jeopardy. What can you do about it? First, you can make sure you understand the risks involved in your business. You can also take precautions to ensure that the risks are minimal. They'll never go away, but, through smart risk management, you can minimize them and prepare for the worst.

When to minimize risk

It's obvious that the best time to minimize the risk of business disasters is before they happen, and the first step to minimizing risk is identifying the risks that can occur. Business risks that electrical contractors typically face are:

- Acts of nature (fire, flood).
- Acts of people (theft, vandalism, vehicle accidents).
- Personal injury (employee or user).
- Legal problems (liens, unfair trade practices, torts).
- Financial (loss of income, funding, or assets).
- Taxation (judgments, tax liens).
- Management (loss of owner's capacity to manage or partner's ownership).

Of course, every method of reducing risk—attorneys, bonds, insurance, binding agreements, security systems, fire alarms, etc.—cost money. So when is it more cost-effective to accept the risk rather than pay for products or services that eliminate the risk? It's a simple question with a simple answer: it all depends.

Actually, the best time to minimize risk in your business is right now. The real answer lies in balancing the cost of loss against the cost of security. For example, if your work vehicle is a beat-up 1972 Ford pickup with a pinto paint job, collision insurance that costs an extra $300 a year is more expensive than absorbing the cost of body damage from minor accidents.

In the coming pages, you'll learn how to minimize risks to your business that come from the previously described situations, and you'll do so with the help of others: insurance agents, lawyers, accountants, and other professionals.

How to minimize risk

You can reduce the risks involved in owning and operating your electrical contracting business by using the knowledge and skills of others. You can select an insurance agent, a lawyer, and an accountant whom you trust and let them guide you toward cost-effectively minimizing risks without spending too much time and money doing so.

A good insurance agent is as valuable to your success as any other professional consultant. A good insurance agent can ensure that your exposure to risk is low and keep your insurance costs to a minimum.

Insurance agent

As with other advisers, ask around among other contractors and professionals for recommendations for a good insurance agent. If possible, search for one who primarily serves the business community rather than families or individuals. Such agents will better know your problems and concerns.

Ask prospective agents for some advice on a specific problem. Don't tell them what you think the solution is. Their responses can help you determine which are the best at cost-effective problem solving.

There are some things you can do to reduce insurance costs. For example, you can save money over the long term by increasing your vehicles' deductible. In fact, the best way to save on all insurance costs—auto, fire, theft, health—is to increase your deductible to an amount that's manageable. A guideline is whether paying the higher deductible annually would significantly change your premiums. That is, if your deductible was increased from $50 to $200, would you save the $150 in annual premiums?

To find a lawyer who is familiar with a business of your size and trade, ask for a referral from a business colleague, your accountant, your banker, your local chamber of commerce, or other tradespeople in your area. Some local bar associations run a lawyer referral and information service; check your local telephone book's yellow pages under Attorneys' Referral and Information Services. Some referral services give you names; others actually give information on experience and fees to help you match your needs to the lawyer's background and charges.

Finding a lawyer

As discussed earlier, a lawyer can help you decide which is the most advantageous business structure to reduce risks. He or she can also help you with zoning, permit, or licensing problems, unpaid bills, contracts and agreements, trademarks, and some tax problems.

Because there's always the possibility of a lawsuit, claim, or other legal action against your business, it's wise to have a lawyer lined up who is already familiar with your business before a crisis arises. A lawyer with experience serving contractors, and especially electrical contractors, can also advise you on federal, state, and local laws, programs, and agencies to help you through loans, grants, procurement set-asides, and tax problems. Your attorney might also be able to advise you about unexpected legal pitfalls and opportunities that might affect your business.

In choosing a lawyer, experience and fee should be related. One lawyer might charge an hourly rate that, at first glance, looks cheaper than another lawyer's. However, because of a lack of experience in solving legal problems for contractors, the less expensive lawyer might cost more to solve the same problem. If you feel overwhelmed with the selection process, take a trusted friend to your initial meeting with the lawyer to help you keep on track as you interview the attorney about services and fees.

If you retain a law firm, be sure you understand who will work on your projects and who will supervise the work. If junior partners or paralegals handle your work, the fees should be lower. That's okay as long as you know that an experienced attorney will review and be ultimately responsible for the work done.

Let your lawyer know that you expect to be informed of all developments and consulted before any decisions are made on your behalf. You might also want to receive copies of all documents, letters, and memos regarding your project. If this isn't practical, you should at least have the opportunity to read such correspondence at your lawyer's office.

Whenever giving your lawyer a project—defending a lawsuit, reviewing a contract, consulting on tax matters—ask him or her to estimate the costs and time required to adequately complete the project. You might want to place a periodic ceiling on fees, after which your lawyer needs to call you before proceeding with work that will add to your bill.

Your lawyer can save you a lot of time and bad debts by explaining local and state laws regarding liens. There are numerous types of liens that you can file or that can be filed against you. A mechanic's lien is a legal action taken to collect just compensation for labor performed or materials provided in construction, improvement, or repair of real property.

One way of reducing the need to file a lien against a job is to never let a customer go past 90 days overdue without taking some sort of action. Talk to your attorney or to a collection service about your options and the process.

One more point for working with an attorney: if you hire an attorney on retainer, make sure that you have a written agreement between you that clearly describes just what you and the lawyer expect from each other.

A lawyer is a valuable resource as you start and build your business, but a good accountant is even more important. As noted earlier, most businesses fail not for lack of good ideas or good intentions, but rather for lack of financial expertise and planning.

Finding an accountant

Look for an accountant as you would an attorney. Get referrals from trusted friends, business associations, professional associations, and other contractors. Discuss fees in advance and draw up a written agreement about how you'll work together. Your accountant can advise you about initial business decisions, will help you set up your records, draw up and analyze income statements, advise on financial decisions involving the purchase of capital assets, and give advice on cash requirements for the successful continuation of your venture. He or she can make budget forecasts, help prepare financial information for a loan application, and handle tax matters.

Accounting firms offer a variety of services. If this is not an easy area for you, the fees you pay will be well worth it. Most accounting firms will maintain books of original entry, prepare bank reconciliation statements and post the general ledger, prepare quarterly and semiannual balance sheets and income statements, and design and implement various accounting and record-keeping systems. Accounting firms will also get your federal and state withholding numbers for you, instruct you on where and when to file tax returns, prepare tax returns, and do general tax planning for your small business.

Your accountant is your key financial adviser. He or she should alert you to potential danger areas and advise you on how to handle growth spurts, how to best plan for slow business times, and how to financially mature and protect your business future from unnecessary risk.

Risk management

Risk management consists of identifying and analyzing the things that might cause loss, and choosing the best way to deal with each of these potentials for loss. You've worked hard to build your business, and you've poured a lot of time, effort, and money into building it up. Spend some time looking at the best ways of reducing risk.

The best way to reduce risk in your growing electrical contracting business is to continue the learning process. You've been a student for all of the years you've worked in your trade, learning how to do your job better, faster, and more efficiently. Now you're starting your own business and have learned about dozens of new topics. Here are three things you can do to continue the learning process, increasing in knowledge, reducing risks, and growing your business.

First, work closely and creatively with your professional advisers—your lawyer, your accountant, and your insurance agent. As you periodically review your business records, you'll see ways that you can do things better the next time. You'll begin to develop your skills in planning and managing your business.

Second, continue to learn about all aspects of business operations, constantly acquiring new ideas and new skills. Sign up for intermediate and advanced business courses at your local community college or through seminars sponsored by regional business development centers. Also, continue to learn more and more about the electrical contracting trade through association books, tapes, seminars, courses, and conventions.

Third, get to know other business owners with similar needs or problems. Your business has little in common with retailers, but your business has much in common with other service businesses. Talking with others can help you avoid repeating mistakes they've made; you'll benefit from their experiences and they from yours. Local and national associations offer membership, social events, networking opportunities, newsletters, conventions, and seminars for electrical contractors. Through some organizations, you can often advertise your product or service to potential customers. These organizations also provide a way to learn about services you might need, such as accounting, advertising, or secretarial services. In their newsletters and workshops, these organizations also offer updates in such areas as taxes and zoning.

Exposures to loss

Identifying exposures to loss is a vital step to reducing your risks. Until you know the scope of all possible losses, you won't be able to develop a realistic, cost-effective strategy for dealing with them. The last thing you want to do is come up with a superficial Band-Aid approach that might cause more problems than it solves.

It's not easy to recognize the hundreds of hazards or perils that can lead to an unexpected loss. Unless you've experienced a fire, for example, you might not realize how extensive fire loss can be. Damage to the building and its contents are obvious exposures. However, related losses include damage or destruction caused by smoke and water, damage to employees' property, damage to customers' or suppliers' property, the loss of income during the time it takes to get the business back to normal, and the loss of customers who might not return when you reopen for business.

What's the solution? You begin the process of identifying exposures by taking a close look at each of your business operations and asking yourself: What could cause a loss to my business operation? How serious is that loss to the continuation of my business?

Many business owners use a "risk analysis" questionnaire or survey as a checklist. These are available from insurance agents, most of whom will provide the expertise to help you with your analysis. With their expertise and experience, you're less likely to overlook any exposures. Most risk analysis questionnaires and surveys look at potential for property losses, business interruption losses, liability losses, key person losses, and automobile losses.

Property losses

Property losses stem from physical damage to property, loss of use of property, or criminal activity.

Physical damage

Property damage can be caused by many common perils: fire, windstorm, lightning, and vandalism might be the first that come to mind, and it's a rare business that doesn't buy insurance to protect against these. However, to cope effectively with the possibility of physical damage to property, the business owner should consider more than just damage to or destruction of a building.

Contents might be even more susceptible to loss. Your contracting business could lose valuable accounting records, making it difficult to bill customers or to collect from customers who owe money. Vital equipment might become inoperable because of fire and, if replacements can't be found and installed immediately, your business might even be forced into a temporary shutdown.

Loss of use

Your business could lose the use of property without suffering any physical damage. A government agency can close a contractor's office down as part of a lawsuit, for delinquent taxes, or other causes. If your contracting business is all in your truck, a mechanical malfunction can virtually place your business in the repair shop.

Criminal activity

Small businesses are very susceptible to crimes committed by others. Burglary and robbery are obvious perils, but don't overlook possible exposure to "white-collar" crime, employee theft, embezzlement, or forgery. An experienced insurance agent can help you define the types of risks your contracting business faces in your region.

You've already seen how a direct loss from a fire can temporarily shut down your business. Although property insurance provides money for repairing or rebuilding physical damage that's a direct result from a fire, most property policies don't cover indirect losses such as the income lost while your business is interrupted for repairs.

Business interruption losses

A special kind of insurance will cover indirect losses that occur when a direct loss forces a temporary interruption of business. For example, a contractor whose truck and tools were stolen during the height of the busiest season lost nearly a month's income because the truck and tools weren't available. Business interruption insurance will reimburse policyholders for the difference between normal income and the reduced income earned during the forced shutdown period.

Not only is income reduced or cut off completely during such interruptions, but also many business expenses continue. These include taxes, loan payments, salaries to key employees, interest, depreciation, and utilities. Without income to pay for these expenses, your business is forced to dip into reserves.

In addition, business interruption often triggers extra expenses. For example, you might have to authorize overtime to shorten the interruption period, or you might have to rent office space or equipment for the period in order to perform your services. These extra expenses put an additional strain on finances at a time when little if any income is being produced.

A contractor can even buy business interruption coverage to protect against interruptions triggered by direct loss on someone else's property. If your key supplier is shut down by fire and can't deliver required materials to you, you could suffer a business loss. Or if your tools and materials are stored at the customer's job site as it suffers physical or criminal damage, you can lose income as if it were a direct loss to you.

Loss of key people

What would happen to your business if an accident or illness made it impossible for you to work? What if one of your partners or your sales manager were to die suddenly? Most of us would rather not think about such a "what if." Nevertheless, it's important for you to prepare your business for survival, long before a key person dies or is disabled. Unfortunately, it's a step that's often overlooked.

Here are some of the questions you should consider regarding the loss of people who are key to your electrical contracting business:

- How will the business survive if the owner becomes seriously ill or disabled?
- What will the owner's source of income be?
- Who would take over his or her job so the business can continue?
- What if the heir is not qualified or is a minor?
- What will happen to the business if the owner dies?
- If a will is not in place before the owner's death, what happens to the business?
- If the owner's life savings have been invested in the business, will the surviving family receive any cash to help them continue?
- What will the surviving family's source of income be while the future of the business is being decided?
- If the business is to be sold, where will working capital come from for the transition period?
- How is the fair market value of the business to be determined?
- Would the fair market value be apt to change because of the loss of a key person?
- If the business forms the bulk of the estate, what are the income and inheritance tax implications for the surviving spouse and heirs?
- Is there some predeath strategy that could minimize that tax liability?
- If the business is a partnership, is there a binding agreement in place that will allow a continuation of the business?

- What are the duties of the surviving partner regarding winding up the affairs of the partnership?
- Will the surviving partner be personally liable for losses that the business' assets are insufficient to cover?
- If your business is a corporation, how does the death or disability of a major stockholder affect your business?

Once again, planning is essential. Your attorney, accountant, and insurance agent can develop a legally binding strategy to reduce losses and to prevent outsiders from taking over your business during a catastrophe.

There are a number of ways that you can keep your losses to a minimum. They include preventing or limiting exposure to loss, risk retention, transferring risk, and insurance.

Loss control

One principle of loss prevention and control is the same in business as it is in your personal life: avoid activities that are too hazardous. For example, if you have little knowledge or experience applying sensitive finishes, avoid taking jobs that require these finishes. Or, if you can't avoid an exposure completely, minimize it. Find someone with experience with these finishes and hire him or her to train or assist you.

A business owner might decide that the firm can afford to absorb some losses, either because the frequency and probability of loss are low or because the dollar value of loss is manageable. Maybe your contracting business owns several older vehicles and their drivers have excellent safety records, so you decide to drop the collision insurance on these vehicles but retain it on newer vehicles.

Another method of managing exposure to loss is by transferring the risk. Although many businesses do this by buying insurance—transferring some of the risk to the insurance company—there are other options. Your firm might decide to eliminate collision exposure completely by only hiring subcontractors who will supply their own vehicles. Or you might decide to not stock any inventory of electrical supplies, but rather purchase materials only as you need them. Then have them delivered to the job site.

Insurance as a risk strategy

The most common method of transferring risk is by purchasing insurance. By insuring your business, equipment, and employees, you've transferred much of the risk of loss to the insurance company. You pay a relatively small amount in premiums rather than run the risk of not protecting yourself against the possibility of a much larger financial loss.

Of course, you can be overinsured or pay more than is necessary for the amount of risk that you transfer. In business insurance, only you can decide which exposures you absolutely must ensure against. Some decisions, however, are already made for you: those required by law and those required by others as a part of doing business with them. Workers' Compensation is an example of insurance that's required by law. Your bank probably won't lend you money for equipment, real estate, or other assets unless you ensure them against loss.

Today, very few businesses—and especially electrical contractors—have sufficient financial reserves to protect themselves against the hundreds of property and liability exposures that they face. What those exposures are, what their dollar value is, and how much is enough, are difficult questions. That's why, as you build a team of business professionals to help you effectively manage your business, you should hire an insurance professional.

The insurance agent

The agent is the insurance industry's primary client representative. Typically, the independent agent is a small business owner and manager. By using this distribution system, insurance companies are represented by agents who receive a commission for selling the companies' products and services. An independent agent might represent more than one insurance company.

The professional independent insurance agent has been trained in risk analysis. She or he is familiar with the insurance coverages and financial strategies available in your state, and with regulations that govern them. With this experience, the agent can point out exposures that you might otherwise overlook.

Finally, your insurance professional can help you develop possible solutions. You make the final decisions, but your agent can suggest options from a vast menu of risk-management strategies. He or she has the technical knowledge to amend a basic policy by adding special coverages and endorsements. The resulting policy will be custom-tailored to your business' unique protection needs.

There are a number of related services that insurance companies provide to policyholders. As a small business person who wants to reduce both risk and costs, you should consider these services made available to you.

The insurance company

Liability insurance coverages, particularly for property damage and bodily injury, usually include legal defense at no additional charge when the policyholder is named a party to a lawsuit that involves a claim covered by the policy. Litigation is costly, whether the claimant's suit is valid or frivolous. The legal defense provision greatly reduces these costs to you.

Insurance companies that write a lot of Workers' Compensation insurance might have rehabilitation services available. Generally, these services help return injured workers to useful employment and, in some cases, might even help train the worker for a different job.

Many cities require businesses to conduct regular inspections of machinery in commercial buildings. Boiler and machinery insurance policies not only protect against certain kinds of damage to energy equipment, but also provide for inspection by the insurance company's specialists. The insurance company issues a certificate of inspection to the policyholder as proof that the inspection requirement has been met. As an electrical contractor, you might be able to subcontract to the insurance company as a machinery inspector for your region. Ask your agent.

Some commercial insurance policyholders might also qualify for consulting services of the insuring company's Loss Control department. This department is staffed with engineers and safety experts who specialize in inspecting business premises, identifying hazards, perils, and possible trouble spots, and recommending solutions.

Essential insurance coverage

Four kinds of insurance are essential to your business: fire, liability, automobile, and Workers' Compensation. Selecting from among the dozens of available policies and options can be somewhat confusing to most business people. However, the following information will guide you in making the right decisions for the right reasons.

Fire insurance

Here are some tips on buying fire insurance coverage: You can add other perils—such as windstorm, hail, smoke, explosion, vandalism, and malicious mischief—to your basic fire insurance at a relatively small additional fee.

If you need comprehensive coverage, your best buy might be one of the all-risk contracts—such as the $1 million umbrella policy—that offers the broadest available protection for the money.

Remember that the insurance company might compensate your losses by paying the actual cash value of the property at the time of the loss; it might repair or replace the property with material of like kind and quality, or it might take all the property at the agreed or appraised value and reimburse you for your loss.

You can ensure property that you don't own, such as a job site, for potential loss of assets at that site. You can't assign an insurance policy along with property you sell unless you have the permission of the insurance company. Even if you have several policies on your property, you can still collect only the amount of your actual cash loss. All the insurers share the payment proportionately.

Special protection other than the standard fire insurance policy is needed to cover the loss by fire of accounts, bills, currency, deeds, evidence of debt, and securities. If you increase the hazard of fire, the insurance company might suspend your coverage even for losses not originating from the increased hazard (such as renting part of your building to a cleaning plant).

After a loss, you must use all reasonable means to protect the property from further loss or run the risk of having your coverage canceled. In most cases, to recover your loss you must furnish within 60 days a complete inventory of the damaged, destroyed, and undamaged property, showing in detail quantities, costs, actual cash value, and the amount of loss claimed.

If you and your insurer disagree on the amount of the loss, the question can be resolved through special appraisal procedures provided for in the fire insurance policy. You can cancel your policy without notice at any time and get part of the premium returned. The insurance company can also cancel at any time within a specified period, usually five days, with a written notice to you.

You can get a substantial reduction in premiums by accepting a co-insurance clause in your fire insurance policy. A co-insurance clause states that you must carry insurance equal to 80 or 90 percent of the value of the insured property. If you carry less than this, you can't collect the full amount of your loss, even if the loss is small. What percent of your loss you can collect will depend on what percent of the full value of the property you've insured it for.

If your loss is caused by someone else's negligence, the insurer has the right to sue this negligent third party for the amount it has paid you under the policy. This is known as the insurer's right to subrogation. However, the insurer will usually waive this right on request. For example, if you've leased your insured building to someone and have waived your right to recover from the tenant for any insured damages to your property, you should have your agent request that the insurer waive the subrogation clause in the fire policy on your leased building. A building under construction can be insured for fire, lightning, extended coverage, vandalism, and malicious mischief.

Here are some important considerations when purchasing liability insurance: You might be legally liable for damages, even in cases where you used "reasonable care." Under certain conditions, your business might be subject to damage claims, even from trespassers.

Liability insurance

Most liability policies require you to notify the insurer immediately after an incident on your property that might cause a future claim. This holds true no matter how unimportant the incident might seem at the time it happens.

Even if the suit against you is false or fraudulent, the liability insurer pays court costs, legal fees, and interest on judgments in addition to the liability judgments themselves. You can be liable for the acts of others under contracts you've signed with them, such as subcontractors. This liability is insurable.

Automobile insurance

One of the most common types of risk transference is purchasing automobile or vehicle insurance. Here are some pointers on making an informed decision: When an employee or a subcontractor uses a car on your behalf, you can be legally liable, even though you don't own the car or truck.

Five or more automobiles, trucks, or motorcycles under one ownership and operated as a fleet for business purposes can generally be insured under a low-cost fleet policy against both material damage to your vehicles and liability to others for property damage or personal injury.

You can often get deductibles of almost any amount—$250, $500, $1,000—thereby reducing your premiums. Automobile medical-payments insurance pays for medical claims—including your own—arising from vehicular accidents, regardless of the question of negligence.

In most states, you must carry liability insurance or be prepared to provide a surety bond or other proof of financial responsibility when you're involved in an accident. You can purchase uninsured motorist protection to cover your own bodily injury claims from someone who has no insurance. Personal property stored in a car or truck and not attached to it (such as electrical supplies in your work truck) is not covered under an automobile policy.

Workers' Compensation insurance

Workers' Compensation insurance is required in most states if you have employees. You can reduce the cost of this mandatory insurance by knowing the following: Federal laws require that an employer provide employees a safe place to work, hire competent fellow employees, provide safe tools, and warn employees of existing danger. If an employer fails to provide these things, he or she is liable for damage suits brought by an employee and possible fines or prosecution.

State law determines the level or type of benefits payable under Workers' Compensation policies. Not all employees are covered by Workers' Compensation laws. The exceptions are determined by state law and therefore vary from state to state.

You can save money on Workers' Compensation insurance by seeing that your employees are properly classified. Rates for Workers' Compensation insurance vary from 0.1 percent of the payroll for "safe" occupations to about 25 percent or more of the payroll for very hazardous occupations.

Most employers can reduce their Workers' Compensation premium cost by reducing their accident rates below the average. They do this by using safety and loss-prevention measures established by the individual state.

Some types of insurance coverage, while not absolutely essential, will add greatly to the security of your business. These coverages include business interruption insurance and crime insurance. Whether these coverages are vital to your business depends much on how and where your business operates. A small firm with two partners who have identical skills might not require business interruption insurance. However, a multimillion-dollar, one-person band might require extensive insurance against business interruption. The same applies to crime insurance: some business locations require it, while others might not.

Desirable insurance coverage

Business interruption insurance was described earlier in this chapter. Once you're ready to consider this form of risk transference for your business, consider the following: You can purchase insurance to cover fixed expenses that will continue— such as salaries to key employees, taxes, interest, mortgage, utilities, loss of profits—if a fire shuts down your business.

Business interruption insurance

Under contingent business interruption insurance, you can also collect if fire or other peril closes down the business of a supplier or customer and this interrupts your business. The business interruption policy provides payments for amounts you spend to hasten the reopening of your business after a fire or other insured peril.

You can get coverage for the extra expenses you suffer if an insured peril seriously disrupts your business rather than closes it down. Some business interruption policies indemnify you if your operations are suspended because of failure or interruption of the supply of power by a public utility company.

Crime insurance
To nearly every business in the country, crime insurance is a cost of doing business. Unfortunately, in several areas it's a major expense. Here are some facts to consider when purchasing crime insurance for your contracting business: Burglary insurance excludes such property as accounts receivable files. If you lose them to a burglary, you'll have problems collecting from them or from your insurance company.

With many policies, coverage is granted under burglary insurance only if there are visible marks of the burglar's forced entry. If the burglar somehow found your keys, you might not be protected. Burglary insurance can be written to cover damage incurred in the course of a burglary, in addition to valuables stolen.

Burglary insurance covers theft on your property. Robbery insurance protects you from loss of property, money, and other assets by force, trickery, or threat of violence on or off your premises.

Consider purchasing a comprehensive crime policy written specifically for small business owners. In addition to burglary and robbery, these policies cover other types of loss by theft, destruction and disappearance of money and securities, and theft by employees.

If your business is located in a high-risk area and you can't get insurance through normal channels without paying excessive rates, you might be able to get help through the federal crime insurance plan. Your agent or state insurance commissioner can tell you where to get information about these plans.

Bonds are required for bidding many large or governmental jobs. A *bond* is an insurance policy that ensures that you'll do what you promised to do. The cost of the bond is based on the type of bond and the total dollar value of the contract requiring bonding.

As you start your electrical contracting business, you might not be able to bid on jobs that require bonds. Bonds aren't usually available to new businesses, except through guarantees from the Small Business Administration. Later, as your business grows, contact your business insurance agent or a trade association about bonding.

What types of bonds are typically required? The three most common types of bonds are the bid bond, the performance bond, and the payment bond. A *bid bond* is a guarantee that the bid given to a customer is good and that the contractor will enter into a contract if awarded the job for the amount of the proposal. A *performance bond* is a guarantee to the customer that the contractor will complete the work as outlined in the specifications and terms of the contract. A *payment bond* is a guarantee that the bonded contractor will pay for specified goods or services.

In each case, it's the bonding or insurance agent that will pay the customer if the contractor doesn't fulfill the contract requirements. Defaulting on a contract will forever make it almost impossible to get another bond.

The Miller Act requires that a contractor must furnish a performance and payment bond before any public works construction, alteration, or repair contract of more than $25,000 is begun. If the contract is for less than $1 million, the payment bond must be for 50 percent of the value. Public

Bonding

The Miller Act

works projects valued between $1 million and $5 million require a payment bond of 40 percent of the total amount payable. For contracts of more than $5 million, the bond must be for $2.5 million.

The Miller Act is a federal law regarding federal public works projects. However, most states have what they call the "little Miller Act." Of course, the specifics vary from state to state, but the principles are the same.

There are numerous ways that an informed electrical contractor can improve profits by reducing risk in business. By selecting qualified advisers and by following their direction, you can ensure that your business will survive the countless risks you'll face.

Managing your electrical contracting business

CONGRATULATIONS! You've started your electrical contracting business. You've researched the local need for your specialized services, equipped your new business, acquired the funds to operate, begun building your business skills, found prospects, and converted them into customers. You've also learned how to reduce costs and risk. Now you're ready for the day-to-day management of your business. That's what this chapter is all about.

In the coming pages, you'll learn how to manage your electrical contracting business better. You'll learn about equipment and whether you should lease or buy it; you'll learn more about budgets and how to make them work for you, and you'll learn how to solve common—and uncommon—business problems. The information and skills that you learn in this chapter will assist you in successfully managing your firm for many years.

Small businesses have difficulty raising capital. That's no secret. This difficulty has caused many to look at leasing as an alternative financing arrangement for acquiring assets. All types of equipment used by electrical contractors—from motor vehicles to computers to equipment to office furniture—have become easier to lease. Smart business owners are learning more about leases and how they can help them manage their business more efficiently.

A *lease* is a long-term agreement to rent equipment, land, buildings, or any other asset. In return for most—but not all— of the benefits of ownership, the user (lessee) makes periodic payments to the owner of the asset (lessor). The lease payment

Leasing versus buying equipment

covers the original cost of the equipment or other asset and provides the lessor a profit.

Types of leases

There are three major types of leases: the *financial lease*, the *operating lease*, and the *sale and lease-back*. Financial leases are most common by far. A financial lease is usually written for a term not to exceed the economic life of the equipment. A financial lease usually requires that periodic payments be made, that ownership of the equipment reverts to the lessor at the end of the lease term, that the lease cannot be canceled, that the lessee has a legal obligation to continue payments to the end of the term, and that the lessee agrees to maintain the equipment or other asset.

The operating or maintenance lease can usually be canceled under conditions spelled out in the lease agreement. Maintenance of the asset is usually the responsibility of the owner or lessor. Computer equipment is often leased under this kind of arrangement with the lessor, who takes care of maintenance or repairs to the computer as required.

The sale and lease-back is similar to the financial lease. The owner of an asset sells it to another party and simultaneously leases it back to the party, who uses it for a specified term. This arrangement lets you free up the money tied up in an asset for use elsewhere. Buildings are often leased in this way. Your corporation buys a building, then leases it back to you.

You might also hear leases described as net leases or gross leases. Under a net lease, the lessee is responsible for expenses such as maintenance, taxes, and insurance. The lessor pays these expenses under a gross lease. Financial leases are usually net leases.

Finally, you might run across the term "full payout lease." Under a full payout lease, the lessor recovers the original cost of the asset during the term of the lease.

As the use of leasing has increased as a method for businesses to acquire equipment and other assets, the number of companies in the leasing business has increased dramatically. Leasing is now a billion-dollar industry.

Types of lessors

Commercial banks, insurance companies, and finance companies do most of the leasing. Many of these organizations have formed subsidiaries primarily concerned with equipment leasing. These subsidiaries are usually capable of making lease arrangements for almost anything. Ask your lender whether it offers leases for equipment that you require.

In addition to financial organizations, there are companies that specialize in leasing. Some are engaged in general leasing, while others specialize in particular equipment such as commercial trucks, computers, or construction equipment. Some equipment manufacturers are also in the leasing business. They often lease their equipment through their sales reps. As you consider leasing equipment, ask your sales rep about leases that are available through the manufacturer.

The obvious advantage to leasing is acquiring the use of an asset without making a large initial cash outlay. Compared to a loan arrangement to purchase the same equipment, a lease usually requires no down payment, requires no restriction on a company's financial operations, spreads payments over a longer period than most loans, and provides protection against the risk of equipment obsolescence.

Advantages and disadvantages of leasing

There might also be tax benefits in leasing. Lease payments are deductible as operating expenses if the arrangement is a true lease (as defined by the Internal Revenue Service). Ownership, however, usually has greater tax advantages through the investment tax credit and depreciation. Naturally, you need to have enough income and resulting tax liability to take advantage of these two benefits.

The investment tax credit might work to the benefit of the lessee as well as the lessor. The credit is a dollar-for-dollar reduction in federal income taxes, equal to 10 percent of the cost of the equipment in the year the equipment is put into use. While the lessor usually takes the tax credit, it can pass part of the benefit on to the lessee in the form of a reduced lease payment.

With leasing firms that specialize in equipment used by electrical contractors, leasing has the further advantage that the leasing firm has acquired considerable knowledge about the kinds of equipment it leases. Thus, it can provide expert technical advice based on experience with the leased equipment.

Finally, there's one further advantage of leasing that you should hope won't ever be necessary. In the event of your firm's bankruptcy, the lessor's claims to your assets are more restricted than those of general creditors.

So, what's the downside of leasing? In the first place, leasing usually costs more because you lose certain tax advantages that go with ownership of an asset. However, leasing might not cost more if you can't take advantage of ownership benefits because you don't have enough tax liability for them to come into play.

Obviously, you also lose the economic value of the asset at the end of the lease terms because you don't own the asset. Lessees have been known to grossly underestimate the salvage value of an asset. If they had known this value from the outset, they might have decided to buy instead of lease.

Finally, never forget that a lease is a long-term legal obligation. Usually, you can't cancel a lease agreement. So, if you were to end an operation that used leased equipment, you might find you'd still have to pay as much as if you had used the equipment for the full term of the lease.

Leases and taxes   Full lease payments are deductible as operating costs. You can make these deductions only if the Internal Revenue Service finds that you have a true lease. You can't take a full deduction for a "lease" that's really an installment purchase.

Although each lease arrangement might be different, here are some general guidelines:

- In no way should any portion of the payment be construed as "interest."
- Lease payments must not be large compared to the cost of purchasing the same asset.
- Any renewal option at lease end must be on terms equivalent to what a third party would offer.
- Purchase options must be at amounts comparable with fair market value.

Accounting for leases

Historically, financial leases were "off-the-balance-sheet" financing. That is, lease obligations often were not recorded directly on the balance sheet, but were listed in footnotes instead. Not explicitly accounting for leases sometimes resulted in a failure to state operational assets and liabilities fairly.

In 1977, the Financial Accounting Standards Board (FASB), the rule-making body of the accounting profession, required that capital leases be recorded on the balance sheet as both an asset and a liability. This was in recognition of the long-term nature of a lease obligation.

Cost analysis

You can analyze the cost of the lease versus purchase problem through discounted cash flow analysis. This analysis compares the cost of each alternative by considering the timing of the payments, tax benefits, the interest rate on a loan, the lease rate, and other financial arrangements.

Even if you plan to have your accountant work up these numbers for you, follow through this exercise so that you'll better understand what this cost analysis tells you about buying versus leasing equipment. After all, it's you not your accountant who will make the decision.

To make the analysis, you must first make certain assumptions about the economic life of the equipment, salvage value, and depreciation. Let's work through a sample problem to illustrate the process. The assumptions for the sample problem are included in the table below. Shown at top of following page is the analysis of the lease alternative, and the full page illustration on page 206 is an analysis of the borrow and buy options.

Example assumptions

Equipment cost: $60,000
Estimated economic life: 10 years
Lease terms: 8 annual* payments of $10,363.94 (Apr 10.5%). First payment due upon delivery. Investment tax credit to lessor. Lessee maintains equipment.
Loan terms: 5 years, 75% financing at 10% (Apr.). 5 annual* payments of $11,870.89. First payment due at end of first year.
Taxes: Lessee tax rate 50%. Method of depreciation for tax purposes is straight line.
Other: Equipment needed for term of lease, 8 years. If firm purchases equipment, it can be sold at end of 8 years for book value. Average after tax cost of capital for lessee is 9%.

*Payments have been annualized to simplify calculations. Payments are usually made monthly.

To evaluate a lease, you must first find the net cash outlay (not cash flow) in each year of the lease term. You find these amounts by subtracting the tax savings (at 50 percent in the example) from the lease payment (as shown at top of following page, column 3). This calculation gives you the net cash outlay for each year of the leases (as shown at top of following page, column 4).

Each year's net cash outlay must next be discounted to take into account the time value of money. This discounting gives you the present value of each of the amounts. The present value of an amount of money is the sum you'd have to invest today at a stated rate of interest to have that amount of money at a specified future date. For example, if someone offered to give you $100 five years from now, how much could you take today and be as well off? Common sense tells you that you could take less than $100 because you'd have the use of the money for the five-year period. Naturally, how much less you

Evaluation of lease cost

(1) End of year	(2) Lease payment	(3) (0.50×2) Tax saving	(4) (2–3) net cash outlay	(5) Discount factor	(6) (4×5) Net present value
0	$ 10,363.94	$ 5,181.97	$ 5,181.97	1.000	$ 5,181.97
1	10,363.94	5,181.97	5,181.97	0.952	4,933.24
2	10,363.94	5,181.97	5,181.97	0.907	4,700.05
3	10,363.94	5,181.97	5,181.97	0.864	4,477.22
4	10,363.94	5,181.97	5,181.97	0.823	4,264.76
5	10,363.94	5,181.97	5,181.97	0.784	4,062.66
6	10,363.94	5,181.97	5,181.97	0.746	3,865.75
7	10,363.94	5,181.97	5,181.97	0.710	3,684.38
8	—	—	—	—	—

Net present value of costs of leasing   **$ 35,170.03**

could take depends on the interest rate you thought you could get if you invested the lesser amount. To have $100 five years from now at 6 percent compounded annually, you'd have to invest $74.70 today. At 10 percent, you could take $62.10 now to have the $100 at the end of five years.

Thus, the present value of the net outlay under the lease ($5,181.97 after-tax savings) at the end of year six of the lease term, for example, is something less than $5,181.97. Here, let's use 5 percent as the appropriate interest rate for discounting the lease payment (after-tax cost of 50 percent times the loan interest of 10 percent). This low rate of interest is used because of the certain nature of the payments under a lease contract. So, at an annually compounded 5 percent interest rate, you'd have to invest $3,865.75 today to have $5,181.97 at the end of six years.

Fortunately, there are tables (see page 207) that provide the discount factors for present-value calculations. In this table, the factor for the present value of $1 six years from now at 5 percent is .746. This factor (.746) times the after-tax lease payment outlay ($5,181.97) equals $3,865.75, or exactly the amount you'd have to invest today at 5 percent interest compounded annually to have $5,181.97 six years hence.

Evaluation of loan cost

(1) End of year	(2) Payment	(3) Interest	(4) (2-3) Principal repayment	(5) (5-4) Out-standing balance	(6) Depreciation	(7) .05 × (6 + 3) Tax savings	(8) (2-7) Net cash flow	(9) Discount factor	(10) (8×9) Net present value
0	$15,000.00			$45,000.00		$ 6,000.00*	$9,000.00	1.000	$ 9,000.00
1	11,870.89	$4,500.00	$ 7,370.89	37,629.11	$6,000.00	5,250.00	6,620.89	0.952	5,303.09
2	11,870.89	3,726.91	8,107.98	29,521.13	6,000.00	4,881.46	6,989.43	0.907	6,339.41
3	11,870.89	2,952.11	8,918.78	20,602.35	6,000.00	4,476.06	7,394.83	0.864	6,389.13
4	11,870.89	2,060.24	9,810.66	10,791.69	6,000.00	4,030.12	7,840.77	0.823	6,452.95
5	11,870.86	1,079.17	10,791.69		6,000.00	3,539.59	8,331.27	0.784	6,531.72
6					6,000.00	3,000.00	(3,000.00)	0.746	(2,238.00)
7					6,000.00	3,000.00	(3,000.00)	0.711	(2,133.00)
8	(12,000.00)**				6,000.00	3,000.00	(3,000.00)	0.677	(2,031.00)
							(12,000.00)	0.502***	(6,024.00)

Net present value of cost of purchasing $28,590.30

* Investment tax credit = 0.10 × $60,000–$6,000.

** Salvage value = book value = $60,000–8 × $6,000 = $12,000.

*** Discount factor using average after tax cost of capital.

There are also relatively inexpensive "business" calculators programmed to make these calculations for you.

Present value of future dollars

Year*	1%	2%	3%	4%	5%	6%	7%	8%	9%	10%
1	.990	.980	.971	.962	.952	.943	.935	.926	.917	.909
2	.980	.961	.943	.925	.907	.890	.873	.857	.842	.826
3	.971	.942	.915	.889	.864	.840	.816	.794	.772	.751
4	.961	.924	.889	.855	.823	.792	.763	.735	.708	.683
5	.951	.906	.863	.822	.784	.747	.713	.681	.650	.621
6	.942	.888	.838	.790	.746	.705	.666	.630	.596	.564
7	.933	.871	.813	.760	.711	.665	.623	.583	.547	.513
8	.923	.853	.789	.731	.677	.627	.582	.540	.502	.467
9	.914	.837	.766	.703	.645	.592	.544	.500	.460	.424
10	.905	.820	.744	.676	.614	.558	.508	.453	.422	.386

*Periods can be any time period; they do not have to be years.

Why bother with making these present-value calculations? They're necessary in order to compare the actual cash flows over the time periods. You simply can't realistically compare methods of financing without taking into account the time value of money. It might seem confusing and complex at first, but if you work through the example, you'll begin to see that the technique isn't difficult—just sophisticated.

The table on page 205 shows you the present value calculations over the full term of the proposed lease. The sum of the discounted cash flows, $35,170.03, is called the net present value of the cost of leasing. It's this table that will be compared with the final sum of the discounted cash flows for the loan and purchase alternative.

Evaluation of the borrow/buy option is a little more complicated because of the tax benefits that go with ownership through the investment tax credit, loan interest deductions, and depreciation. In the table on page 206, the steps in the calculation are shown above each column head. The interest portion of each loan payment is found by multiplying the loan interest rate (10 percent in the example) by the outstanding loan balance for the preceding period.

Note that in the last three years of the analyzed period the cash flow is positive, coming from the tax savings on depreciation and, in the eighth year, from depreciation and the assumption that the asset could be sold for a salvage value of $12,000. Because these amounts in the last three years are coming in, they're subtracted after discounting from the amounts in the first five years (cash flowing out) to get the net present value of costs of purchasing.

As noted earlier, the salvage value is one of the advantages of ownership. It must be considered in making the comparison. However, it's discounted at a higher rate (the firm's assumed average cost of capital, 9 percent). This rate is used because the salvage value is not known with any certainty, as are the loan payment, depreciation, and interest payments.

When you compare the two alternatives, you see that the buy option looks like the least costly approach. The major difference in cost, of course, comes from the salvage value. If you ignore that value, the alternatives are very close in their net present value of costs. Naturally, it's possible that salvage cost for real assets could be very high or be next to nothing. So, salvage value assumptions need to be made carefully because they can greatly impact your decision.

Thus, while this sort of analysis is useful, you can't make a lease/buy decision solely on cost analysis figures. The advantages and disadvantages discussed earlier in this chapter, while tough to qualify, might outweigh the differences in cost. This is especially true if costs between leasing and buying are reasonably close.

Signing a lease

A lease agreement is a legal document. It's a long-term obligation. You must be thoroughly informed of just what you're committing yourself to. Find out the lessor's financial condition and reputation. Be reasonably sure that the lease arrangements are the best you can get, that the equipment is what you need, and that the term is what you want.

Remember, once the agreement is signed, it's just about impossible to change it.

The lease document will spell out the precise provisions of the agreement. These provisions will probably include the nature of the financial agreement, the payment amount, terms of the agreement, disposition of the asset at the end of the term, schedule of asset value (for insurance and settlement purposes in case of damage or destruction), who gets the investment tax credit, who is responsible for maintenance and taxes, renewal options, and cancellation penalties. In addition, the lease might include special provisions required by either you or the lessor. As with any legally binding document, make sure that your attorney—and even your accountant—review it before you sign it to ensure that they don't have to defend it later.

Managing your operating budget

Managing your electrical contractor business requires that you manage your budget so you can continue to provide service, support, and employment to others as well as profit to yourself. When you first started your business, you established a preliminary budget. Now that your business is operating, you must establish an operating budget.

A *budget* is a forecast of all cash sources and cash expenditures. It's organized in the same format as a financial statement and most commonly covers a 12-month period. At the end of the year, the anticipated income and expenses developed in the budget are compared to the actual performance of the business as recorded in the financial statement.

A budget can greatly enhance your chances of success by helping you to estimate future needs and to plan profits, spending, and overall cash flow. A budget allows you to perceive problems before they occur and alter your plans to prevent those problems.

In business, budgets help you determine how much money you have and how you'll use it, as well as help you decide whether you have enough money to achieve your financial goals. As part of your business plan, a budget can help convince a loan officer that you know your business and have anticipated its needs.

A budget will indicate the cash required for necessary labor and materials, day-to-day operating costs, revenue needed to support business operations, and expected profit. If your budget indicates that you need more revenue than you can earn, you can adjust your plans by:

- Reducing expenditures (hiring fewer employees, purchasing less-expensive furniture, eliminating a telephone line).
- Expanding sales (offering additional services, conducting an aggressive marketing campaign, hiring a salesperson).
- Lowering profit expectations (not my first choice!).

There are three main elements to a budget: sales revenue, total costs, and profit.

Sales revenue

Sales are the cornerstone of a budget. It's crucial to estimate anticipated sales as accurately as possible. Base estimates on actual past sales figures. Once you target sales, you can calculate the related expenses necessary to achieve your goals.

Total costs

Total costs include fixed and variable costs. Estimating costs is complicated because you must identify which costs will change—and by how much—and which costs will remain unchanged as sales increase. You must also consider inflation and rising prices as appropriate.

Variable costs are those that vary directly with sales. Electrical supplies and subcontractor expenses are examples of variable costs. Fixed costs are those that don't change, regardless of sales volume. Rent is considered a fixed cost, as is your salary. Semivariable costs, such as office salaries, labor wages, and telephone expenses, have both variable and fixed components. So, part of the expense is listed as fixed (telephone line charges) and part is variable (long-distance charges).

Profit should be large enough to make a return on cash investment and a return on your work. Your investment is the money that you put into the firm when you started it and the profit of prior years that you've left in the firm (retained earnings). If you can receive 10 percent interest on $25,000 by investing outside of your business, then you should expect a similar return when investing $25,000 in equipment and other assets within the business. In targeting profits, you also want to be sure you're receiving a fair return on your labor. Your weekly paycheck should reflect what you could be earning elsewhere as an employee.

As you develop your budget, you'll be working with the budget equation. The basic budget equation is:

Sales = Total costs + Profit

This equation shows that every sales dollar you receive is made up partly of a recovery of your costs and partly of profit. Another way to express the basic budgeting equation is:

Sales − Total costs = Profit

This equation shows that, after reimbursing yourself for the cost of producing your service, the remaining part of the sales dollar is profit. For example, if you expect $1,000 for a specific job and you know that it will cost $750 to market and perform this service, your profit will be $250.

In calculating an operating budget, you'll often make estimates based on past sales and cost figures. You'll need to adjust these figures to reflect price increases, inflation, and other factors. For example, for the past three years, a contractor spent an average of $3,500 on advertising costs. For the coming year, the owner expects a price increase of 3 percent (.03). To calculate next year's advertising costs, the owner multiplies the average annual advertising costs by the percentage price increase ($3,500 × .03 = $105) and adds that amount to the original annual cost ($3,500 + $105 = $3,605). A shortcut method is to multiply the original advertising cost by one plus the rate of increase ($3,500 × 1.03 = $3,605).

Profit

Establishing an operating budget

If your contracting business is a new venture and has no past financial records, rely on your own experience and knowledge of the industry to estimate demand for and costs of your service. Your accountant or trade association might also be able to help you develop realistic estimates.

The budgeting process

Before you create an operating budget, you must answer three questions:

- How much net profit do you realistically want your business to generate during the calendar year?
- How much will it cost to produce that profit?
- How much sales revenue is necessary to support both profit and cost requirements?

To answer these questions, consider expected sales and all costs, either direct or indirect, associated with your electrical contracting service. To make the safest estimates when budgeting, most companies prefer to overestimate expenses and underestimate sales revenue.

Start constructing your budget with either a forecast of sales or a forecast of profits. For practical purposes, most small businesses start with a forecast of profits. In other words, decide what profit you realistically want to make and then list the expenses you'll incur to make that profit. The steps to creating an operating budget are: target desired profit, determine operating expenses, calculate gross profit margin, estimate sales revenues, and adjust figures.

A sample operating budget for ABC Electrical Contractors illustrates the main steps in budget preparation. As you follow the steps, calculate all the figures yourself. Once you've calculated projected sales, expenses, and profits, organize the figures into the format of an income statement as shown on pages 214 and 215. Refer to page 214 for ABC Electrical Contractors' income statements for the past three years.

Step one: target desired profit

During the three-year period, the company averaged an annual net profit of $63,100. During year two, the company had its highest net profit of $65,000. In year three, sales were up, but net profit declined. For the coming year, year four, the company is targeting a net profit of $65,000.

ABC Electrical Contractors estimates that it will have many additional expenditures in year four. It will award a five percent wage increase to its two employees and purchase a more comprehensive medical insurance package for them at an additional annual cost of $2,400. The company also plans to install additional telephone services at a cost of $1,500.

Step two: determine operating expenses

In addition, the company's accountant has advised it to plan on a three percent overall inflation rate next year. Taking these factors into consideration, ABC Electrical Contractors figures its expenses as shown in the preliminary budget. (See bottom of page 215.) Under fixed costs, the company estimates that:

- Rent will remain unchanged at $24,000 per year.
- Depreciation will remain unchanged at $4,000 per year.
- Salaries will be raised by five percent (.05).

The annual insurance expense of $1,700 will be increased by $2,400 to provide for additional medical coverage, so annual insurance expense will now be budgeted at $4,100.

The company calculates variable costs as follows:

- Telephone and utilities expenses will be budgeted for $7,683 (average annual cost plus the $1,500 expected increase).
- Advertising, repair, maintenance, and miscellaneous expenses will increase by the 3 percent inflation factor.
- Due to company growth, office expenses increased 10 percent each year plus the 3 percent inflation factor.
- Legal and accounting expenses increased by 6 percent each year, to which the 3 percent inflation factor should be added.

Step three: calculate gross profit margin

Gross profit margin is the sum of net profit and total operating expenses, computed by working the preliminary budget backwards. ABC Electrical Contractors' gross profit margin is obtained by adding net profit of $65,000 to operating expenses of $95,119, equalling $160,119.

Income statements for years one, two, and three

	Year 1	Year 2	Year 3	Total	Average	Average percent of sales
Sales	$490,000	$508,333	$513,233	$1,511,566	$503,855	100%
Cost of goods sold	$343,000	$355,833	$359,263	$1,058,096	$352,698	70%
Gross profit margin	$147,000	$152,500	$153,970	$ 453,470	$151,157	30%
Operating expenses:						
Advertising	$ 3,200	$ 3,700	$ 3,600	$ 10,500	$ 3,500	0.7%
Depreciation	$ 4,000	$ 4,000	$ 4,000	$ 12,000	$ 4,000	0.8%
Insurance	$ 1,700	$ 1,700	$ 1,700	$ 5,100	$ 1,700	0.3%
Legal and accounting expenses	$ 3,400	$ 3,605	$ 3,800	$ 10,805	$ 3,602	0.7%
Office expenses	$ 2,200	$ 2,400	$ 2,650	$ 7,250	$ 2,417	0.5%
Rent	$ 24,000	$ 24,000	$ 24,000	$ 72,000	$ 24,000	4.8%
Repair and maintenance	$ 300	$ 550	$ 420	$ 1,270	$ 424	0.1%
Salaries	$ 33,000	$ 33,000	$ 33,000	$ 99,000	$ 33,000	6.6%
Telephone and utilities	$ 6,000	$ 6,350	$ 6,200	$ 18,550	$ 6,183	1.2%
Miscellaneous	$ 9,200	$ 8,195	$ 10,300	$ 27,695	$ 9,231	1.8%
Total operating expenses	$ 87,000	$ 87,500	$ 89,670	$ 264,170	$ 88,057	17.5%
Net profit	$ 60,000	$ 65,000	$ 64,300	$ 199,330	$ 63,100	12.5%

Final budget for year four

	Amount ($)	Percent of sales
Sales	523,063	100%
Cost of goods	366,144	70%
Gross profit margin	156,919	30%
Operating expenses:		
Advertising	3,605	0.7%
Depreciation	4,000	0.8%
Insurance	2,900	0.6%
Legal and accounting expenses	4,142	0.8%
Office expenses	2,995	0.6%
Rent	24,000	4.6%
Repair & maintenance	437	0.1%
Salaries	34,650	6.6%
Telephone and utilities	6,683	1.3%
Miscellaneous	8,507	1.6%
Total operating expenses	91,919	17.6%
Net profit	65,000	12.4%

Preliminary budget for year four

	Amount ($)	Percent of sales
Sales	533,730	100%
Cost of goods sold	373,611	70%
Gross profit margin	160,119	30%
Operating expenses:		
Advertising	3,605	0.7%
Depreciation	4,000	0.8%
Insurance	4,100	0.8%
Legal and accounting expenses	4,142	0.8%
Office expenses	2,995	0.6%
Rent	24,000	4.5%
Repair and maintenance	437	0.1%
Salaries	34,650	6.5%
Telephone and utilities	7,683	1.4%
Miscellaneous	9,507	1.8%
Total operating expenses	95,119	17.8%
Net profit	65,000	12.2%

Step four: estimate sales revenue

To target sales, the gross profit margin should be analyzed. Income statements (see page 207) show that ABC Electrical Contractors has experienced a gross profit margin equal to 30 percent of sales for three consecutive years. Because a gross profit margin of $160,119 is expected to equal 30 percent of net sales, then targeted sales should equal $533,730.

Step five: adjust figures

If the preliminary figure for targeted net sales seems realistic, the budget is complete. If generating the amount of targeted net sales will be a problem, the preliminary budget must be reviewed and adjusted. In the example, the management of ABC Electrical Contractors is uncomfortable with the preliminary results. They don't believe that the firm can realistically generate sales of more than $525,000. To derive a more realistic operating budget, the owner decides to:

- Delay installing additional telephone services to reduce telephone expenses by $1,000.
- Carefully monitor expenses to reduce miscellaneous expenses by $1,000.
- Choose a similar but less expensive employee benefit package with a higher employee deductible for medical insurance to reduce benefit expenses by $1,200.

After making those adjustments to its budget (see page 215), ABC Electrical Contractors' new gross profit margin is $156,919 ($65,000 + $91,919). To compute the targeted sales, the company divides the gross margin by 30 percent for a targeted sales of $523,063. This figure is within the company's limit of $525,000.

The annual operating budget might have to be altered during the year to reflect changing circumstances. There might be a sharp rise or drop in one or more variable expenses or in revenues. Often, annual operating budgets are divided into smaller monthly or quarterly operating budgets. Monthly budgets are used to measure actual results against budgeted goals.

For large contractors with several departments or work functions, the annual operating budget should be expanded into a master budget. A master operating budget consists of a group of separate but interconnected operating budgets. These budgets will depend on and contribute to the company's overall plans.

An operating budget is an indispensable tool for converting plans into a successful reality. The budget helps focus your efforts on the direction in which you're headed. It indicates how much cash you have to spend, your expenses, and how much you need to earn. By planning on paper first, you minimize some of the risks of owning and operating an electrical contracting firm. A good operating budget can also build morale by helping you organize, communicate, and motivate employees to do their part in achieving the company's financial goals.

Solving business problems

As the owner of your own electrical contracting business, you deal with problems on a daily basis. So, learning how to effectively solve problems can dramatically affect the growth and success of your business. Most business owners solve problems by intuition. By learning the "skill" of problem solving—just as you'd learn the skill of installing an electrical apparatus—you'll become more comfortable with solving problems and you'll reduce the inherent stress of your job.

What's a problem? A problem is a situation that presents difficulty to your desire to move ahead. Here are a few examples:

- An electrical controller doesn't function as it should.
- A part you need for an important job is unavailable.
- An employee is undermining your authority at the job site.
- New job contracts are down.
- A customer is complaining about shoddy work.
- You're two payments behind on a lease, and they've threatened to sue.

Where do problems come from? Problems arise from every facet of human and mechanical functions, as well as from nature. Some problems we cause ourselves (hiring an untrainable employee). Other problems are caused by forces beyond our control (inclement weather at a job site). Problems are a natural, everyday occurrence of life. However, if mismanaged, they cause tension and frustration that only compounds the problem. You must learn how to deal with problems in a logical, rational fashion.

Steps to solving any problem

The solutions to some problems, such as how to plan next week's work schedule, are typically simple and will require only a few moments of contemplation and planning. However, some problems, such as how to increase income by $100,000 in the next six months, are more crucial to your operation and will require more time and effort. For crucial problems, you might want to set aside a full day for analyzing the problem and finding the best solutions.

Before a problem can be solved, you must first recognize that a problem exists. Here's where your approach to problem solving is crucial. You shouldn't allow the problem to intimidate you. Don't take it personally. Approach it rationally and remind yourself that every problem is solvable if it's tackled appropriately.

Fear of failure can block your ability to think clearly. You can overcome this natural fear if you:

- Follow a workable procedure for finding solutions.
- Accept the fact that you can't foresee everything.
- Assume that the solution you select is your best option at the time.
- Accept the possibility that things might change and your solution might fail.

Define the problem

Once you recognize that a problem exists, your next step is to identify or define the problem itself. You can do so by asking yourself questions like:

- What exactly happened?
- What started the problem?
- Did something occur that wasn't supposed to?
- Did something break that was supposed to operate?
- Were there unexpected results?

Ask questions that help you identify the nature of the problem:

- Is this a person, equipment, or operational problem?
- What product or service does it involve?
- Is the problem tangible or intangible?
- Is the problem internal or external to the firm?

Determine type

How important is this problem to the scheme of things? Ask yourself:

- Is this problem disrupting operations?
- Is this problem hampering sales?
- Is this problem causing conflict among people?
- Is this problem affecting personnel and their productivity?
- Is this problem affecting business goals and, if so, which ones?
- Is this problem affecting customers, suppliers, subcontractors, or any other external people?

Evaluate significance

Some problems are "100-year floods" that don't occur often enough to warrant extensive attention. Ask these questions:

- Is it basically a problem that occurred in the past and the main concern is to make certain that the problem doesn't occur again?
- Is it a problem that currently exists and the main concern is to clear up the situation?
- Is it a problem that might occur in the future and the basic concern is planning and taking action before the problem arises?

Estimate frequency

The answers to these questions will help you focus on the true problem. You can't effectively research the causes of a problem until you have a clear definition of what the problem is. Sometimes, managers spend many hours on what they perceive as the problem only to learn, after seeking the causes, that something else was really the problem.

To appropriately identify the problem and its causes, you might need to do some research. If the solution is worthwhile to the goals of your business, you'll invest the required time and resources. If it isn't, you won't.

Before beginning your search for a defined problem, consider what has previously been done by your firm (if anything) regarding this problem, what other firms have done, what knowledge you might need to acquire, what has been learned from past experience, and what experts say about the problem.

Also, make sure that, as you travel your road toward a solution, you don't trip on common roadblocks:

- Bad habits.
- Perceptions.
- Fears.
- Assumptions.
- Affinity.
- Procrastination.
- Reactiveness.
- Rashness.
- Sensitivities.

At this point, you have a clear understanding and a definition or diagram of the problem. You understand what it is and maybe even the cause, but you've refrained from answering the next question: What should I do about it? It's now time to look for a solution.

How to find solutions

There are a number of methods for finding solutions. Try each of them out and select the best solution developed by these methods.

Analytical thinking

The analytical thinking method is based on analysis. It's the most conventional and logical of all the methods and follows a step-by-step pattern. First, examine each cause of the problem. Then, for each cause, based on your direct knowledge and experience, list the solutions that logically would seem to solve the problem. Next, arrive at possible solutions and check them against research on how the problem was solved by others. Analytical thinking is often used in troubleshooting equipment for electrical and other equipment.

There are three types of *associative thinking*. This type of thinking is basically a process that links things, either through similarity, difference, or contiguity. For example, contiguity finds solutions from things that are connected through proximity, sequence, and cause and effect. The process works like this: List as many parts of the problem as you can think of. Then, giving yourself a short time limit, list as many ideas that have either proximity, sequence, or related cause and effect to the ones you've listed. For example, a contiguous association might be:

Association

- Misplaced files = cluttered desk (proximity).
- Misplaced files = rushing (sequence).
- Misplaced files = irate customer (cause and effect).

Associative thinking taps the resources of the mind. It brings into focus options you might not have considered if you stuck to ideas only directly related to the problem. As a result of associative thinking, you might find other relationships embedded in the problem, and those relationships might lead to a better solution. Using association might help you solve the problem of a shrinking marketplace by helping you discover related markets for your contracting services.

The *analogical method* of thinking is a way of finding solutions through comparisons. The process is based on comparing the different facets of the problem with other problems that might or might not have similar facets. An analogy might go like this:

Analogy

Employees have been coming in late to work quite often. How can I get them to be at work on time? This to me is like soldiers being late for a battle. Would soldiers come late to a battle? Why not? Because their future as a soldier depends on being there, and because there will be severe penalties for soldiers who are AWOL.

By comparing the situation of workers to the situation of soldiers, you might find a solution for a way to motivate employees to come to work on time.

Brainstorming

Brainstorming is based on a free, nonthreatening, anything-goes atmosphere. You can brainstorm alone or with a group of people. Most often, a group of people from different departments of your firm or from diverse backgrounds is preferable. The process works like this: The problem is explained to the group and each member is encouraged to throw out as many ideas for solutions as he or she can think of, no matter how ridiculous or far-fetched they might sound.

All the ideas are discussed, written down on a large pad of paper, then discussed among the group, revised, tossed out, combined, and expanded. Based on the group's recognition of the effectiveness of each idea, the best ones are selected for closer review. For example, a group of all of your employees might throw out for consideration any thoughts they might have on how to increase sales or improve profits for the firm.

Intuition

Intuition is based on "hunches." It's not, as some think, irrational. Intuition is built on a strong foundation of facts and experiences that are buried somewhere in the subconscious. All the things you know and have experienced can lead you to believe that something might be true, although you've never actually experienced that reality. Use your intuition as much as possible, but check it against the reality of the situation. Intuition is often used by experienced electricians in solving a particularly difficult problem.

Selecting the best solution

You've now developed a long list of solutions. Now go through this list and cross out those that obviously won't work. These ideas aren't wasted, for they influence those ideas that remain. In other words, the best ideas you select might be revised using ideas that you originally thought wouldn't work.

With the remaining solutions, use what's called the *Force Field Analysis Technique*. This is an analysis technique that breaks the solution down into its positive effects and negative effects. To do this, write each solution you're considering on a separate piece of paper. Below the solution, draw a vertical line down the center of the sheet. Label one column "Advantages" (or "+") and the other column "Disadvantages" (or "–"). Finally, analyze each facet of the solution and its effect on the problem, listing each of the advantages and disadvantages you can think of.

One way to help you think of the advantages and disadvantages is to role-play each solution. Call in a few of your employees and play out each solution. Ask them for their reactions. Based on what you observe and on their feedback, you'll have a better idea of the advantages and disadvantages of each solution you're considering.

After you complete this process for each solution, select those solutions that have the most advantages. At this point, you should be considering only two or three options. In order to select the most appropriate solution from these, consider:

- Cost-effectiveness.
- Time constraints.
- Availability of personnel and materials.
- Your own intuition.

Before you actually implement the chosen solution, you should evaluate it. Ask yourself:

- Are the objectives of the solution sound, clear, and simple?
- Will the solution achieve the objectives?
- What are the possibilities that it will fail and in what way?
- How can I reduce the possibility of failure?

Finding the solution doesn't mean that the problem is solved. Now you need to design a plan of action so that the solution gets carried out properly. Designing and implementing the plan of action is equally as important as finding the solution. The

Taking action

best solution can fail because it isn't implemented correctly. When designing the plan of action, consider:

- Who will be involved in the solution?
- Who will be affected by the solution?
- What course of action will be taken?
- How should this course of action be presented to employees, customers, suppliers, and others?
- When will the action start and be completed?
- Where will this action happen?
- How will this action happen?
- What's needed to make it happen?

Design a plan-of-action chart that includes all the details you need to consider to implement the plan and when each phase should happen. Keep in mind, though, that the best plans have setbacks for any number of reasons. A key person might be out for illness, or a supplier might ship materials late, or a change at the customer's site might require that the timetable be changed.

As each phase of your plan of action is implemented, you should ask yourself whether your goals were achieved, how well they were achieved, and did it work smoothly. To check your own perceptions of the results, get as much feedback as possible from your managers and employees. What you might think is working might not be considered so by those closer to the action. Always remember that they're one of your most valuable tools in successfully carrying out your solution.

To manage your business effectively, you must manage your employees effectively, which is the topic of the next chapter.

Managing employees

A BUSINESS IS ONLY as good as the people in it. This is true whether you're an electrical contractor or you manage a Dairy Queen. So, one of the most important skills that you can develop is learning how to find and keep good people in your business.

In this chapter, you'll learn how to define jobs, find applicants, interview applicants, determine "fair" pay, hire, set personnel policies, and fire. In addition, you'll learn how other successful electrical contractors manage employee benefits and hire temporary employees.

The trick to getting the right person for the job is in deciding what kind of skill is needed to perform the job. Once you know what it takes to do the job, you can match the applicant's skills and experience to the job's requirements. This step will probably come easy for you if you're hiring an electrician or an electrician's helper, but how about office help or other support functions?

The first step in analyzing a job is to describe it. Suppose that, as the owner of a growing electrical contracting business, you decide to hire someone to relieve you of some of your administrative or sales duties. Look at the many functions you perform and decide what your stronger and weaker areas are.

Further suppose that you've decided you'll need help in the office. The phone is always ringing. Letters that need answering are piling up. Bids must be typed and mailed.

Once you have a job description on paper, decide what skills the person must have to fill the job. What's the lowest level of skill you'll accept? In this example, let's assume that you initially decide to hire a secretary, but you discover that secretaries are scarce and expensive. Likewise, in your area, stenographers are almost as hard to find and nearly as

Finding the right employee

expensive as secretaries. Perhaps you could get by with a typist. Hiring a typist might be both easier and cheaper than hiring a secretary or stenographer. Many high-school students are well qualified as typists, and many are seeking part-time work.

When you start looking for someone to fill your job, make sure you describe exactly what you want. As an "office manager," what do you want this person to do? Answer the telephone and take messages? Contact you at the job site? Type correspondence? Write correspondence? Sort mail? Pay bills? Prepare bills for payment? Keep accounting records? Produce invoices? Mail monthly statements? Manage collection of past-due accounts? Read trade journals and mark important articles for you? Order supplies and materials? Manage payroll? Prepare the books for your accountant? Make quarterly tax payments? Make good coffee?

Finding job applicants

When you know the kinds of skills you need in your new employee, you're ready to contact sources that can help you recruit job applicants. If you're a union shop, you can work with the union to find skilled journeymen and apprentice electricians. An advantage to apprentices is that their pay ranges from 35 to 85 percent of the wage of a journeyman, depending on the union, the apprenticeship program, and the time served in the apprenticeship. Most union employees are members of a local of the International Brotherhood of Electrical Workers (IBEW).

Each state has an employment service (Department of Employment, Unemployment Bureau, or Employment Security Agency). All are affiliated with the United States Employment Service, and local offices are ready to help businesses with their hiring problems. The state employment service will screen applicants for you by giving aptitude tests (if any are available for the skills you need). Passing scores indicate the applicant's ability to learn the work. So, be as specific as you can about the skills you want.

Private employment agencies will also help in recruitment. However, the employee or the employer must pay a fee to the private agency for its services. This fee can be from a month's to as much as a year's salary.

Another source of applicants is a "Help Wanted" sign in your own office window (if you have one). Of course, a lot of unqualified applicants might inquire about the job, and you can't simultaneously interview an applicant and talk on the phone to a customer.

Newspaper advertisements are another source of applicants. You reach a large group of job seekers, and if you used a blind box address, you can screen them at your convenience. If you list an office phone number, you might end up on the phone with an applicant instead of with a customer.

Newspaper advertisements are another source of applicants. You can reach a large group of job seekers, and if you used a blind box address, you can screen them at your convenience. If you list an office phone number, you might end up on the phone with an applicant instead of with a customer.

Job applicants are readily available from local schools. The local high school might have a distributive or cooperative education department where the students work in your office part time while taking business courses at school. Many part-time students continue with their employer after they finish school. Consider local and regional business schools as well. The students are often more mature and more motivated than high-school students.

You might also find job applicants by contacting friends, neighbors, customers, suppliers, current employees, local associations, service clubs, or even a nearby armed forces base where people are leaving the service. However, don't overlook the problems of such recruiting. What happens to the goodwill of these sources if they recommend a friend whom you don't hire, or if you have to fire the person they recommend?

Your choice of recruitment method depends on what you're looking for, your location, and your method of managing your business. You have many sources available to you. A combination might serve your best needs. The important thing is to find the right applicant with the correct skills for the job you want to fill, whatever the source.

Labor laws

As you begin the search for qualified employees, there are certain laws, federal and state, that come into play. Your local state employment office can assist you in learning the requirements of these laws. The Social Security Act of 1935, as amended, is concerned with employment insurance laws as well as retirement insurance. The Fair Labor Standards Act of 1938, as amended, establishes minimum wages, overtime pay, record keeping, and child labor standards for most businesses. The Occupational Safety and Health Act (OSHA) of 1970 is concerned with safety and health in the workplace and covers almost all employers. There are specific standards, regulations, and reporting requirements that must be met.

There are other laws that might concern your business. Contact your local state employment office to determine the requirements for hiring disadvantaged workers, federal service contracts for work on public buildings or other public projects, employee pension and welfare benefit plans, and the garnishment of employee's wages.

In addition, the Immigration Reform and Control Act of 1986 prohibits employing illegal aliens. Employers must require every employee to fill out the Employment Eligibility Verification Form (Form 19) within three days of the date of hire (if hired after November 7, 1987). Fines are levied for noncompliance. For more information, contact the nearest office of the Immigration and Naturalization Service.

The application form

The hardest part of the hiring process, once you've listed the required skills, is in finding and hiring the one right employee. You need some method of screening the applicants and selecting the best one for the position.

The application form is a tool that you can use to make your tasks of interviewing and selection easier. The form should have blank spaces for all the facts you need as a basis for judging the applicants.

You'll want a fairly complete application so you can get sufficient information. However, keep the form as simple as you can. The form can be photocopied as needed. Have the applicants fill out the application before you talk to them. It makes an excellent starting point for the interview. It's also a written record of experience and former employers' names and addresses.

The Civil Rights Act of 1964 prohibits discrimination in employment practices because of race, religion, sex, or national origin. Public Law 90-202 prohibits discrimination on the basis of age with respect to individuals who are between 40 and 70 years of age. Federal laws also prohibit discrimination against the physically handicapped. Your state employment office can help you in understanding the laws regarding applicants and employment. In addition, firms like G. Neil (720 International Parkway, Sunrise, FL 33345) offer catalogs of human relations supplies: job applications, personnel folders, labor law posters, attendance controllers, employee awards, and related materials.

When an applicant has had work experience, other references are typically not as important. However, if the level of work experience is limited, additional references might be obtained from other individuals such as school counselors, who can give objective information.

Personal references are almost useless because an applicant would only list people who have a kind word for them. Some employers will use them, though, to open a discussion: What would this reference say were your greatest skills and traits? What would this reference say were skills and traits that you needed to work on?

The objective of the job interview is to find out as much information as you can about the job applicant's work background, especially work habits and skills. Your major task is to get the applicants to talk about themselves and about their work habits. The best way to go about this is to ask each applicant specific questions:

The interview

- What did you do on your last job?
- How did you do it?
- Why was it done?
- What were the results?

As you go along, evaluate the applicants' replies. Do they know what they're talking about? Are they evasive or unskilled in the job tasks? Can they account for discrepancies?

When the interview is over, ask the applicant to check back with you later, if you think you might be interested in that applicant. Never commit yourself until you've interviewed all likely applicants. You want to be sure that you select the best available applicant for the job.

Next, verify the information you've obtained. A previous employer is usually the best source. Sometimes a previous employer will give out information over the phone. However, if you have the time, it's usually best to request your information in writing and get a written reply.

To help ensure a prompt reply, you should ask previous employers a few specific questions about the applicant that can be answered by a YES or NO or with a very short answer. For example:

- How long did the employee work for you?
- Was his or her work: __poor __average, or __excellent?
- Why did the employee leave your employment?

Also make sure that you include a self-addressed, stamped envelope for the reply.

After you've verified the information on all your applicants, you're ready to make your selection. The right employee can help you make money. The wrong employee will cost you much wasted time and materials, and might even drive away your customers.

More and more, the government is requiring written personnel policies, even for the smallest firms. As an owner/manager, a written personnel policy manual will make your life easier as well. Fortunately, there are specific books and computer programs that will make your job easier and help you write your personnel policies to conform with current laws.

The first rule of writing personnel policies is: know yourself. Know your business. Know your own personal abilities and weaknesses, and try to anticipate how you'll deal with the situations that you expect to arise in the daily operation of your contracting business. Then, formulate your policies in writing. Include all matters that would affect employees, such as wages, promotions, vacations, time off, grievances, fringe benefits, and even retirement policies.

Once you've developed your personnel policies, write down the policy on all matters that affect your employees and give each one a copy. For a small contracting office, this statement might consist of just one or two typed pages. Matters such as these shouldn't be left to whim: hours of work, time record keeping, paid holidays, vacations, dress regulations, wage payment system, overtime, separation procedure, severance pay, pension and retirement plan, hospitalization and medical care benefits, and grievance procedures.

Employment and training procedures must be established so that you have a better chance of getting the job done the way you want it done. Your policy manual will probably cover policy decisions in the following areas.

Consider the number of hours to be worked per week, the number of days per week, evening and holiday work, and the time and method of payment for both regular and overtime work. Unnecessary payment of overtime at premium rates is a source of needless expense. By planning ahead, you might be able to organize your employees' work to keep overtime to a minimum. When peak periods do occur, you can often handle them by using part-time help paid at regular rates.

Personnel policies

Writing the policy manual

Hours

Compensation   Most of your employees will be paid a salary or commission that's competitive with the pay offered by other similar local firms. Try to relate the incentive to both your goals and the goals of your employees. Whatever plan and level of compensation you use, be sure each employee understands them completely.

Fringe benefits   You might consider offering your employees free life insurance, health insurance, pension plan, and tuition payments at schools and colleges. You might also look into joining with other contractors in a group disability plan and a group Workers' Compensation plan. Such a plan could mean a considerable savings in your premium costs. I'll cover fringe benefits in greater detail later in this chapter.

Vacations   Your policy manual should answer: How long will vacations be? Will you specify the time of the year they may be taken? Are vacations with or without pay?

Time off   Will you allow employees time off for personal reasons, emergencies in the family, holidays, Saturday or Sunday holidays?

Training   You must make sure that each employee is given adequate training for the job. In a small contractor's office, the training responsibility normally falls to the owner/manager. However, if you have supervisors, each one should recognize the importance of being a good teacher and should schedule time to teach or review the requirements of the job with new employees.

Retirement   What are your plans for retirement benefits such as Social Security, pension plans, and annuity plan insurance?

Grievances   You can expect conflicts with employees, regardless of the quality of the employment you offer. The best course of action is to plan for grievances and establish a procedure for handling them. Considering the employee's rights to demand review, you should establish provisions for third-party arbitration.

You'll want to consider such promotion matters as normal increases in wages and salaries, changes of job titles, and the effects that your business' growth will have on your employees and their careers.

Promotion

Will you periodically review your employee's performance? If so, what factors will you consider? Will you make salary adjustments or training recommendations?

Personnel review

Even though this is a distasteful matter to many business owners, it would be wise to have a written policy regarding layoffs, seniority rights, severance pay, and the conditions that warrant summary discharge.

Termination

Pay administration is just a fancy term for something you do without naming it: defining jobs and pay. Pay administration is a management tool that enables you to control personnel cost, increase employee morale, and reduce work-force turnover. A formal pay system provides a means of rewarding individuals for their contributions to the success of your firm while making sure that your firm receives a fair return on its investment in employee pay.

Paying a fair wage

If you're hiring union members, the local labor union will assist you in defining job descriptions and establishing pay levels and incentives. Many electrical workers are members of the International Brotherhood of Electrical Workers (IBEW).

There are two good reasons to establish a fair employee pay plan: your business and your employees. A formal pay plan, one that lets employees know where they stand and where they can go as far as take-home pay is concerned, won't solve your employee relations problems. It will, however, remove one of those areas of doubt and rumor that might keep your work force anxious and unhappy—and less loyal and more mobile than you'd like them to be.

What's in it for you? Let's face it: in an electrical contracting business, it's good employees who can make the difference between success and failure. Many people enjoy a good "mystery," but not when it's about how their pay is established. If employees are under a pay plan that they can understand, they'll also see that it's fair and consistent rather than at the whim of the owner. They'll know what to expect and what they can hope to shoot for. So, a good pay plan will help you recruit, keep, and motivate employees. It can help you build a solid foundation for a successful business.

Overtime

In most cases, overtime shouldn't be required because the typical job will be bid based on a normal workday. However, as business increases seasonally or as modified schedules require, you might want to consider overtime.

To do so, first consider your employment policy or union requirements regarding payment for overtime hours. Depending on the standard workday and the number of hours required beyond that day, overtime can typically cost from 25 to as much as 200 percent more than standard pay.

In addition, efficiency decreases as overtime increases. By how much? One contractor's group developed a table of overtime efficiency rates. With five 10-hour days on the same job, the efficiency rate for the last two hours of the day is reduced to 87.5 percent. With five 12-hour days on the same job, the efficiency rate for the last four hours of the day is reduced to 75 percent. If the worker of five 12-hour days must move to another job after 8 hours, the efficiency rate for the 4 hours at the second job drops to 68.8 percent.

If overtime is required to complete a job, make sure that you consider the costs of both overtime pay and reduced efficiency as you bid, schedule, and manage the job. Also make sure that your employee handbook communicates your policies regarding overtime.

Writing the pay plan

As your electrical contracting business grows beyond a single employee, you'll need to take time to consider a formal pay plan. Developing a written pay plan doesn't have to cost you a lot of time and money. In fact, an elaborate plan is more difficult to put into practice, communicate, and manage.

The most important aspect of setting up a formal pay administration plan is to gain the acceptance, understanding, and support of your management and supervisory employees. Of course, for a small contracting office, that's you. The steps in setting up a successful pay plan are:

- Define the jobs.
- Evaluate the jobs.
- Price the jobs.
- Install the plan.
- Communicate the plan to employees.
- Appraise employee performance under the plan.

Defining the jobs

Unless you know each job's specifications and requirements, you can't compare them for pay purposes. It's no surprise, therefore, that the initial step in installing a formal pay plan is preparing a job description for each position.

You might be able to write these job descriptions yourself, because in many small businesses the owner-manager at one time or another has worked at just about every job. However, the best and easiest way to put together such job information is simply to ask employees to describe their jobs. Supervisors, if you have them, should be asked to review these descriptions. Prepare a simple form to be filled out by the employee or by someone interviewing the employee. The form should include:

- Job title.
- Reporting relationship.
- Specifications.
- Primary function.
- Main duties (by importance and percent of time spent).
- Other duties.
- Job requirements (training, experience, responsibilities, unusual working conditions).

It will probably take some time to prepare job descriptions from the information you get from your employees, but what you learn might have other uses besides comparing jobs for pay purposes. For one thing, you might discover that some employees aren't doing what you thought they were, or what they were hired to do. You might find you want to make some changes in their work routines. The information might also be useful for hiring, training, and developing employees; realigning duties in your firm; comparing job data for salary surveys; assuring compliance with various employment practice and pay rate laws; and evaluating job performance based on assigned duties.

Evaluating the jobs

Nobody has yet come up with a precise way of deciding exactly how much a particular job is worth to a company. Human judgment is the only way to put a dollar value on work. A good job evaluation method for smaller firms is called *simple ranking*.

Under the simple-ranking system, job descriptions are compared against each other. They're ranked according to difficulty and responsibility. Using your judgment, you end up with an array of jobs that shows the relative value of each position to the company.

After you've ranked the job descriptions by value to the firm, the next step is to group jobs that are similar in scope and responsibility into the same pay grade. Then you arrange these groups in a series of pay levels from highest to lowest. The number of pay levels depends on the total number of jobs and types of work in your organization, but for a small firm, 6 to 12 pay levels is the typical range and covers everyone from the janitor to the president.

Pricing the jobs

So far, you've looked only inside the company itself to establish a pay system. To put an accurate dollar value on each of your pay levels, you should look outside at the going rates for similar work in your area. Because you've ranked and grouped your jobs in pay levels, you won't have to survey each job. Survey those on each level that are easiest to describe and are most common in the industry.

A survey of who's paying how much for what in your locality is the best way of finding out how much you ought to pay for each of your jobs. You probably have neither the time nor the money to spend on making such a survey yourself. That shouldn't be a problem; you should be able to get the data you need from sources such as a local contractor's association, a union local, the local chamber of commerce, major firms in your area, or from national sources such as the National Electrical Contractors Association, the Independent Electrical Contractors, the U.S. Bureau of Labor Statistics, or the American Management Association.

After you're satisfied that you're comparing apples and apples, you can compute an average rate for each job and enter it on a work-sheet. The average rates in the figure are purely arbitrary and for example only.

You might need to adjust the average rates somewhat to keep a sufficient difference between pay levels to separate them. The going rates you find for each pay level can then become the midpoints of your pay level ranges. You can, of course, set your midpoints above or below the survey averages, based on your firm's ability to pay, the length of your work week, the type and value of your firm's benefits program, and the local job market.

You'll then build a pay range for each pay level, with a minimum, a midpoint, and a maximum. Typically, the minimum rate in a level is 85 percent of the midpoint rate, and the maximum rate is 115 percent of the midpoint. With this arrangement, a new employee can increase his or her earnings by 30 percent without a job change, thus having performance incentives even if the employee is not promoted.

Such a pay range will enable you to tell where your employees' pay and pay potential stand in relation to the market rates for their kinds of work. The pay range should show you at a glance where you need to make changes to achieve rates that are fair within your organization and pay that's competitive with similar businesses in your community. With a planned pay structure, you can tie the individual rates of pay to job performance and contribution to company goals while providing enough flexibility to handle special situations.

Installing the plan

At this point, you have a general plan, but you don't, of course, pay in general. You pay each employee individually. You must now consider how the plan will be administered to provide for individual pay increases.

In administering the pay increase feature of your plan, you can use several approaches:

- Merit increases, granted to recognize performance and contribution.
- Promotion increases for employees assigned to different jobs in higher pay levels.
- Progression to minimum for employees who are below the minimum or hiring rate for the pay level.
- Probationary increases for newer employees who have attained the necessary skills and experience to function effectively.
- Tenure increases for time with the company.
- General increases, granted to maintain real earnings as economic factors require and to keep pay competitive.

Those are the most common approaches, but there are many variations. Most annual increases are made for cost of living, tenure, or employment market reasons. Obviously, you might use several, all, or combinations of the various increase methods.

Communicating the plan

After you've set your pay administration plan into place, you have to consider how to tell employees about it. Setting up a good pay administration program is almost useless if you don't communicate it to your employees.

How you tell them is your decision. Some of the more successful methods include personal letters to each employee, and staff meetings to explain the plan and answer general questions. However you tell your employees, you must clearly, honestly, and openly explain the way the plan works. This is a prime opportunity for you to enhance good relations with your employees. Be sure that your supervisors understand and can explain the plan to their people. Explaining the plan to new hires is also essential, as well as reviewing the plan periodically with all employees to handle questions and concerns.

The majority of employees in the labor force are under a merit increase pay system, though most of their pay increases result from other factors. This approach involves periodic review and appraisal of how well employees perform their assigned duties.

Appraising the employee

An effective employee appraisal plan improves two-way communications between the manager and the employee. It also relates pay to work performance and results, while showing the employee how they can improve by helping them understand job responsibilities and expectations. An employee appraisal plan also provides a standardized approach to evaluating job performance.

Such a performance review helps not only the employee whose work is being appraised, but also helps the manager doing the appraising to gain insight into the organization. An open exchange between employee and manager can show the manager where improvements in equipment, procedures, or other factors might improve employee performance. Try to foster a climate in which employees can discuss progress and problems informally at any time throughout the year.

To get the best results, use a written form for appraisals. A typical appraisal form should cover the results achieved, quality of performance, volume of work, effectiveness in working with others in the firm and with customers and suppliers, initiative, job knowledge, and dependability.

To keep your pay administration plan in tune with the times, you should review it at least annually. Make adjustments where necessary and don't forget to retrain supervisory personnel. This isn't the kind of plan that can be set up and then forgotten.

During your annual review, ask yourself if the plan is working for you. That's the most important question. Are you getting the kind of employees you want or are you just making do? What's the employee turnover rate? Do employees seem to care about the business? Most important: does your pay administration plan help you achieve the objectives of your business?

Employee benefits

Employee benefits play an important role in the lives of employees and their families, and they have a significant financial impact on your business. Contractors can't be competitive employers if they don't develop a comprehensive benefit program. However, if not managed, an employee benefit program can quickly eat up a small firm's profits.

A comprehensive employee benefit program can be broken down into four components: legally required benefits, health and welfare benefits, retirement benefits, and prerequisites.

Legally required benefit plans are mandated by law, and the systems necessary to administer such plans are well established. These plans include Social Security, Workers' Compensation, and Unemployment Compensation.

Health and welfare benefits and retirement benefits can be viewed as benefits provided to work in conjunction with statutory benefits to protect employees from financial hazards such as illness, disability, death, and retirement. Health and welfare plans are perhaps the most visible of all the benefit program components. They include medical care, dental care, vision care, short-term disability, long-term disability, life insurance, accidental death and dismemberment insurance, dependent care, and legal assistance.

Retirement plans are established to help ensure that employees are able to maintain their accustomed standard of living on retirement. Retirement benefit plans basically fall into two categories: *defined contribution plans* (which provide employees with an account balance at retirement) and *defined benefit plans* (which provide employees with a projected amount of income at retirement).

Prerequisite benefits are any other benefits an employer promises, such as a company automobile or truck, professional association or club membership, paid tuition, sabbatical, extra vacation, personal expense account, credit cards, financial counseling services, or other benefits of employment.

Designing and implementing an employee benefit program can be a complicated process. Many small businesses contract with employee benefit consulting firms, insurance companies, law firms, or accounting firms to assist in this task. As you establish your program yourself or with a professional, ask yourself:

Selecting an employee benefit program

- What should the program accomplish in the long run?
- What's the maximum amount you can afford to spend on a program?
- Are you capable and knowledgeable in administering the program?
- What kind of program will best fit the needs of your employees?
- Should you involve your employees in the design and selection of the benefit program? If so, how much and at what stage?

When purchasing a health and welfare plan, select a professional whose clientele is made up primarily of small businesses. If you can find one in your area, select an insurer that's used and recommended by other contractors. Your insurer needs to be aware of the special problems that face small businesses, especially in your trade. Generous plans that look attractive and logical today might become a financial burden for your growing company. Remember that it's much easier to add benefits than it is to take them away.

Health and welfare plans

Medical plans are usually the greatest concern of employers and employees. There are essentially two kinds of traditional medical plans. *Major medical plans* cover 100 percent of hospital and inpatient surgical expenses, as well as a percentage (typically 80 percent) of all other covered expenses. *Comprehensive medical plans* cover a percentage (again, generally 80 percent) of all medical expenses.

In both types of plans, the employee is usually required to pay part of the premium, particularly for dependents, as well as a deductible. Deductibles often range from $100 to $200 for single coverage and from $200 to $500 for family coverage. A comprehensive medical plan is typically less expensive because more of the cost is shifted to the employee. Any plan you design should include features for containing costs.

As an alternative to a traditional medical plan, an employer can contract with a Health Maintenance Organization (HMO) to provide employees with medical services. The main difference between a traditional medical plan and an HMO is that the traditional plan allows employees to choose their medical providers, while HMOs often provide medical services at specified clinics. HMOs trade this flexibility for lower costs that are often passed on to the employee through reduced or eliminated deductibles. If your electrical contracting firm has 25 or more employees, you might be legally required to offer your employees the option of coverage under an HMO. Discuss current requirements with your insurer.

Disability insurance is an important but often overlooked benefit in small businesses. Disability insurance prevents a drain of financial resources to support a principal in the event that he or she can't continue working.

Group life insurance is a benefit employees have come to expect in many regions and trades. Such insurance is usually a multiple of an employee's salary. Be aware that an amount of insurance over a legally specified amount is subject to taxation as income to the employee.

Recent legislation provides that employers who maintain medical and dental plans must provide certain employees the opportunity to continue coverage if they otherwise become ineligible through employment termination or other causes. In addition, new rules state that if a firm's health and welfare plan discriminates in favor of key employees, the benefits to those employees are taxable as income. Talk to your plan administrator about current laws and requirements.

Retirement benefit plans are either qualified or unqualified plans. A plan is qualified if it has met certain standards mandated by law. It's beneficial to maintain a qualified retirement plan because contributions are currently deductible, earnings on plan assets are tax-deferred, benefits earned aren't considered taxable income until received, and certain distributions are eligible for special tax treatment. Of the various qualified plans, profit sharing plans, 401(k) plans, and defined benefit plans are the most popular.

Retirement benefit plans

A *profit-sharing plan* is a defined contribution plan in which the sponsoring employer has agreed to contribute a discretionary or set amount to the plan. Any contributions made to the plan are generally allocated pro rata to each participant's plan account, based on compensation. The sponsoring employer makes no promise as to the dollar amount a participant will receive at retirement.

Profit-sharing plans

The focus in a profit sharing plan, and in defined contribution plans, is on the contribution. What a participant receives at retirement is a direct function of the contributions made to the plan and the earnings on such contributions during the participant's employment with the plan sponsor. At retirement, profit sharing plan participants receive an amount equal to the balance in their account. Profit sharing plans are favored by employers because they allow employers the ability to retain discretion in determining the amount of the contribution made to the plan.

Another type of defined contribution is the *401(k) plan*. In a 401(k) plan, participants agree to defer a portion of their pretax salary as a contribution to the plan. In addition, the sponsoring employer might decide to match all or a portion of the participant's deferrals. The employer might even decide to make a profit-sharing contribution to the plan.

401(k) plans

As described earlier, the focus is on the contribution to the plan. At retirement, participants will receive an amount equal to their account balance. Special nondiscrimination tests apply to 401(k) plans. These tests might reduce the amount of deferrals that highly compensated employees are allowed to make, and that can somewhat complicate plan administration. The 401(k) plans are popular because they allow employees the ability to save for retirement with pretax dollars, and they can be designed to be relatively inexpensive.

Defined benefit plans

In direct contrast to a defined contribution plan, a *defined benefit plan* promises participants a benefit that's specified by a formula in the plan. The focus of a defined benefit plan is the retirement benefit provided instead of the contribution made. Plan sponsors must contribute to the actuarially determined amounts necessary to meet the dollar amounts promised to participants. Generally, benefits are paid at retirement during the remainder of the employee's life, so a defined benefit plan guarantees a certain flow of income at retirement.

Selecting the right plan

As you can see, certain plans are more suitable for electrical contractors than others, based on the employer's financial situation and the demographics of the employee group. Employers who aren't confident of their future income might not want to start a defined benefit plan, which will require a specific level of contributions.

However, if the employees are fairly young, a profit-sharing plan or 401(k) plan can result in a more significant and more appreciated benefit than a defined benefit plan. The 401(k) plans are very popular now that IRAs have been virtually eliminated. However, the nondiscrimination tests make it more difficult for small businesses to maintain 401(k) plans. If your work force is composed mainly of older employees, a defined benefit plan will be more beneficial to them but more expensive for you to maintain.

Remember that while a qualified plan has many positive aspects, the qualified retirement plan area is complicated and well monitored by the government. Make sure you have adequate counsel before you decide on the most appropriate plan for your business.

How does your electrical contracting business cope with unexpected personnel shortages? Many businesses are facing this question, whether the cause is seasonal peaking, several employees on sick leave, or an unexpected increase in business. For electrical skills, many contractors hire and use subcontractors. However, for office work, a growing number hire temporary personnel. In fact, many new contractors will start up their business renting part-time, temporary office personnel instead of hiring full-time employees.

A temporary personnel service (listed in your phone book's yellow pages under Employment Contractors—Temporary Help) is not an employment agency. Like many service firms, a temporary personnel service hires people as its own employees and assigns them to companies requesting assistance. This means that when you use a service, you aren't hiring an employee; you're buying the use of their time. The temporary personnel firm is responsible for payroll, bookkeeping, tax deductions, Workers' Compensation, fringe benefits, and all other similar costs connected with the employee. You're relieved of the burden of recruiting, interviewing, screening, and basic skill training.

Most national temporary personnel companies also offer performance guarantees and fidelity bonding at no added cost to their clients. Just as important, you're relieved of the need for government forms and for reporting withholding tax, Social Security, and unemployment compensation.

If you need temporary personnel for a period of six months or more, it's usually more cost-effective to hire a full-time employee. If the task requires skills or training beyond basic office skills, it might be more cost-effective to pay overtime to an employee with those skills.

The key to successful use of temporary employees is in planning what type of help you'll need, how much, and when. The accurate information you give to the temporary service firm will improve the efficiency they'll have in supplying the correct person for your needs.

Hiring temporary help

Before your temporary employee arrives on the job, there are a few things you should do. First, appoint one of your permanent employees to supervise the temporary employee and check on the progress of the work. Be sure this supervisor understands the job to be done and just what the responsibilities are. Next, let your permanent staff know that you're taking on extra help and that it will be temporary. Explain why the extra help is needed and ask them to cooperate with the new employee in any way possible.

Have everything ready before the temporary employee arrives. The work to be done should be organized and laid out so that the employee can begin producing with a minimum of time spent in adjusting to the job and the surroundings. Also, don't set up schedules that are impossible to complete within the time you allot. Try to stay within the time limits you gave the temporary help service, but plan to extend the time period if necessary rather than hurry the employee.

Finally, furnish detailed instructions. Describe your type of business and the services you offer. Help the temp feel comfortable and a part of your team. Most temporary employees have broad business experience and can easily adapt to your requirements—if they know what they are.

Hiring salespeople

If you've been your own salesperson, as you expand you might want to consider hiring a professional salesperson who can take this task from you and let you get on with other things. Unfortunately, most contractors don't know how to hire a good salesperson. Here are some ideas.

First, there are three main types of sales personnel, ranging in creativity. The first is the order handler. A knowledgeable person with a pleasant personality is a good choice for this job, maybe an employee who has worked in the field but now must move to a desk job, for whatever reason.

The second type is the order taker. Technical knowledge, again, is important. However, this position requires that the employee know and apply some of the skills of sales. The request for a bid might be called in and the order taker will ask, for example, if there are other jobs that your firm can bid on.

The third type of salesperson is the order getter. This position requires someone who knows people and how to sell to them. In fact, sales skills are often as important as technical knowledge. An order getter will develop and qualify prospects, rank them by interest and opportunity, then work with them in order to develop them into customers. Once a prospect has developed into a customer, management can turn continued service over to an order taker or order handler.

So, how do you hire salespeople? First, you determine which type you need: order handler, order taker, or order getter. Then consider your budget. The more creative the salesperson, the more he or she must be paid. Many electrical contractors offer order getters a base salary plus a commission. Terms are quite negotiable. However, don't make the mistake that many business managers make: don't complain when you write a commission check that's larger than your own salary. Remember that every sales dollar is another potential profit dollar for you.

What should you look for in an order getter? Common sense, maturity, intelligence, tact, a positive attitude, personal hygiene, and stability. Your salesperson must be a people person.

Hiring subcontractors

Depending on your business structure, your work load, and your specialty, you might decide to hire subcontractors for specific jobs. How can you do this effectively? Much like you hire an employee. Here are some of the questions you should ask the sub and yourself:

- How long have you been in business?
- Are you reliable and prompt?
- How would you manage the job?
- Have you done this type of work before?
- What size crew will be working on the job?
- Do you have references? May I contact them?

- What warranties do you provide?
- Do you have the necessary tools and equipment?
- Do you have quick access to materials?
- What's the rate for your services?
- Why do you want to be hired to subcontract this job?
- Are you efficient? How?
- How do you expect to be paid?

If selected carefully, a subcontractor can not only help you during a busy time but can also furnish you with an alliance that can help you in your growing electrical contracting business.

Managing employees and subs is one of your greatest challenges as the owner of a successful electrical contracting firm. The next chapter will give you additional skills in solving communications problems with employees, subcontractors, clients, prospects, inspectors, regulators, suppliers, and other people who can impact the success of your business.

Solving communication problems

WHAT DOES COMMUNICATION have to do with becoming a successful electrical contractor? Plenty! Without good communication, you soon won't have your business. Your customers won't know what you can do for them or why your service is better than others; your banker won't know why you need the expansion loan; local regulators won't issue you required licenses and permits; employees won't know what you want them to do. Get the point? Communication is vital to the success of your business.

Of course, most business people do communicate with customers, bankers, regulators, and employees. The problem is that many business people don't communicate well enough to avoid problems: misunderstandings, incorrect specifications, hurt feelings, puzzling responses, inaccuracies, and delays.

This chapter is about solving communication problems. That might not seem like the most fascinating topic to would-be electrical contractors, but there are many reasons why this might be the most important chapter in this book. Powerful communication can:

- Change prospects into long-time clients.
- Appease disgruntled customers.
- Clearly direct unproductive employees.
- Gain support from powerful decision-makers.
- Simplify training new employees.
- Define subcontractors' responsibilities.
- Encourage customers to pay their bills swiftly.

- Help you negotiate better pricing from suppliers.
- Acquire low-cost funding from lenders.
- Improve community and media relations.
- Develop better public relations.
- Improve the effectiveness of your advertising.

Sold yet? Your electrical contracting business thoroughly depends on effective communications. It's actually the "secret" ingredient that separates journeyman electricians from successful electrical contractors. So, read this chapter carefully. It can be very profitable to you.

Communication basics

On a ledge in central Africa sits the smartest rock in the world. This rock not only understands the true meaning of life, it knows how to enhance the quality of life on this planet to a level far beyond any civilization that has ever lived. It understands the concepts of math beyond a hundred Einsteins, compassion greater than a thousand Mother Teresas, and the wisdom of a million Judge Wapners. Yet, it can't talk. It can't write. It can't communicate with animate beings. So, what good is it? It's good for skipping across ponds! The point is that being successful requires communicating well with others. Communication is the key to your success as an electrical contractor—and as a person.

Yet, the concept of communication is very simple. Any communication requires three things:

- A thought: some information that you want someone else to have or that you want from them.
- A transmission: a method of getting this thought from you to someone else.
- A receiver: someone whom you want to acquire your thought.

It's that simple. Remember, you use basic communication every day of your life:

- Telling a subcontractor when and where to start a specific job.
- Asking a supplier when the next shipment of materials will arrive.

- Reading a book about starting a successful electrical contracting business.
- Ordering a hamburger at a drive-up window.
- Calling up an old friend to share some common experiences.

In each case, there's a thought (either a statement or a question), a transmission (oral speech, writing, or graphic image), and a receiver (subcontractor, supplier, reader, restaurant clerk, or friend). The thought(s) you want to transmit to a receiver might be a fact (the status of a job) or an emotion (expression of your concern). By nature, business normally involves factual thoughts. The transmission might be conveyed in person, over the phone, on a written fax, with a letter or invoice, with a diagram or drawing, or in a recorded message. The receiver might get your message instantaneously, in a few moments over a fax machine, in a few days via the mail, or months or even years from now in a published document. In each case, you must decide who your receiver is, what the receiver needs to know, and how best to present this information to the receiver.

How to think

Clear writing requires clear thinking. So, what is "thinking?" It's simply the process of asking ourselves questions and then answering them. "How do I adjust this sprayer tip? I know: I first . . .," or "How am I going to meet payroll this month? Let's see, my bank balance is $13,500 and I have $8,700 in recurring bills . . ."

You can clarify your thinking by simply becoming more aware of the questions you ask yourself. The better the question, the better the answer. "Do I want to know how to solve this specific problem, or all similar problems?" So, the key to clear thinking is simply asking questions of your questions, or redefining your question until it accurately states what you want to know. Then the answer comes easier.

Saying what you mean

Every day, successful electrical contractors speak to many people in person or on the telephone. These people are prospects, customers, suppliers, employees, subcontractors, inspectors, government employees, bank employees, professionals, salespeople, agents, and others. Contractors might speak to different people in different ways with a distinct vocabulary. The words they use to explain the finishing of a surface are very different from those used to transact business at the bank.

So, what's different? Why does a communicator speak differently to various people? Because each is a unique audience. Each needs different information and has a distinct vocabulary. For example, the terms "gun," "base," and "lap" mean different things to hunters, ball players, and nursery workers, respectively, than they do to electricians.

Audience The first rule for saying what you mean is: consider your audience. Consider your listener. This is such an obvious rule that we automatically follow it—most of the time. We walk into the bank and automatically switch our jargon to what's understood by the audience: the teller, loan officer, or banker. If, on the way out of the bank, we see a customer, we automatically return to trade jargon—but only at the level the customer will probably understand. We don't get too technical. Then, seeing another electrical contractor in the parking lot, our vocabulary changes again, this time to highly technical terms. In each case, we've automatically considered our audience.

However, it's the exceptions to this "automatically" considering the audience that makes the most trouble. A prospect calls you. If you begin speaking in highly technical terms, the prospect might be impressed, but he or she will more probably be confused (though the prospect might never say so). Or the prospect who has extensive knowledge in your trade might keep up with you.

How can you know the prospect's level of understanding? By asking. You shouldn't embarrass the prospect by asking "how much of this do you understand?" Instead, ask the prospect "tell me about the problem you're trying to solve." Then, by listening to the response, you'll be able to determine the prospect's knowledge of electrical contracting and adjust your vocabulary.

Hint: you can always keep people talking by repeating their last few words in question form. The prospect says, "I really need someone to rewire my dairy barn." You respond, "Rewire your dairy barn?" and the prospect will probably continue feeding you clues to help you determine his or her knowledge. Remember that a good communicator is first a good listener.

Once you've determined your audience's understanding of the problem and its solution, you can start asking more questions to find out what he or she needs. Is the audience looking for some technical information, for pricing, for an immediate solution, for a reason to buy from you, or for something else?

Need

The best way to learn need is, again, to ask. Many electrical contractors simply ask, "How can I help you?" and take their cue from the response. "Well, I'm not sure . . ." tells you to ask more questions until the problem is fully defined in the person's mind. "What I need is some pricing . . ." says that you need to review the benefits of your service and promise to work up an estimate. "I need someone to stop my electrical switch from shooting sparks . . ." says you need to jump in your truck and get over there.

In some cases, people will call you to pick your brain. "I have this problem. How can I solve it?" If it's a problem to which you sell the solution, don't give it away. That might sound unfair, but, with some research and trial-and-error, callers can find solutions on their own. What they pay you for is to save them time and trouble, so let them pay you. You can simply explain that, "I would have to see the situation before I could give you a comprehensive answer." To summarize the point: determine need. Ask yourself, what does this person need to know?

How can you best present the solution to this person? If the audience is a prospective customer and he or she needs an estimate of costs for a specific job, your presentation is a quote or a bid. If your audience is a loan officer and he or she needs information about your business, your presentation is a thorough loan application. If your audience is a disgruntled customer and he or she wants a resolution to problems he or

Presentation

she feels you caused, your presentation is an immediate and factual response and solution.

To easily present a solution, first define the problem. Once you've clearly defined the actual problem, the solution usually becomes obvious. As an example, a client says he or she is angry with you because the new materials ordered from your firm didn't arrive in time. So you begin asking questions: "Didn't arrive in time?" "When was it scheduled to arrive?" "Was someone there to receive the shipment?" "Is that a time that you normally receive shipments?" By probing, you learn that the shipping dock is normally closed from 1 to 3 p.m. on Friday afternoons, but that the shipper was not informed because you weren't informed. So the real problem is: the customer didn't tell you that the shipping dock would be closed during part of the day on which he or she expected the shipment.

The solution, quite obviously, is to resend the shipment when the dock will be open. Now you can present the solution by asking the exact hours when the dock is open and ensuring that the shipper follows them. Defining the problem doesn't blame anyone, it just makes sure that all the facts are used in developing a solution. It's nothing personal to you or to your customer.

So, the best way to communicate or present a solution to someone is to:

1. Know what they know (audience).
2. Know what they need to know (need).

By understanding these two things, you can easily present what customers need in a way that they'll understand.

Measurement Communication, like electricity, is a loop. There must be a return path. In the case of communication, it's feedback in one of many forms. As you speak to someone in person, you can usually evaluate whether your audience is understanding what you say by watching their "body language": eye movement, hands and arms, smiles, and frowns.

On the phone, it's more difficult to measure feedback. So you ask questions: "Does that make sense?" "Did I explain that clearly?" After such a clarifying question, leave a long pause for a response after the "yes" or "no." If you successfully communicate your thought, listeners will usually rephrase it in their own terms. If they don't, or if they repeat your own exact words back to you, consider that you might not have been sufficiently clear. Rephrase what you said. "That's right. To put it another way . . ."

So, the four steps to saying what you mean are: know your audience; know what they need to know; give them what they need, and make sure they understand it.

In general, writing what you mean is the same as saying what you mean. The same four principles apply: audience, need, presentation, and measurement. Of course, they're applied somewhat differently.

Writing what you mean

The best and worst aspect of written communication is that it gives you time to come up with a response—and gives the reader time to ponder your response. So, even more than oral communications that drift away with the wind, written communications require more time and thought. For many, this is what's so intimidating about writing: its permanence. However, its permanence is also what makes the written word so powerful: write it once, clearly and accurately, and be done with it.

Here are the three steps to writing that are guaranteed to make you more comfortable and more successful with written communications in your contracting business:

Writing secrets

- Prewrite.
- Write.
- Rewrite.

That's it! No written document, including this book, is written in a single draft. All successful writing evolves through these three stages—by these or other names—once the audience, need, presentation, and measurement have been defined. In the coming pages, I'll cover these three stages, with examples, until you're comfortable with them—even enjoy them.

Prewrite Prewriting is simply preparing to write. You make notes about the topic you want to cover, you put them in a logical order, and you look for ways to make your ideas as clear as possible. For example, if you need to write a letter to a customer about the Friday delivery problem mentioned earlier, you'd first list the topics you want to cover:

- Dock was closed when delivery was made.
- Shipper didn't expect that dock would be closed.
- Customer didn't mention to you that dock would be closed.
- We're very sorry that the important delivery was missed.
- You're a valued customer and we apologize for the misunderstanding.
- Shipper agreed to attempt redelivery if they're sure dock will be open.
- We want to make all of our customers happy with our service.
- In the future, I'll specifically ask all customers for times that their dock will be open and keep them on record.

Once you have all the topics written down, simply put them in the logical order in which the reader wants to see them. Following our example, the order would be:

1. We're very sorry that the important delivery was missed.
2. We want to make all of our customers happy with our service.
3. Dock was closed when delivery was made.
4. Shipper agreed to attempt redelivery if they're sure dock will be open.
5. Shipper didn't expect that dock would be closed.
6. Customer didn't mention to you that dock would be closed.
7. In the future, I'll specifically ask all customers for times that their dock will be open and keep them on record.
8. You're a valued customer and we apologize for the misunderstanding.

Finally, look for ways to make your ideas as clear as possible. Help your reader visualize the problem and the solution. Here are a couple of comments that you could weave into your letter to make it more visual:

- "I can fully imagine what you must have thought about our firm when Friday ended and your supplies hadn't arrived."
- "The delivery driver, Bob Haskins, has promised to make sure you get this shipment as quickly as possible."

How do you develop a list of topics that you want to cover in your written communication? You simply "think" about it. Thinking, as we discussed earlier, is merely asking questions, then answering them. Typical questions would include:

- What's the purpose of this correspondence?
- What does the reader want to know?
- What are the facts of this situation, in random order?
- What's the most logical order for these facts?
- What does the reader want to know first?
- What single point do I want to leave in the reader's mind?

Find the answers to these and related questions, and you'll have prewritten your correspondence.

Now that you've prewritten what you want to say, the writing comes very easy. You simply elaborate on each point, in order. As an example, the above outline started with:

Write

1. We're very sorry that the important delivery was missed. That's the first topic you want to cover. You can amplify it like this: "Bob, I'm very sorry that the important delivery on invoice #12345 was not made last Friday afternoon when you expected it. I can fully imagine what you must have thought about our firm when Friday ended and your supplies hadn't arrived." Then you lead into the second point on the prewrite outline.

2. We want to make all of our customers happy with our service. You continue the correspondence with, "All of our customers are very important to us, and your business is

especially important, Bob, because you were one of our first clients. If you're not happy with our service, then we're not happy." Then you bring the third point into your correspondence.

3. Dock was closed when delivery was made. However, you say it more positively: "The delivery driver arrived at your loading dock Friday afternoon at 2:30 p.m. with the shipment on his truck. Unfortunately, he discovered that deliveries weren't accepted between 1 and 3 p.m. on Fridays." Then develop the fourth point.

4. Shipper agreed to attempt redelivery if they're sure dock will be open. "The shipper called me later that day, but it was too late in the day to redeliver, so he brought the merchandise back to their warehouse. He offered to redeliver the shipment at your convenience."

Get the point? Once you've prewritten your correspondence, the writing is very easy. It's simply a matter of turning independent thoughts into smooth sentences. Don't worry about spelling, punctuation, or sentence structure at this point. Just develop each thought into a sentence or two.

Rewrite Now comes the cleanup. If you're not a proficient speller, refer to a dictionary, a spelling computer, or a spell-checker in your computer's word processing system. Don't worry too much about "proper English." The best English is conversational English, so simply read your sentences out loud and you'll probably spot any major errors. If you're still uncomfortable with tenses and phrasing, ask someone with those skills to review your draft before you complete it.

You can also dress up your writing by adding transitions such as "However," "In addition," "By the way," "As we discussed," and others. They'll make your correspondence sound more like conversation as well as signal the reader that you're changing thoughts or want to emphasize a specific point.

One more point about writing: if you've decided to purchase and use a computer in your business, consider a word processing program such as WordPerfect, Microsoft Write or

Word, XyWrite, AmiPro, WordStar, or others. Writing on a word processor allows you to prewrite, write, and rewrite quickly and easily. You can readily move words, sentences, and paragraphs around until you're satisfied with them. Then, you can store them on your computer so that future correspondence can reuse these well-written thoughts.

Some word processors include an outliner, a spell checker, a thesaurus, and even a grammar checker. If yours doesn't include these features, you can purchase them separately and add them to your system. A word processor lets you continually improve your written communications until they say exactly what you want them to say.

Your business plan, discussed earlier in this book, might be the most important document you'll ever write. It includes specific information on the structure and direction of your electrical contracting firm. It not only tells others—bankers, investors, partners—what your business is about, it also helps you think about and focus your business ideas.

Writing your business plan

As noted earlier, thinking is simply asking yourself questions then answering them. A business plan compiles the answers to the basic business questions:

- Why am I in business?
- What business am I in?
- What's my market?
- How will I make a profit?
- How much do I need to start and operate this business?
- How will I find customers?
- Who is my competition?
- How will I sell my service?
- How will I plan my work?
- Who will do the actual work?
- What tools and materials do I need?
- Will I have employees, use subcontractors, or do all of the work myself?

You began a business notebook in chapter 2. This notebook was a place to record your answers to these and related business questions. As you've read this book, maybe you've answered many of these questions for yourself. Some might need additional information from other sources. Once you gather this information, you can develop your business plan by following the three steps of writing what you mean: prewrite, write, and rewrite.

A successful business plan will include the following information, as appropriate to your business:

- Description of your business and a statement of its purpose.
- Table of contents of your business plan.
- Description of the services or products your business will provide.
- Information on the location of your business and, if necessary, plans for expansion of the physical plant.
- Definition of the management of the business, their job descriptions and qualifications.
- List of personnel who will initially be employed.
- Description of your business' marketing plan (explained later in this book).
- Information on your competition and market share.
- Outline of your price structure and the philosophy behind it.
- Facts on short- and long-term trends in the market.
- Discussion of quality and how you expect to obtain and retain it in your business.
- Description of the sources and requirements of funds, including inside and outside investors, and their participation in the financial and control aspects of your business.

You should also include a capital equipment and capital improvement list, an opening balance sheet, and a break-even analysis. Incorporate monthly income projections for the first three years of business, and include a list of the independent professionals hired to assist you in the establishment and management of your business: accountants, lawyers, financial consultants, etc.

A *marketing plan* is simply a description of how you plan to market or develop customers for your electrical contracting business. You can incorporate your marketing plan into your business plan, or you can make it a separate document. That decision depends on how you'll use your marketing plan. If you'll implement your own marketing plan, incorporate it into your business plan. If you'll hire a marketing consultant or an advertising agency to implement your marketing plan, make it a separate document that doesn't require a copy of your business plan to be understood.

A typical marketing plan will include the following:

- Executive Summary: overview of the plan, short description of your service and how it differs from services offered by other electrical contractors, the required investment, and a summary of anticipated sales and profits.
- Introduction: a full description of your service and how it fits into the marketplace.
- Situation: an analysis of local demand and trends for your service, laws and regulations, financial requirements, competitors, and structure of your company, including key employees.
- Market: describe in more specifics your target market, its size and requirements, its needs, and the problems that your electrical contracting service will solve for this market.
- Strategy: explain how you'll reach this target market, the promotional tools you'll need, the image you'll present, and how you'll react (or not react) to competitors.
- Control: specify how you expect to manage your electrical contracting firm to improve your services and increase your market share.

A marketing plan can be as long or as short as required by its purpose. If you're planning to bring on a big-bucks investor, you'll want to develop a detailed marketing plan. However, if you're both the writer and the implementer of the marketing plan, a few pages might be sufficient. In either case, the act of writing will help you clarify your intentions and help you to visualize the outcome.

Writing your marketing plan

Writing your employee handbook

If you plan to hire employees in your business, you'll need an employee handbook. Fortunately, there are model employee handbooks that you can modify for your own use. There are also employee handbook software programs that will help you both write and publish your firm's employee handbook.

A typical employee handbook for an electrical contractor will include information on:

- Work hours (office, field personnel, service department, warehouse personnel, etc.).
- Time reports.
- Salaries and wages.
- Overtime.
- Absence.
- Lateness.
- Vacations.
- Holidays.
- Sickness and disability benefits.
- Health insurance.
- Life insurance.
- Bonding.
- Union.
- Confidentiality of company information.
- Outside work.
- Benefits and profit-sharing.
- Personal telephone calls and use of office equipment.
- Personal appearance.
- Safety.

How to negotiate

Many people fear the face-to-face confrontation of negotiating. They don't like to buy cars because they know that not negotiating the price is considered un-American. In fact, it is. Very few things are nonnegotiable. With just a little practice, you can actually enjoy negotiating with others.

To remove any fear of negotiating, remember that it's just a game. You wouldn't be fearful of playing a checkers game or a basketball game. In fact, many products and services you purchase include a percentage of the price set aside for those who negotiate. It ranges from 2 percent to 20 percent or more of the price. In most cases, the higher the price, the higher the available discount. Many larger ticket items such as cars and houses can be negotiated to a discount of 10 to 20 percent— even if the owner says, "My price is firm."

You're not fearful of chess or many sports games because you understand the rules. There will always be unsportsmanlike players who break these rules, but the majority of players follow them. Here are a few of them:

- Don't negotiate unless you're willing to buy. If you're looking at a $500 item and you offer $450, the seller might accept and you're stuck with something you didn't want—or you have to explain that you weren't serious.
- Don't fall in love. There are few unique items in this world. If you can find it once, you can probably find it again. If you tell yourself that you must have this item, then you must have it—at any price.
- Apologize for your low offer. "I'm embarrassed to offer $200, but that's all I can pay for it." This doesn't say $200 is all you have or all you'll pay for it if necessary, so it still leaves you room to negotiate. A few sellers will walk away, but most will make a counter-offer that's lower than the original asking price . . . so you win.
- Don't be afraid to walk away. Once you've determined what the product or service is worth to you, set the realistic limit that you'll pay. If it isn't met, walk away. Some sellers will call you back and reopen negotiations, and others will let you go. Of course, you can always come back later and reopen negotiations yourself.

What products and services can you negotiate? Just about any of them. Electrical suppliers will often negotiate prices or terms on items or orders valued at more than a few hundred dollars.

Some subcontractors will negotiate their hourly fees if you can keep them busy during normally slow times. Car/truck dealers are notoriously adept negotiators, but you can often get the best deal by determining wholesale value (what they probably paid for the vehicle) and adding a standard commission and sales costs plus a little profit. Ask your banker for the wholesale blue book value for the vehicle you're considering.

The other side of the table

Learning how to negotiate with sellers will also help you when you face customers who want to negotiate. Set up your own pricing structure with this in mind. However, always ask for a trade. If customers ask for a 5 percent discount, you might want to give it to them if they pay cash in advance. For a 10 percent discount, you might ask for cash in advance and a letter of recommendation from the customer's firm when the job is done. The rule is: never give away a discount; trade it for something you want. Most important, never sell your services for less than they cost you to furnish.

As you can see, effective communication can set you apart from your competitors as a concerned, thoughtful, knowledgeable, and professional electrical contractor. How you communicate impresses others—positively or negatively. You now have the tools to profitably communicate with prospects, customers, suppliers, lenders, and other people who are important to your success. In the next and final chapter, you'll learn advanced techniques for magnifying the influence of your business.

CHAPTER 12

Growing your electrical contractor business

THROUGHOUT THIS BOOK you've learned how to plan, start, and manage your electrical contracting business. You've developed business skills to complement your knowledge and training as an electrician. You're on the road to success.

However, there are many more skills that you can learn to make the trip along this road go faster. You can learn how to improve your cash flow, gain additional capital, and cope with recessions; you can also learn more about your trade through conventions. Most important, you can review the basic rules for making your business an important component of a successful life. Finally, you can learn how to look toward a profitable retirement.

I'll elaborate on these and other topics in this final chapter. In addition, I recommend two other excellent books written for established electrical contractors. The first is *Electrical Contracting Business Handbook* by Ralph Edgar Johnson (McGraw-Hill, 1986). It covers administration and management functions, a comprehensive electrical estimating system, job management, application of claims to job costs, marketing electrical contracting services, and purchasing and warehousing procedures. The other book is *Successful Business Operations for Electrical Contractors* by Ralph E. Johnson and Gene Whitson (McGraw-Hill, 1993). Topics include business management, using computers, financial management, marketing, claims determination, and operations. Both will help you grow your electrical contracting business.

What works for you?

Even though this book offers hundreds of worthwhile tips for growing your electrical contracting business, there's one primary rule that supersedes all others: Do what works best for you. If your business is growing through telephone marketing while other contractors are using direct mail, do what works for you. You're certainly wiser to at least try the other methods, but there are so many variables among local markets, customer types, client needs, and your own skills and personality, that the "best" way to do something is relative. What works well for you might not work at all for someone else.

That doesn't mean that you should always follow the easiest path. A good business manager always looks for new and better ways to complete the "process," discussed earlier. That better way might be a new computer program that automates credit collections, or searching for a niche market that isn't being served. However, just because something is new doesn't always mean that it's better. Be aggressive in your learning and conservative in your changing. Know what works for you.

One way to know what works is to continually rethink how you manage your business and serve your customers. Remember that to "think" is simply to ask yourself questions, then answer them. The better the question, the better the answer. So, as you go about your daily business, ask yourself: How can I do this job better, more efficiently, faster, more profitably, more safely, or with more quality? Here are some examples:

- How can I better handle incoming calls from prospects who want "information and pricing" in a hurry?
- Without spending too much money on advertising and promotion, how can I get more prospects to call me for a quote?
- How can I get my employees to stop spending so much time at the coffee shop and more time at the job site?
- How can I encourage my banker to extend me more credit during the slower winter months?
- How can I find out if customers are happy or unhappy with my service?

- How can I get my customers to tell others about my service in a positive way?
- How can I ensure that my employees and subs are working as safely as possible?
- How can I reduce my insurance costs without increasing my risk?
- How can I cut costs without cutting my quality of service?

A successful manager is always rethinking the way he or she does everything, from maintaining an office to purchasing materials to serving customers. To make your business grow, you must rethink your business every day.

One more tip: if you're a better tradesperson than you are a business manager, then hire a manager. If you become a better business manager, hire a trades person to do the work. Do what you do best—and what you enjoy most.

If it ain't broke

Here's a seeming contradiction to the rule I just stated: If it ain't broke, break it! Actually, the two rules work together. Do what works for you, but make sure it's really working. Also, to test its strength, try to break it from time to time.

Here's what I mean: New customers are coming to you faster than you can handle them, so you take some time to plan what you'll do when the customers aren't coming at all. Or you've set up a front office that smoothly handles incoming calls, handles messages in a timely fashion, and manages the paperwork without problems; consider what you'll do if this gem-of-an-office-manager decides to move to the competition or leaves the area. What would you do to ensure that valuable records aren't lost, that proven procedures are documented, that your next office manager is as efficient as the one you have? Plan now as if it already happened, because it will. Murphy was an electrical contractor!

Improving cash flow

All businesses, no matter how small or large, function on cash. Many businesses become insolvent because they don't have enough cash to meet their short-term obligations. Bills must be paid in cash, not profits. Sufficient cash is, therefore, one of the keys to maintaining a successful business. Thus, you must understand how cash moves or flows through the business and how planning can remove some of the uncertainties about future requirements.

Cash cycle

Electrical contractors face a continual cycle of events that can increase or decrease the cash balance. Cash is decreased in the acquisition of materials and services. Cash is reduced in paying off the amounts owed to suppliers (accounts payable). Services or inventory are sold, and these sales generate money owed from customers (accounts receivable). When customers pay, accounts receivable is reduced and the cash account is increased. However, the cash flows aren't necessarily related to the sales in that period because customers might pay in the next period. Electrical contractors must continually be alert to changes in working capital accounts, the cause of these changes, and their implications for the financial health of the company.

Net working capital

As discussed earlier in this book, current assets are those resources of cash and those assets that can be converted to cash within one year or as a normal business cycle. These include cash, marketable securities, accounts receivable, and inventories. Current liabilities are obligations that become due within one year or a normal business cycle. Those include accounts payable, notes payable, and accrued expenses payable. Consider current assets as the source of funds that reduce current liabilities.

One way to measure the flow of cash and the firm's ability to maintain its cash or liquid assets is to compute working capital. That's the difference between current assets and current liabilities. The change in this value from period to period is called *net working capital*.

For example, see page 269. Net working capital increased during the year, but you don't know how. It could have been all in cash or all in inventory, or it might have resulted from a reduction in accounts payable.

Example of net working capital

	Year 1	Year 2
Current assets	$110,000	$200,000
Less current liabilities	–70,000	–112,000
Working capital	40,000	88,000
Net working capital increase		$48,000

Cash-flow statement

While net working capital shows only the changes in the current position, a "flow" statement can be developed to explain the changes that have occurred in any account during any time period. The cash flow statement is an analysis of the cash inflows and outflows.

The ability to forecast cash requirements is indeed a means of becoming a more efficient contractor/manager. If you can determine the cash requirements for any period, you can establish a bank loan in advance, or you can reduce other current asset accounts so that the cash will be made available. Also, when you have excess cash, you can put this cash into productive use to earn a return.

The change in the cash can be readily determined if you know net working capital and the changes in current liabilities and current assets other than cash. For example, let:

NWC = Net working capital
CA = Change in current assets other than cash
CL = Change in current liabilities
cash = Change in cash

Because net working capital is the difference between the change in current assets and current liabilities:

$$NWC = CA + cash - CL$$
$$Cash = NWC - CA + CL$$

This relationship states that if you know the net working capital (NWC), the change in current liabilities (CL), and the change in current assets less cash (CA – cash), you can calculate the change in cash. The change in cash is then added to the beginning balance of cash to determine the ending balance.

Suppose you forecast that contracting income will increase $50,000 and the following will correspondingly change:

- Receivables increase by $25,000.
- Inventory increases by $70,000.
- Accounts Payable increases by $30,000.
- Notes Payable increases by $10,000.

Using net working capital of $48,000, what's the projected change in cash?

$$cash = NWC - CA + CL$$
$$= 48,000 - 25,000 - 70,000 + 30,000 + 10,000$$
$$= -7,000$$

The answer is that, over this period of time, under the condition of increasing sales volume, cash decreases by $7,000. Is there enough cash to cover this decrease? This will depend on the beginning cash balance.

At any given level of sales, it's easier to forecast the required accounts payable, receivables, and inventory, than net working capital. To forecast this net working capital account, you must trace the sources and application of funds. Sources of funds increase working capital. Applications of funds decrease working capital. The difference between the sources and applications of funds is the net working capital.

The following calculation is based on the fact that the balance sheet is indeed in balance. That is, the total assets equal total liabilities plus owner's equity.

Current assets + Noncurrent assets = Current liabilities + Long-term liabilities + equity

Rearranging this equation:

Current assets – Current liabilities = Long-term liabilities + Equity – Noncurrent assets

Because the left side of the equation is working capital, the right side must also equal working capital. A change in either side is the net working capital. If long-term liabilities and equity increase or noncurrent assets decrease, net working capital increases. This change would be a source of funds. If noncurrent assets increase or long-term liabilities and equity decrease, net working capital decreases. This change would be an application of funds. Typical sources of funds or net working capital are: funds provided by operations, disposal of fixed assets, issuance of stock, and borrowing from a long term source.

To obtain the figure for "funds provided by operations," subtract all expense items requiring funds from all revenues that were sources of funds. You can also obtain this result in an easier manner: add back expenses that don't result in inflows or outflows of funds to reported net income.

The most common nonfund expense is depreciation, the allocation of the cost of an asset as an expense over the life of the asset against the future revenues produced. Adjusting net income with depreciation is much simpler than computing revenues and expenses that require funding. Again, depreciation is not a source of funds. The typical applications of funds or net working capital are: purchase of fixed assets, payment of dividends, retirement of long-term liabilities, and repurchase of equity.

Cash flow can be used not only to determine how cash flowed through the business but also as an aid to determine the excess or shortage of cash. Suppose your analysis of cash flow forecasts a potential cash deficiency. You might then do a number of things, such as increase borrowings (loans, stock issuance), reduce current asset accounts (receivables, inventory), and reduce noncurrent asset accounts (sell fixed assets, postpone expansion).

Planning for cash flow

By using a cash flow statement, you can determine if sufficient funds are available from financing activities, show funds generated from all sources, and show how these funds were applied. Using and adjusting the information gained from this cash flow analysis will help you to know in advance if there will be enough cash to pay suppliers' bills, bank loans, interest, and dividends. Careful planning will ensure a sufficient amount of cash to meet future obligations on schedule, which is essential for the successful electrical contractor.

Increasing cash flow

As you can see, you need cash to grow your electrical contracting business. Once you've analyzed cash flow and determined that you need more of it, what can you do? Depending on the specific type of electrical contracting business you own, you can find increased cash in your accounts receivable and in your inventory.

Accounts receivable represents the extension of credit to support sales. In your business, the types and terms of credit you grant are set by established competitive practices. As an investment, the accounts receivable should contribute to overall return on investment (ROI).

Excessive investment in accounts receivable can hurt ROI by tying up funds unnecessarily. One good way to judge the extent of accounts receivable is to compare your average collection period with that of rivals or the industry average. If your average collection period is much higher than your competitors' or the industry norm, your accounts receivable might be excessive.

If they are excessive, it might be that you aren't keeping tight control of late payers. You can check this by developing an aging schedule. An aging schedule shows the distribution of accounts receivable with respect to being on time or late.

Failure to closely monitor late payments ties up investment and weakens profits. The more overdue accounts become, the greater is the danger that they'll be uncollectable and will have to be written off against profits.

If the aging schedule doesn't reveal excessive late accounts, your average collection period might be out of line simply because your credit policy is more liberal than most. If so, it should translate into more competitive sales and greater profits. Otherwise, you should rethink your credit program.

Not all electrical contractors have significant inventory—or even require standing inventory. However, those who do can improve cash flow by improving their management of inventory. Excessive inventory will reduce your return on investment. One way to determine whether your inventory level is excessive is to compare the inventory turnover ratio with the industry norm. If your inventory turnover (the times per year that you replace your inventory) is much lower than the average, your ROI will obviously suffer.

If inventory is much higher than it should be for your level of sales, it might be that you're holding items that are obsolete or that simply don't move fast enough to justify their cost. You might also be speculating on price increases, or perhaps for competitive reasons you think a full line of inventory items is essential, even if some items are in very low demand. In any case, you should reevaluate your policy and make sure that the gains outweigh the costs of the higher investment. Which is more valuable to the success of your business: the excess inventory or the equivalent cash?

As you consider your level of inventory, also consider the cost associated with maintaining inventory. *Carrying costs* are the expenses associated with inventory storage, handling, and insurance. *Ordering costs* are the clerical and administrative costs incurred when an order is placed for an item in inventory. If you expect to use 51 gallons of undercoating during the next thirty days, you could simply buy it all now and carry it in inventory until it's all used up, or you could buy 17 gallons every ten days. The more frequently you place orders for inventory, the less inventory you have to keep on hand and the less carrying costs you have. However, more frequent orders also result in greater ordering costs. Remember, the bottom line is: the bottom line.

Where to get more money

Electrical contractors never seem to have enough money. Bankers and suppliers, naturally, are important in financing small business growth through loans and credit, but an equally important source of long-term growth capital is the venture capital firm.

One way of explaining the different ways in which banks and venture capital firms evaluate a small business seeking funds is: Banks look at its immediate future, but are most heavily influenced by its past. Venture capitalists look to its longer-run future.

Of course, venture capital firms are interested in many of the same factors that influence bankers in their analysis of loan applications from smaller companies. All financial people want to know the results and ratios of past operations, the amount and intended use of the needed funds, and the earnings and financial condition of future projects. However, venture capitalists look much more closely at the features of the service and the size of the market than do commercial banks.

Banks are creditors. They're interested in the market position of your company to the extent that they look for assurance that your service business can provide steady sales and generate sufficient cash flow to repay the loan. They look at projections to be certain that the owner has done his or her homework.

Venture capital firms are owners. They hold stock in your company, adding their invested capital to its equity base. Therefore, they examine existing or planned services and the potential markets for them with extreme care. They invest only in firms they believe can rapidly increase sales and generate substantial profits.

Why? Because venture capital firms invest for long-term capital, not for interest income. A common estimate is that they look for three to five times their investment in five to seven years.

Of course, venture capitalists don't realize capital gains on all of their investments. Certainly, they don't make capital gains of 300 or 500 percent, except on a very limited portion of their total investments. However, their intent is to find venture projects with this appreciation potential to make up for investments that aren't successful.

As you can imagine, venture capital is a risky business because it's difficult to judge the worth of early-stage companies. So, many venture capital firms set rigorous policies for venture proposal size, maturity of your company, and requirements and evaluation procedures to reduce risks. Venture capitalists are cautious because their investments are unprotected in the event of failure.

There are several types of venture capital firms:

- Traditional partnerships, which are often established by wealthy families to aggressively manage a portion of their funds by investing in small companies.
- Professionally managed pools, which are made up of institutional money and which operate like the traditional partnerships.
- Investment banking firms, which usually trade in more established securities, but occasionally form investor syndicates for venture proposals.
- Insurance companies, which—as protection against inflation—often require a portion of equity as a condition of their loans to smaller companies.
- Manufacturing companies, which have sometimes looked on investing in smaller companies as a means of supplementing their research and development programs.
- Small Business Investment Corporations (SBICs), which are licensed by the Small Business Administration and can provide management assistance as well as venture capital.

In addition to these venture capital firms, there are individual private investors and finders. Finders, which can be firms or individuals, often know the capital industry and might be able to help the small company to locate capital.

Most venture capital firms are interested in investment projects requiring an investment of $250,000 to $1,500,000. Projects requiring less than $250,000 are of limited interest because of the high cost of investigation and administration. However, some venture firms will consider smaller proposals if the investment is intriguing enough.

The venture proposal

The typical venture capital firm receives more than 1,000 proposals a year. As many as 90 percent of these will be rejected quickly because they don't fit the established geographical, technical, or market-area policies of the firm, or because they've been poorly prepared.

The remaining 10 percent are investigated with care. These investigations are expensive, costing the venture firm $2,000 to $3,000 per company investigated. Of these, 10 or 15 proposals per year will earn a second investigation. Finally, the venture firm will select one or two in which to invest.

Most investment capital firms' investment interest is limited to projects proposed by companies with some operating history, even though they might not yet have shown a profit. Companies that can expand into a new product line or a new market with additional funds are particularly interesting. The venture capital firm can provide funds to enable such companies to grow in a spurt rather than gradually, as they would on retained earnings.

Most venture capital firms concentrate primarily on the competence and character of the proposing firm's management. They feel that even mediocre products or services can be successfully developed, promoted, and distributed by an experienced, energetic management group.

Finally, most venture capital firms seek a distinctive element in the strategy, market, or process of the firm. This distinctive element might be a new feature or a particular skill or technical competence. They're looking for something that will provide a competitive advantage for the firm in which they'll invest.

Writing the venture proposal

A successful venture proposal must convince the venture capitalists that their investment is worthwhile for them. Here are the components of a typical venture proposal:

- Purpose and objectives: a summary of the what and why of the project.
- Proposed financing: the amount of money you'll need from the beginning to the maturity of the project proposed, how

the proceeds will be used, how you plan to structure the financing, and why the amount designated is required.

- Marketing: a description of the market segment you have or plan to get, the competition, the characteristics of the market, and your plans (with costs) for getting or holding the market segment you're aimed at.

- History of the firm: a summary of significant financial and organizational milestones, description of employees and employee relations, explanations of banking relationships, and a recounting of major services or products your firm has offered during its existence.

- Description of the product or service: a detailed description of the product (process) or service offered by the firm and the costs associated with it.

- Financial statements: both for the past few years and pro forma projections (balance sheets, income statements, and cash flows) for the next three to five years, showing the effect anticipated if the project is undertaken and if the financing is secured. This should include an analysis of key variables affecting financial performance, showing what could happen if the projected level of revenue is not attained.

- Capitalization: a list of shareholders, how much is invested to date, and in what form (equity or debt).

- Biographical sketches: the work histories and qualifications of key owners and employees.

- Principal customers and suppliers.

- Problems anticipated and other pertinent information: a candid discussion of any contingent liabilities, pending litigation, tax or patent difficulties, and any other contingencies that might affect the project you're proposing.

- Advantages: a discussion of what's special about your service, product, marketing plans, or channels that gives your project unique leverage.

How venture capitalists participate

What happens when, after the exhaustive investigation and analysis, the venture capital firm decides to invest in your company? Most venture firms prepare an equity financing proposal that details the amount of money to be provided, the percentage of common stock to be surrendered in exchange for these funds, the interim financing method to be used, and the protective covenants to be included.

Venture capital financing is not inexpensive for the owners of a small business. The partners of the venture firm buy a portion of the business' equity in exchange for their investment. They become part of the ownership.

This percentage of equity varies, of course, and depends on the amount of money provided, the success and worth of the business, and the anticipated investment return. It can range from a 10-percent interest in an established and profitable business to as much as 80 or 90 percent for a young or financially troubled firm.

Most venture firms, at least initially, don't want a position of more than 30 to 40 percent because they want the owners to have the incentive to keep building the business. If additional financing is required to support business growth, the outsiders' stake might exceed 50 percent, but investors realize that small business owners/managers can lose their entrepreneurial zeal under these circumstances. The venture firm wants to leave control in the hands of the company's managers because it's really investing in that management team more than in the business.

Control is a much simpler issue to resolve. Unlike the division of equity, over which the parties are bound to disagree, control is an issue in which they have a common, though perhaps unapparent, interest. While it's understandable that the management of a small company will have some anxiety in this area, the partners of a venture firm typically have little interest in assuming control of the business. They have neither the technical expertise nor the managerial personnel to run a number of small companies in diverse industries. They much prefer to leave operating control to the existing management.

The venture capital firm does, however, want to participate in any strategic decision that might change the basic product/market character of the company and in any major investment decisions that might divert or deplete the financial resources of the company. They will, therefore, generally ask that at least one partner be made a director of your company.

The investment of the venture capital firm might be in the final form of direct stock ownership, which doesn't impose fixed charges. More likely, it will be an interim form—preferred stock or convertible subordinated debentures. Financing might also be straight loans with options or warrants that can be converted to a future equity position at a preestablished price.

Venture capital firms generally intend to realize capital gains on their investments by providing for a stock buy-back by the small firm, by arranging a public offering of stock of the company invested in, or by providing for a merger with a larger firm that has publicly traded stock. They usually hope to do this within five to seven years of their initial investment. Venture capital might be just the source of the funding you require to successfully grow your electrical contracting business.

Coping with business recessions

No businesses are truly recession-proof. All businesses have cycles in which sales become easier or harder to make. Electrical contractors are subject to the same business cycle that most building and general contractors face. Even so, there are steps you can take to minimize the market's down-swing and extend its up-swing.

First, determine the construction or business cycle for your market. Reviewing income and financial records from prior years—or checking with the local building permits office, or from other contractors—you can draw a chart illustrating the local business cycle. In your region, it might be that most of the market for your service occurs in the spring and summer, or maybe in the winter and fall. Or the cycle might be fairly equal across the year, but alternate years might fluctuate up or down. The first step to coping with recessions in the local business cycle is to determine exactly what and when that cycle is.

The next step is to begin planning for it. If you're coming up to a typically slower period, determine what you need to do. In past years, how much has income dropped? For how long? Can you find income sources in other specialties where the cycle is moving up? What expenses can you cut back? Do you have employees who would prefer a seasonal layoff so they can catch up on other interests?

Maybe you need to dramatically cut back on your expenses and debts for this period. If so, list them out now and determine which will naturally diminish and which will need to be reduced.

One successful electrical contractor, while in a busy period, decided that times would be much slower six months hence. So, he talked with his bank and other creditors, offering to prepay debts and expenses now so he could cut back payments later. It worked. When times got rougher, he reduced his expenses and wintered the problem. If you aren't into your slow season yet, you can also talk to your banker about building a line of credit now that will help you get through the tougher times ahead.

One more option for those who are facing a downturn in business: trade out your services. If your bank or a major creditor is beginning to pressure you, offer to perform electrical services for them in lieu of partial or complete payment. Even if they don't require your service now, you can either promise future services as required or learn if they have other customers who might want to hire or trade. Many creditors would rather work out a trade rather than absorb a bad debt. Of course, much depends on your relationship with them.

Some creditors, such as the Internal Revenue Service and other governmental agencies, will not consider service trades. However, they can sometimes develop terms for a business person who has an otherwise good financial record and the opportunity for growth once the local economy turns around. However, don't expect compassion; it's purely business.

Another source for cash to tide you through a recession is available from a second mortgage on your building, your home, or other large asset. One more: consider widening your market. Travel to a nearby metropolitan area and study whether you can expand your services to reach it. If so, you can pick up additional sales by either subcontracting your services or by promoting your services in the expanded market. It certainly beats starving at home.

Conventions

Trade conventions offer electrical contractors an opportunity to get out of the house. Actually, they do much more. They update you on the latest tools, methods, and opportunities. They inspire and entertain you. They train you.

The National Electrical Contractors Association holds its annual exposition every October. In 1993, it's in San Diego. In 1994, it moves to Chicago, then in the following years to Anaheim, Boston, and Denver.

Planning for business continuation

The electrical contracting business you've started, nourished, managed, and expanded has become a part of you. For many firms, the owner is the business, and vice versa. So, what happens to your business when you or your partner dies or is disabled? That's up to you.

Life insurance and good planning can provide significant amounts of cash to help employees and family members cushion the financial impact of the death or retirement of the owner/manager of a sole proprietorship, partnership, or a closely held corporation. Life insurance and good planning can also help attract and retain valuable employees.

Sole proprietorships

The personal skills, reputation, and management ability of the sole proprietor help to make the business successful. Without these human-life values, the business is worth only the liquidation value of the tangible assets.

The sole proprietor's personal and business assets are one and the same. When death occurs, the loss can become a financial disaster to the proprietor's estate and fatal to the business. The business that was producing a good living for the owner and family will become a defunct business. What are the options?

Family continuation

The business can be transferred to a capable family member as a gift through provisions in the proprietor's will or by a sale provided through a prearranged purchase agreement effective at death. Cash is needed to offset losses to the business caused by the owner's death, to equalize the value of bequests made to other family members if the transfer is a gift, and to provide the sale price if the transfer is through sale.

New owner   If the buyer is a key employee, competitor, or other person, the business might be transferred at death, pursuant to a prearranged sale agreement. However, cash is needed to provide a "business continuation fund" to meet expenses and perhaps to offset losses until the business adjusts to the new management.

Liquidation   If future management is not available, then the business must be liquidated. Cash is needed to offset the difference between the business' going-concern value and its auction-block liquidation value to provide a fund for income replacement to the family and to pay outstanding business debts.

Partnerships   Unless there's a written agreement to the contrary, the death of a partner automatically dissolves the firm. In the absence of an agreement to the contrary, surviving partners have no right to buy the deceased's partnership interest. Surviving partners can't assume the goodwill or take over the assets without consent of the deceased's estate. If the deceased was in debt to the partnership, the estate must settle the account in full and in cash.

The surviving partners act as liquidating trustees. They have exclusive possession of firm property but no right to carry on the business. If the business is continued, the surviving partners must share all profits with the deceased's estate and are liable for all losses. They must convert everything into cash at the best price obtainable. They must make an accounting to the deceased's estate and divide the proceeds with the estate. They must liquidate themselves out of their business and income. What are the options a business has on the death of a partner?

If the surviving partner and deceased's heirs do nothing, the business is liquidated, resulting in "auction-price" value for the salable assets. The business might receive nothing for goodwill. This is a disastrous solution for both the dead partner's family and the surviving partners. It means termination of jobs for the surviving partners and employees.

Liquidation

The surviving partners might attempt to reorganize the partnership by taking the heirs into the partnership. However, if heirs are incapable of working, the survivors must do all the work and share the profits. The surviving partners can also accept a new partner picked by the heirs; the surviving partners can also sell their interest in the business to the heirs, or they can buy out the interest now controlled by the deceased partner's heirs.

Reorganization

Of course, there are some preparations that can be made prior to the death of a partner that will make a reorganization smoother. Buy-and-sell agreements funded with life insurance should be entered into while all partners are alive. Such an agreement, drafted by an attorney, will typically include a commitment by each partner not to dispose of his or her interest without first offering it at an agreed sale price to the partnership. The agreement will also include a provision for the partnership to buy a deceased partner's interest. The funding of the purchase will typically be from the proceeds of a life insurance policy written for that specific purpose.

The death of a stockholder who has been active in the operation of a closely held corporation allows the business entity to continue its legal structure, but not its personal structure. The interests of the heirs of the deceased inevitably come in conflict with the interests of the surviving associates. What options are available to surviving stockholders?

Corporations

The deceased's family might retain the stock interest. If the heirs have a majority interest, they might choose to become personally involved in management in order to receive income. Or they might choose to remain inactive, elect a new board of directors, and force the company to pay dividends. In either

Retention of stock by heirs

case, the surviving stockholders might lose a voice in management and possibly their jobs, while the deceased's family might become heirs to a business on the brink of failure. If the heirs have a minority interest and aren't employed by the surviving associates, their only means of receiving an income from the corporation will be through dividends.

Sale of stock by heirs

After the death of a stockholder, the deceased's heirs or estate might offer to sell the stock interest to the surviving stockholders, or an outside buyer might be interested in purchasing stock in the corporation. While all of the interested parties are alive, they can enter into a binding buy-and-sell agreement funded with life insurance. This is done with a stockholder's buy-and-sell agreement, which is drawn up with the assistance of your corporate attorney and accountant.

Key employees

Many growing firms develop key employees who are assets that the firm can't afford to be without. Even though these key employees might not own an interest in the firm, they're nonetheless valuable to its continuation. So, what happens if a key employee dies?

Electrical contractors who have key employees should consider life insurance payable to the firm on the death or disability of one of these human assets. How much life insurance? It should be an amount sufficient to offset financial losses during the readjustment period, to retain good credit standing, and to assure customers and suppliers that the company will continue as usual. In addition, key-employee insurance could retire loans, mortgages, and bonds; attract and train a successor; or carry out ongoing plans for expansion and new developments.

Talk to your insurance agent about the appropriate policy for insuring your business against the loss of a proprietor, a partner, a stockholder, or a key employee. It's one of the costs of growth.

Managing time and stress

A growing electrical contracting business will soon take up at least 24 hours of your day. Maybe more. Some contractors spend most of their day fighting fires. Others let the fires burn each other out. The smart contractor manages available time by prioritizing the jobs to be done. Those that are vital to the success of the business get done first. Important jobs come next. Then those that are of limited value fill up the remainder of the time, if there is any.

Many successful electrical contractors start their day with a planning session of up to a half hour. During this time, the contractor plans out the events of the day to ensure that the vital jobs get done and that the important jobs are handled as time is available. The contractor might schedule "chatter" time with employees or customers, but will ensure that the discussion stay mostly on business or at least on personal topics that will help forge a better business relationship.

How can the contractor ensure that time is well managed? First, by organizing work space so that important papers don't get lost and unimportant papers do. You can also make a rule that you'll avoid handling papers more than once. If you pick up a piece of paper, make a decision regarding it right then, if possible.

Set up a regular work schedule. It might be from 7 a.m. to 6 p.m. or 8 a.m. to 5 p.m. or 6 a.m. to 6 p.m. Whatever it is, try to stick to it. If you manage your time well, you'll be able to stick to the schedule. If you have one time of the day that seems more productive for you than others, plan your most important functions around it.

What about travel and waiting time? Take work with you in a briefcase or purchase a cellular phone that you can use to stay productive every minute. As your time management skills improve, you'll learn how to do more than one thing at a time. You could be making job notes or talking with the supervisor or gathering information on an upcoming bid while you're waiting to talk with an inspector or a client.

Meetings seem to be one of the biggest time-wasters there are. However, you can change this by organizing all of your meetings. Meetings, to be productive, must have a purpose or agenda and a time limit. Even if you didn't call the meeting, if you see that it has no focus or structure, you can step in and say, "I have another appointment in an hour. What topics do we have to cover in that hour?" Then list those topics as the agenda.

One more time-management tip: use one of the popular time management planning systems to help you get the most out of your day. They include Day Timer (Day Timers, Inc.) and Day Runner (Harper House, Inc.). These and other systems give you a place to record appointments, daily to-do lists, special projects and their steps, as well as a contact book for names and addresses. If you spend most of your time in the office at a computer, there are numerous contact management and scheduling programs that will help you manage your time. If you use a portable computer, you can install these programs on it and carry this information wherever you go.

Time and stress are closely related. The lack of time to do what you need to do often increases personal stress. How do you manage both? Here are some ideas from successful contractors:

Plan your time and establish priorities on a daily "to-do" list. Decide what your prime time is and do your most important or difficult tasks then. Set business hours, specific times when you're at work and times when you turn on the answering machine because you're on duty but off call. You, your customers, and your family will appreciate knowing your set routine, even though you know that for special events or emergencies you can break that schedule.

Notice what your four or five big time-wasters are and learn techniques to eliminate them or compensate for them. Some common ones are telephone interruptions, visitors, socializing, excessive paperwork, lack of policies and procedures, procrastination, failure to delegate, unclear objectives, poor scheduling, lack of self-discipline, and lack of skill in a needed area.

Stay in contact with people. As you move from a tradesperson to a business owner, you'll naturally spend more time at "the office." Make sure that you get out to talk with your customers, your employees, and for social events. This will help your morale if you feel isolated. Just as important, your contacts will appreciate your visibility and your interest in sharing time with them.

Build a fitness program into your day. As an active trades person, you might have gotten plenty of exercise doing your daily job. However, as a business manager you might not—unless you take time for fitness. Many successful business people exercise in order to think creatively because physical activity sends oxygen to the brain and helps the mind function better. With regular exercise, your health will improve, your stress level will go down, and your trim look will inspire people to have confidence in your abilities.

If you're working from your home, give your business as much of a separate and distinct identity as possible. Although you might save a few dollars by using the dining room table as a desk and a cardboard box as a file cabinet, the stress and strain of operating without proper space and supplies will take its toll. Have a separate room or area for your business, with a separate entrance if customers or suppliers visit. Consider soundproofing so your family won't be bothered by your noise, and vice versa. In addition to the psychological and physical comfort of having a separate office, the IRS requires it in order for you to make a legitimate claim for tax deductions.

Finally, take care of your major business asset: you. Being the boss can be exciting, fulfilling, and rewarding. It can also be lonely, stressful, and demanding. Learn to balance your professional and personal life. Go on vacation. Get a weekly massage. Join a health club. Take a class in meditation or spiritual studies. Attend a business owner's breakfast club. Your business depends on your being at your best.

The primary reason you started your own business is to increase your opportunities to enjoy life. You wanted to offer a needed service; you wanted to help others; you wanted to extend your skills in electricity and in business; you wanted to be able to afford the better things of life. However, you didn't want to spend your entire waking time working. In fact, you

Improving the quality of life

might get so caught up in the chase for success that you miss the opportunities that success brings along the way.

Those who have found success in this and other fields will tell you that success is often empty if isn't shared with others. That doesn't mean waiting until a successful destination—say at $1 million net worth—is reached. It means sharing success with others along the way, on a day-to-day basis. Maybe, for you, this means sharing your success with your family or a few close friends, or even some humanity-serving organization in which you believe. In any case, consider that your financial success will mean much more to you if you can use it to bring physical, emotional, or spiritual success to others.

Manage your life outside your business as you do your time at the business. Look for ways to help others. Find methods of giving yourself the things you most enjoy, whether time with friends, time with hobbies, time with competitive sports, time alone, or all of the above. Especially, take time to recharge your "batteries." You'll use lots of personal energy in starting, managing, and growing your electrical contracting business. Make sure you take the time to reenergize yourself.

When to quit

The failure rate of new businesses is very high. However, the failure rate lowers as time passes. The longer you're in business, the greater the chance that you'll continue in business. Of course, your electrical contracting business can fail at any time. Most fail because they don't have a functioning record-keeping system. They aren't even sure exactly when or how they fail; they just do. So, a key element of continued success is maintaining good records and learning how to use them to manage.

However, there might come a time when business conditions require that you throw in the towel. If you're not making sufficient profit or are reducing your capital to losses, you'll soon be in financial trouble. What to do?

First, cut overhead as much as possible. The sooner this is done, the longer your business will survive—maybe long enough to find a solution. Next, sell unused or inefficient assets. Of course, you must maintain your working tools. However, maybe you can move your office to a less expensive location—even home.

Then talk with your creditors about the situation and what you plan to do. Some might be very helpful in offering a workable solution: an extension of credit, assistance in finding additional contracts, or even purchase of stock in your business.

Finally, as necessary, talk with your attorney about your legal obligations and options. No one wants to declare bankruptcy, but it might be necessary. Or you might decide to set up a payment schedule for all debts and return to the work force as an employee.

There's no shame in failing to succeed—just in failing to try. If there are things you've learned from the experience, you can use them to increase your worth to an employer. Who would be better to manage an electrical contracting business than someone who has learned the hard way how not to manage one?

When should you retire from your profitable electrical contracting business? When you want to. Some tradespeople will hold off retiring until they're no longer physically able to work their trade. Others make plans to retire when they're 65 or even 62 years of age. Still others give their business 10 or 20 years to grow, then sell it to semiretire or to move to a different trade.

Planning to retire

Some successful tradespeople will sell their shares to a partner or to another corporation. Others will sell or give their equity in the business to a son, daughter, or in-law. A few will simply liquidate their assets and keep the proceeds. Some will sell out to a competitor.

How to retire

The business can be sold outright for cash, earning the owner a cash settlement for equity. Or the seller can "carry the paper" or sell it on a contract with a down payment and monthly payments for a specified term. In this case, buyers will often require the seller to sign a "noncompetition" contract that says the seller can't go to work for a competing contractor or start another electrical contracting firm in the same market.

This chapter has presented a number of advanced topics that can help you grow your electrical contracting business into a long-term success for you and for others. I've covered business management, time management, money management, and even life management.

This book is intended to be more than a how-to on electrical contracting. It's also a book about developing and maintaining an attitude of service. Such an attitude is rewarded financially and emotionally as you enhance life for yourself and for those whom you serve. Remember—the quality of life is of greater value than the quantity.

Forms & work-sheets for electrical contractors

ABC ELECTRICAL CONTRACTORS
BANK ACCOUNT

Date	Source/Payee	Check #	Debit	Credit	Adjustment	Balance
	OPENING BALANCE					
	BALANCE FORWARD					

Sample bank account register.

ABC ELECTRICAL CONTRACTORS

CHECK ALLOCATION

SUPPLIER _____

CHECK # _____ DATE _____

Account #	Dept. #	Amount	
	TOTAL:		

DESCRIPTION:

_____

_____

1st Approval:_____

2nd Approval:_____

Prepared By :_____

Sample check allocation form.

Forms & work-sheets for electrical contractors   293

ABC ELECTRICAL CONTRACTORS
CASH RECEIPTS JOURNAL

PAGE ___ OF ___

DATE	DESCRIPTION	AMOUNT
	TOTALS	

Sample cash receipts journal.

ABC ELECTRICAL CONTRACTORS
PETTY CASH REGISTER

Location		Date	

Amount		Paid to: (attach receipt)	Purpose

Remarks:

Signature_____

Sample petty cash register.

Forms & work-sheets for electrical contractors   295

ABC ELECTRICAL CONTRACTORS
ACCOUNTS RECEIVABLE JOURNAL

PAGE _____ OF _____

INVOICE DATE	ACCOUNT/DESCRIPTION	AMOUNT	DATE DUE	DATE RECEIVED

Sample accounts receivable journal.

ABC ELECTRICAL CONTRACTORS
ACCOUNTS PAYABLE JOURNAL

PAGE _____ OF _____

DATE RCVD	ACCOUNT/PROJECT	AMOUNT	DISCOUNT DUE DATE	DATE PAID

Sample accounts payable journal.

Forms & work-sheets for electrical contractors   297

ABC ELECTRICAL CONTRACTORS
LOCAL TRAVEL EXPENSES

NAME:		ID NO:		WEEK ENDING:		

	IN	OUT	IN	OUT	REG	OVER	TOTAL
FRI							
SAT							
SUN							
MON							
TUE							
WED							
THU							
TOT							

DATE	LOCATION	MILEAGE	GALLONS	AMOUNT
TOTAL				

DATE	MISC EXPENSE	AMOUNT
	TOTAL MISC	
	TOTAL GAS	
	TOTAL EXPENSES	

SIGNATURE_____

Sample local travel expenses report.

298   Electrical Contractor

ABC ELECTRICAL CONTRACTORS
TRAVEL EXPENSES

Name:

Expense Center:

Week of:

Day	City	Transpor	Hotel	Meals	Misc	Total
Sunday						
Monday						
Tuesday						
Wednesday						
Thursday						
Friday						
Saturday						
Totals						

INSTRUCTIONS:

1) Complete middle section, listing each expense item seperately. Receipts must be obtained for all expenses over $20.00.

2) Fill in the amount advanced. Sign the form. Have the form signed by your manager and forward to accounting no later than 15 days from the last travel date.

3) Complete top section including department, expense code, and purpose of trip. Expense centers MUST be specified for proper budget allocation.

M U S T   F I L L

Prepaid Tickets:

Amount Advanced:

AMEX #

Signature:

Manager's Approval:

Processing Checklist:

○ Credit Card # ○ Entered in A/P system
○ Claimant's Signature ○ Reimbursement paid
○ Manager's Approval

Sample travel expenses report.

Forms & work-sheets for electrical contractors   299

ABC ELECTRICAL CONTRACTORS
COMMISSION REPORT

YEAR				
NAME			PAGE	

TERMS	RATE	NOTES

DATE	PRODCT.	GROSS SALE	CASH	CHG	LEDGER #	COMMISSION		NAME	PAID
TOTALS									

Sample commission report.

300   Electrical Contractor

ABC ELECTRICAL CONTRACTORS

CREDIT APPLICATION	Account #	
	Date Business Started	
Company:	Phone:	
Industry:	Fax:	
Address:		
City/State/Zip:		

Names of Owners, Partners or Officers	
Name	Title

Trade References		
Name	Address	Phone

Bank Information	
Bank:	Bank:
Branch:	Branch:
Phone: Acct #:	Phone: Acct #:

Authorization:

Date:_____ Signature:_____ Title:_____

Sample credit application.

For:	
Date:	Time:

ABC ELECTRICAL CONTRACTORS
TELEPHONE MESSAGE

M	
of	

Phone	Ext

□Customer   □Prospect   □Supplier

□Telephoned   □Please Call
□Came to See You   □Will Call
□Returned Your Call Again

Message

Taken by:

Sample telephone message form.

ABC ELECTRICAL CONTRACTORS - WEEKLY PLANNER

NAME: WEEK ENDING:

TIME	MONDAY	TUESDAY	WEDNESDAY	THURSDAY	FRIDAY
8:00am					
9:00am					
10:00am					
11:00am					
12:00pm					
1:00pm					
2:00pm					
3:00pm					
4:00pm					
5:00pm					

TO-DO LIST:

1.
2.
3.
4.
5.
6.

ADMINISTRATION:

1.
2.
3.
4.
5.
6.

COMMENTS:

Sample weekly planner form.

Forms & work-sheets for electrical contractors   303

```
+-----------------------------------------------------------+
|              ABC ELECTRICAL CONTRACTORS                   |
|                     PROPOSAL                              |
+---------------------------+----------------+--------------+
| FOR:                      | PHONE:         | DATE:        |
+---------------------------+----------+-----+--------------+
| STREET:                   | CITY:    | STATE:  | ZIP:     |
+---------------------------+----------+---------+----------+
| JOB:                      | LOCATION:                    |
+---------------------------+------------------------------+
| WE HEREBY SUBMIT SPECIFICATIONS AND ESTIMATES FOR:        |
|                                                           |
|                                                           |
|                                                           |
|                                                           |
|                                                           |
|                                                           |
|                                                           |
|                                                           |
|                                                           |
|                                                           |
| WE PROPOSE HEREBY TO FURNISH MATERIAL AND LABOR IN        |
| ACCORDANCE WITH THE                                       |
| ABOVE SPECIFICATIONS FOR THE SUM OF: $_____   |
| PAYABLE AS FOLLOWS:_____    |
|                                                           |
| AUTHORIZED SIGNATURE:_____ DATE:_____    |
+-----------------------------------------------------------+

+-----------------------------------------------------------+
| ACCEPTANCE OF PROPOSAL: THE ABOVE PRICES, SPECIFICATIONS, |
| AND CONDITIONS                                            |
| ARE SATISFACTORY AND ARE HEREBY ACCEPTED.  YOU ARE        |
| AUTHORIZED TO DO THE                                      |
| WORK AS SPECIFIED.  PAYMENT WILL BE MADE AS OUTLINED      |
| ABOVE.                                                    |
|                                                           |
| AUTHORIZED SIGNATURE:_____ DATE:_____    |
+-----------------------------------------------------------+
```

Sample proposal form.

ABC ELECTRICAL CONTRACTORS
ESTIMATE WORKSHEET

CLIENT_____ LOCATION_____
JOB DESCRIPTION:_____
_____
_____
_____

JOB CODE	UNITS	EXTENSION	LABOR	EXTENSION	TOTAL

PREPARED BY:_____DATE:_____ CHECKED BY:_____DATE:_____

Sample estimate work-sheet.

Forms & work-sheets for electrical contractors   305

ABC ELECTRICAL CONTRACTORS
LABOR COST COMPARISON

JOB:_____   SUPERVISOR:_____

JOB CODE	JOB DESCRIPTION	EST. HOURS	ACTUAL HOURS

NOTES:

Sample labor cost comparison work-sheet.

ABC ELECTRICAL CONTRACTORS
CHANGE ORDER

FOR:	PHONE:		DATE:	
STREET:	CITY:	STATE:		ZIP:
JOB:	LOCATION:			

THIS CHANGE ORDER IS HEREBY INCORPORATED INTO THE ORIGINAL CONTRACT AND IS TO BE ATTACHED THERETO. ALL OTHER ITEMS AND CONDITIONS OF THE ORIGINAL CONTRACT AND ANY PRIOR CHANGE ORDERS NOT MODIFIED BELOW REMAIN THE SAME. CHANGES ARE AS FOLLOWS:

ORIGINAL CONTRACT SUM: $ _____
NET CHANGE BY PREVIOUS CHANGE ORDERS: $ _____
NET CHANGE BY THIS CHANGE ORDER: $ _____
REVISED CONTRACT SUM: $ _____
TERMS OF PAYMENT:
THIS CHANGE ORDER INCREASES/DECREASES COMPLETION OF THIS JOB BY ____ DAYS.

CLIENT'S SIGNATURE:_____ DATE:_____

CONTRACTOR'S SIGNATURE:_____ DATE:_____

Sample change order form.

Forms & work-sheets for electrical contractors   307

ABC ELECTRICAL CONTRACTORS
PROJECT SCHEDULE WORKSHEET

PAGE_____ OF_____

CLIENT:		LOCATION:			
ACTIVITY	WORKERS	START DATE	END DATE	NO. OF DAYS	REMARKS

Sample project schedule work-sheet.

ABC ELECTRICAL CONTRACTORS
JOB COST RECORD

PROJECT_____ PAGE ____ OF ____

DATE	DESCRIPTION	MATERIAL	LABOR	EQUIPMENT	MISC.
	TOTALS				

Sample job cost record.

ABC ELECTRICAL CONTRACTORS
BILL OF MATERIALS

PART NAME _____   DATE _____

CUSTOMER PART NUMBER_____   PAGE _____   OF _____

CUSTOMER _____

ITEM NUMBER	DESCRIPTION	QUANTITY

ISSUED BY: _____   ISSUE NUMBER _____

Sample bill of materials.

ABC ELECTRICAL CONTRACTORS

Your Street Address
Your City, State, Zip
Your Telephone Number

STATEMENT

DATE_____

CLIENT:

TERMS:

DATE	INVOICE	DESCRIPTION	CHARGES	CREDITS	BALANCE
		BALANCE FORWARD			

THANK YOU!

PAY LAST AMOUNT
IN THIS COLUMN

Sample statement.

Forms & work-sheets for electrical contractors   311

ABC ELECTRICAL CONTRACTORS
INVENTORY SHEET

INVENTORY DATE_____ TAKEN BY_____ PAGE _____ OF _____

CODE	DESCRIPTION	QUANTITY	UNIT PRICE	EXTENSION

Sample inventory sheet.

ABC ELECTRICAL CONTRACTORS
TIME SHEET

Employee I.D. Number

Date of Birth

Day Month Year

Mr.
Surname: Mrs.
Miss.

Given Names

Address:

Dates Employed	Days	Department	Type of Work	Hours If hourly pay	Days If daily pay
	Monday				
	Tuesday				
	Wednesday				
	Thursday				
	Friday				
	Saturday				
	Sunday				
			TOTAL		

Employee's Signature:

Certified By: _____
Manager

Approved By: _____

Sample time sheet.

ABC ELECTRICAL CONTRACTORS
OVERTIME REPORT

NAME: _____   DEPARTMENT: _____

DAY	DATE	O/T HOURS WORKED	SUP'RS INITIALS	REASON FOR OVERTIME	DAY	DATE	O/T HOURS WORKED	SUP'RS INITIALS	REASON FOR OVERTIME
THURS					THURS				
FRI					FRI				
SAT					SAT				
SUN					SUN				
MON					MON				
TUES					TUES				
WED					WED				

TOTAL HOURS: _____

AUTHORIZATION: _____

NUMBER OF DAY ABSENT IN THESE WEEKS:

FULL DAYS _____   HALF DAYS _____

Sample overtime report.

ABC ELECTRICAL CONTRACTORS
WEEKLY EMPLOYEE ABSENTEE REPORT

Department: _____   Dept. No. _____   Date: _____

Employee Absent	Date	Reason For Absence	Occasional Employee	Full Day	Half Day

_____
Department Manager's signature

Sample weekly employee absentee report.

ABC ELECTRICAL CONTRACTORS
VACATION ENTITLEMENT

Supervisor

Date

(Employee)

	Jan	Feb	Mar	Apr	May	Jun	Jul	Aug	Sep	Oct	Nov	Dec
Entitled												
Taken												
Balance												

(Employee)

	Jan	Feb	Mar	Apr	May	Jun	Jul	Aug	Sep	Oct	Nov	Dec
Entitled												
Taken												
Balance												

(Employee)

	Jan	Feb	Mar	Apr	May	Jun	Jul	Aug	Sep	Oct	Nov	Dec
Entitled												
Taken												
Balance												

(Employee)

	Jan	Feb	Mar	Apr	May	Jun	Jul	Aug	Sep	Oct	Nov	Dec
Entitled												
Taken												
Balance												

Sample vacation entitlement report.

About the author

Dan Ramsey sold his first magazine article at age 17. Since then, he has written more than 50 articles, more than 40 non-fiction books, as well as training manuals, product manuals and brochures, sales literature, marketing collateral, radio commercials, newspaper stories, and other business documents. He has broad experience in the construction trade.

Dan's books are on small business opportunities, part-time business ventures, do-it-yourself home maintenance and repair, trade business start-up guides, and other topics.

Dan earned his Bachelor of Science degree in General Studies from Eastern Oregon State College in La Grande, Oregon. He earned a Certificate in Marketing Management from the American Management Association, and the Certified Business Communicator designation from the Business/Professional Advertising Association. Dan is a member of the National Association of Home and Workshop Writers, and he produces their newsletter.